With Heart and Hand

The Inside Story of Wexford's Hurling Resurgence

With Heart and Hand

The Inside Story of
Wexford's Hurling Resurgence

Tom Williams

BLACKWATER PRESS

Editor
Rosemary Dawson

Design & Layout
Paula Byrne

ISBN
0 86121 721 7

© 1996 Tom Williams

Produced and printed in Ireland by
Blackwater Press,
7/8 Broomhill Business Park,
Tallaght, Dublin 24.

British Library Cataloguing-in-Publication Data
A catalogue record is available from the British Library.

To
my wife, Marie,
to
Mary Griffin
and to
the wives and girlfriends
of the Wexford hurlers.

ACKNOWLEDGEMENTS

My appreciation and thanks are due to many people who helped while this book was in preparation. Liam Griffin and his wife, Mary, showed extreme patience during the days when my persistent presence in their home caused upset to their family life. Seamus Barron and his wife, Anne; and Rory Kinsella and his wife, Gerry were hospitable and helpfully informative at all times. Ger Walsh and his staff at *The People Newspapers;* and the Buttle family and *The Echo* staff very kindly allowed me access to their files and were very supportive of my efforts. A small and effective committee of five people deserve immense credit for their voluntary efforts which helped to bring the project to a successful conclusion. Chairman, Ronan Furlong, led by example and his untiring efforts and attention to detail was an example to us all. Phil Murphy of *The People* put his great experience at our disposal and his expertise in sporting matters was seen to great advantage in his selection of exciting photographs. Phil also made many helpful suggestions in relation to proofs and corrections. John O'Leary and Martin Quigley were tireless and thorough and their enthusiasm was infectious. Barry Kehoe also contributed.

Three members of my family gave me enormous help in research and proof-reading. My brother Dominic, whose knowledge of hurling is immense, spent many hours checking facts, dates and teams. He made my task much simpler. My wife, Marie tirelessly went through each copy and offered many helpful suggestions with phrasing and interpretation. My son, David, delved into his store of match programmes and came up with lists, statistics and facts. Without the help of these three people in particular, it would not have been possible to complete the book in the short time allotted.

There are many others who offered insights and recalled significant events which made 1996 so memorable for Wexford people, in hurling terms. All the members of the Wexford panel were friendly, helpful and enthusiastic towards the project. My particular thanks is due to Wexford GAA Supporters Club. I acknowledge photographs kindly supplied by Adrian Melia, Nick Hayes, Agnes Codd, Paddy Murphy, Pat O'Connor, Ray Flynn, *The People Group* of Newspapers, *The Star* and *The Examiner.* Lastly my thanks is due to John O'Connor, Rosemary Dawson and Anna O'Donovan of Blackwater Press for their help and encouragement.

My sincerest thanks is due to all of the following:

Alan Aherne	Sean Flood	Mick Kinsella	Noel O'Gorman
Anne Barron	Kathleen Flood	Gerry Kinsella	John O'Leary
Seamus Barron	Dr Tom Foley	Rory Kinsella	Mick O'Sullivan
Mark Browne	Gerry Forde	Garry Laffan	Brendan O'Sullivan
Eamonn Buttle	Nicky Furlong	Fan Larkin	Bill Peare
Billy Byrne	Ronan Furlong	Larry Larkin	Brid Quigley
Helen Byrne	Jenny Griffin	Enda Maher	John Quigley
Agnes Codd	Liam Griffin	Pierce Maher	Martin Quigley
Sean Collier	Mary Griffin	Adrian Melia	Ned Quinn
Kevin Cashman	Dave Guiney	Tom Mooney	Billy Rackard
Ger Cushe	Rod Guiney	Larry Murphy	Carmel Redmond
Rosemary Dawson	Nick Hayes	Phil Murphy	Peter Redmond
Tom Dempsey	Christy Heffernan	Rory McCarthy	Richard Roche
Tony Doran	Delia Hunt	Seamus O'Beirne	Eamonn Scallan
Andy Doyle	Barry Kehoe	George O'Connor	Martin Storey
Margaret Doyle	Eamonn Kehoe	John O'Connor	Fr John Sweetman
Liam Dunne	Jim Kehoe	John O'Connor	Ger Walsh
Cyril Farrell	Colm Kehoe	*(Blackwater Press)*	Annette Williams
Adrian Fenlon	Hilda Kenny	Anna O'Donovan	David Williams
Damien Fitzpatrick	Paddy Kenny	Trishie O'Dowd	Catherine Williams
Niamh Fitzpatrick	Christy Keogh	Eoin O'Gorman	Dominic Williams
	Dominic Kiernan	Larry O'Gorman	Marie Williams

CONTENTS

We are the boys of Wexford
Who fought with heart and hand

The Boys of Wexford, Robert Dwyer Joyce

PROLOGUE

The raw emotion that consumed the people of Wexford at the end of the 1996 All-Ireland Final is indescribable. It was difficult to take it all in. A 28-year gap had been bridged with valour, with dignity and with the kind of determination that was the perfect riposte to those national hurling critics, who had the temerity to question the quality of the blood that coursed through the veins of Wexford's representatives on the hurling fields.

All around me in the Hogan Stand, I saw grown men and women unashamedly crying with unqualified joy and elation. Our day of deliverance had come. In the words of Liam Griffin, 'It was as if every Wexford person had been released from gaol at the same time'. People from Cork, Dublin, Kerry and Kilkenny found it hard to comprehend. Only the people from the Banner County truly understood the emotion. They had experienced it all a bare 12 months earlier. The events of the days and weeks that followed are forever etched in the minds of Wexford people.

An unashamed admirer of great sportsmen and great sporting occasions, I have watched the Irish soccer team from the drab terraces of Dalymount Park, in the days of Hurley and Haverty, to the glories of the Charlton era at Landsdowne Road. I have been enthralled by O'Reilly, Hewitt, Gibson, Goodall and Slattery. I marvelled at Delany, Tracey, Coghlan and O'Sullivan. I stood in astonishment at the feats of Kelly and Roche, of Teidt and McGuigan, of Freddie Gilroy and Carruth and recently of Michelle Smith. The deeds of great sporting figures and majestic events are engraved in my subconscious.

My most memorable moments in sport, however, have come from the ancient and noble game of hurling. Nothing stirs the blood like it. A fine day, a clear sky, a green field and 30 fit athletes in a contest of will, of valour and of skill is an experience to light the fires in our souls. Hurling is, indeed, a warrior game. Liam Griffin was correct when, in the sporting phrase of the season, he labelled it 'The Riverdance of Sport'.

Maybe Orwell was also correct when he said that 'Sport is war minus the shooting'. Maybe deep in our subconscious the old tribal differences lie buried waiting to be resurrected by a group of young lads from our area, carrying our colours, going into battle to bring the prize back to our county.

These feelings and more were part of what was felt by the people of Wexford when Liam Griffin's team finally and dramatically bridged the frustrating and ever-widening gap on the 1st Sunday of September, 1996. The experience will hardly be repeated. All-Irelands will be won again by Wexford. But there is unlikely ever to be another period so long and so barren. The intensity of the outpourings of joy, the absolute sense of rapture and happiness that descended on the county was unforgettable.

This indeed was Wexford's 'Field of Dreams'.

This book is an attempt to record the pride, the joy and the emotion that washed like a flood tide through the streets of Gorey and Enniscorthy, through New Ross and Bunclody, along the narrow Viking streets of Wexford town and through every hill and hollow of the Model County in the wake of that memorable sporting year.

Tom Williams
Wexford
November 1996

∞ CHAPTER 1 ∞

THE BARREN YEARS

The Last Great Victory

The September sun shone down on the supporters of the Wexford hurling team as they filed joyfully through the narrow lanes leading from Croke Park. The shouts of 'Up Wexford!' echoed across the streets of North Dublin as the frenzied and ecstatic hordes poured forth their exuberance and exultation in the great victory of their county's hurling team. The Dublin flag sellers had experienced their best day's business of the year. Purple and gold badges, purple and gold hats, bunting, small flags, big flags – they had all been snapped up by the confident and good-humoured people from below the Blackstairs.

It was the first Sunday of September 1968.

A Dual Win

They had just witnessed a dual All-Ireland win. The minor hurlers had supplied the appetiser in the form of the county's third All-Ireland crown, by defeating Cork on a score line of 2-13 to 3-7. The main event, the All-Ireland senior hurling final, was a game to savour. For the Wexford supporters, however, the real enjoyment was confined to the second half. In the first half, the highly-rated Munster champions, Tipperary, took Wexford apart. An unforgettable display by Mick Roche at centre-half back and an equally adept exhibition of power and skill by Babs Keating in the forwards, left Tipperary in control of the game and leading by 1-11 to 1-3 at the interval. But for the heroics of Wexford goalkeeper, Pat Nolan of Oylegate, the gap between the sides would have been farcical. A verbal tour-de-force, of crockery-smashing proportions, by Wexford coach, Padge Kehoe, at half-time, brought about the desired transformation in his team. Aided and abetted by selector, Nick Rackard, he unleashed a torrent of censure and reproach at his charges. The second half was a revelation as Wexford, led by their captain, Dan Quigley, and admirably supported by Paul Lynch, Tony Doran, Jack Berry and an impudent young substitute named John Quigley, overhauled Tipperary and eventually won on a score line of 5-8 to 3-13.

The Celebrations

The supporters were now determined to celebrate a famous victory. Some headed for nearby hostelries while others made for their cars and began the homeward journey to the banks of the Slaney. No sporting followers are as unswerving in their allegiance as the men, women and children who follow the Wexford hurlers. South of the smoky-blue Blackstairs, bonfires were prepared and flags and bunting were strung from gable and pylon as the people prepared for what was becoming a regular event. If some hurling clairvoyant had suggested that it would be 28 long, bitterly disappointing years before the Wexford hurlers were to again experience the joys of such a day, he would have been dismissed as a deranged idiot.

Accustomed to Success

Wexford followers had become accustomed to seeing their favourites playing in All-Ireland finals. Until the mid-1940s, the hopes for All-Ireland Senior success had lain firmly at the feet of the county footballers. Five titles had been won, including a memorable and record-breaking four-in-a-row from 1915 to 1918. A sturdy and inspirational son of Rathnure had other ideas. Following the charismatic Nick Rackard-led revival in the fortunes of the county senior hurling team, the first hurling All-Ireland final for 33 years was contested against Tipperary in 1951. Although beaten, the performance gave hope for the future. A further All-Ireland defeat, in an all-time classic game to Cork in 1954, was followed by victory against Galway in 1955, to bring the ultimate hurling laurels to Slaneyside for the first time since 1910. Another magnificent exhibition saw the county victorious against Cork in 1956. During this period, the Wexford hurlers were the undisputed kingpins of the game. In winning everything that they competed for, from All-Ireland to National League to Oireachtas, they brought a new dimension to the game. Big, powerful men such as Ned Wheeler, the three Rackard brothers, Nick O'Donnell and Jim Morrissey allied to the charming skills of Tim Flood, Jim English and Padge Kehoe ensured that this team would be remembered as long as the caman was wielded across the broad green fields of Ireland.

More Victories in the 1960s

When Kilkenny beat Wexford in the Leinster championship of 1957, retirements hastened the break-up of the great team of the 1950s. A bare four years later, in 1960, only seven of that team remained, when Wexford hammered a hotly fancied Tipperary to win their fourth All-Ireland. Newcomers had matured to take the place of the old 1950s heroes. There followed three more All-Ireland final appearances in that decade – all against Tipperary. The impact of the defeat of 1962 on the Wexford supporters was lessened by the absolute brilliance of the hurling of both sides on that day. 1965 saw Wexford well beaten by a great Tipperary, but now on this day of days, the men from Wexford had won their fifth All-Ireland.

An Optimistic Future

In 1968, Pat Nolan, Tom Neville and Jimmy O'Brien were the only survivors from the winning 1960 team. The supporters were confident that many days of All-Ireland victories lay ahead. The old game of Cuchulainn was alive and well by the banks of the Slaney and the Wexford camogie team confirmed that pre-eminence by also winning the premier title in 1968. The 1968 'Hurler of The Year' was Wexford captain, Dan Quigley. During this same year, St Peter's College, the Wexford town-based secondary school, further emphasised the healthy state of the game in the county by winning the All-Ireland Colleges senior title. It seemed that the future of Wexford hurling was very bright indeed. The people of the county were now hurling mad and they trembled in anticipation of further sporting glories.

Confident Young Men

Some of the younger members of the 1968 senior panel such as, Vinnie Staples, Willie Murphy, Dave Berney, Tony Doran, Christy and Mick Jacob, Ned Buggy and John Quigley accepted that first All-Ireland medal with an assured air. They felt that it represented the first of many. They were not to know that it was also their last. The young guns of the all-conquering minor team of 1968 looked ahead, with understandable confidence, to the day when they too would climb, as victors, up the steps of the Hogan Stand and receive their All-Ireland senior medals to the acclaim of the faithful Wexford followers. Aspiring stars of that minor team, like Martin Quigley, Jack Russell, Liam Bennett, Tom Byrne, Mick Butler and Martin Casey, already totally dedicated to the game of hurling, felt sure that their day was not far off. Their ambition was to get selected on the county senior team and, one day, be part of an occasion that would yield the coveted Celtic Cross.

Their aspirations and dreams went unrealised.

The Beginning of the Drought

No member of the 1968 minor team was to achieve the hurler's ultimate ambition. A National League title was won in 1973 when Wexford beat Limerick by 4-13 to 3-7 and although the county reached three further senior All-Irelands, the supreme prize remained elusive.

And then it all ended.

A major hiatus in Wexford hurling developed. There were no more All-Ireland victories. Not in senior, not in under-21 and not in minor.

The Poor Return of the 1970s

Every Leinster final from 1970 to 1979 was between Kilkenny and Wexford. There were many classic games in this series, with superb hurling and intense rivalry. Leinster final victories over Kilkenny were achieved in 1970, 1976 and 1977 only to fail in the All-Ireland final to Cork on each occasion. The 1976 win was particularly satisfying as Kilkenny, the all-conquering All-Ireland champions, were attempting to win three finals in a row. Wexford hurled Kilkenny off the park and came out winning by the huge margin of 2-20 to 1-6. Still the Model County men failed to cross the final hurdle. From these ten Leinster finals, Wexford won only three and on each occasion the team was beaten in the All-Ireland. The brilliant Kilkenny team of the early 1970s, on the other hand, won All-Irelands in 1972, 1974 and 1975 and had another win in 1979 against Galway. The Wexford team was certainly good enough to win the national title in some of these years. On quite a few occasions they came within a puck of the ball of beating their neighbours, who later went on to win the ultimate prize, sometimes by wide margins.

The Classic Game of 1974

This was particularly true in 1974 when, in an utterly thrilling encounter, Wexford went under by a bare point to a great Kilkenny team. An incident just before half-time resulted in Phil Wilson's dismissal. Kilkenny, leading at the break by 3-8 to 0-10, looked home and dry. Wexford played heroically in the second half and twice took the lead, only to see Kilkenny hit back in determined fashion. The Noresiders were nine points to the good with fifteen minutes remaining. Again Wexford levelled and went ahead with a John Quigley point. Kilkenny, bidding to win four successive Leinster titles for the first time in 86 years, levelled again. It was enthralling stuff as Wexford once more went into the lead, this time courtesy of Tom Byrne. A Nicky Brennan point tied the scores. The winning point was scored, in the last minute of the game, from a difficult free at the sideline under the Hogan Stand,. The greatest freetaker that hurling has ever seen took up his position. Memorably, for all who were watching, the utterly professional Eddie Keher bent down to tie his boot lace before striking unerringly into the breeze and over the bar. To the chagrin of the Wexford crowd, the referee blew the whistle following the puck out, when there were still twenty seconds to go on the clock.

So the 1970s saw Kilkenny play in seven All-Ireland finals and win four. Wexford played only in three and lost them all.

No More Leinster Titles after 1977

To compound matters, there were no more Leinster final victories after 1977. Good teams came and went. Great players played out their careers without an All-Ireland medal. Celebrated hurlers like Martin Quigley, honoured with All-Star selection in 1973, 1974, 1975 and 1976 and Mick Jacob, honoured in 1972, 1976 and 1977 continued, with admirable enthusiasm, to strive for the holy grail of hurling. Although Jacob had won a medal as a sub on the 1968 team, it was not the same as winning on the field of play. The county was still producing wonderful hurlers such as Colm Doran – an All-Star in 1973; John Quigley – honoured in 1974; and Willie Murphy – honoured in 1976. The great Tony Doran was honoured in 1976 and also voted Hurler of The Year. Christy Keogh was honoured in 1977 and Ned Buggy was honoured in 1979. Unfortunately, while these great hurling men contributed much to the cause of Wexford hurling, the much sought after All-Ireland senior victory remained elusive.

Those who joined the team after 1977 never even won a Leinster medal.

Under-Age Neglect

The neglect of under-age hurling was catching up with the county. Despite dire warnings from farseeing Bord-na-nÓg officials, little if anything was done to improve the under-age structures within the county. 1968 marked the last national win at minor level and not since 1965, had the under-21s triumphed. Many people felt that the multitude of different grades at under-age level and the consequent large number of competitions resulted in the neglect of the important aspect of improving basic skills.

The Desert of the 1980s

The 1980s were a barren desert for Wexford.

The introduction of the open draw and a dramatic improvement in the hurling skills of the Offaly men resulted in Wexford dropping down to third in the pecking order in Leinster. Kilkenny, with a better under-age structure and an excellent conveyor belt of handy stickmen, continually frustrated the efforts of the Model County to win a Leinster title and challenge for the ultimate prize. The sight of spindly, but amazingly skilful, Kilkenny men, the vertical stripes of their black and amber jerseys emphasising their lack of physique, continually outfoxing the purple and gold clad Wexford men was becoming too much to take.

The Arrival of Offaly

A new, immense hurdle had materialised to create another hazard which began, with distressing regularity, to frustrate Wexford's attempt to gallop through Leinster. On the few joyous occasions when Kilkenny was vanquished, and Wexford was in sight of the Promised Land (of Leinster, at least) the county hurlers were ambushed by Offaly, whose team invariably included young boys who hardly knew how to use a razor. That they knew how to wield a camán, with purpose and dexterity, was never in doubt. They left the Wexford dreams of returning to former glories in tatters. Offaly had truly arrived as a hurling force and a combination to be wary of, even before their breakthrough first All-Ireland in 1981. From 1980 onwards, the Faithful County began to assume the role formerly played by Wexford. Although their selection was confined to a few hurling clubs in pockets of the county, their diligence at under age had resulted in a string of impressive successes. These young players now began maturing into fine adult exponents of the game. The county contested every Leinster final from 1980 to 1990. Out of eleven appearances, victory went to Offaly on seven occasions. Kilkenny won the other four finals and Wexford had nothing to show from 1980 to 1990 but three losing Leinster final appearances. While the exciting emergence of Offaly was undoubtedly a great boost for hurling in general, it was a dark cloud on the horizon of Wexford's hopes of a return to the winner's enclosure.

Bad Habits

It is generally acknowledged that the standard of the Wexford teams in the 1980s fell somewhat below the level of other eras. Fewer real stars were coming forward. A glance at the make-up of the All-Stars selections confirms this. While Wexford men such as George O'Connor – in 1981 and 1988; John Conran – in 1987; and Eamonn Cleary in 1989; were honoured with selection, no Wexford hurler received the ultimate accolade in 1982, 1983, 1984, 1985 or 1986. Nevertheless the Leinster finals of 1981 and 1984, both against Offaly, could and should have been won.

Bad habits however, had crept into the Wexford style. Whether these were the result of frustration, borne out of continual defeat, is a moot point. The legacy of overdependence on a big full-forward was still very much in evidence. From 1967 to 1984, Tony Doran had manned the position, with utter distinction, for Wexford. His scoring record was phenomenal and the Wexford team profited by the many high balls hit towards the dynamic leader of the attack. On many occasions, the redheaded firebrand from Boolavogue, possessed of a right hand that could catch a homing pigeon, and an indomitable spirit, rescued his team with important goals. High balls struck from the half-back line or centre-field became a way of life for the Wexford men. When Tony's powers began to wane, the team was left with no attacking plan. The skyscraper deliveries no longer bore fruit. In vain did they search for the ghosts of Doran and Rackard. This fuelled other discrepancies. The Wexford hurlers became known for witless clearances from defence, the conceding of needless frees, aimless solo running, scandalous levels of wide balls hit and ridiculous scoring attempts from impossible angles. Their followers were in despair.

The method of picking the men to take charge of the senior hurlers was often haphazard. It rarely got the attention it deserved and club representation was more important than the suitability of the candidates for the job in hand. A marked tendency by some selectors to favour players from their own clubs was another important factor that militated against success. The best players were not always selected. Players from lower profile junior or intermediate clubs did not always get the chance that their talents deserved. This is not as it should have been.

The selection of Michael O'Grady to oversee team matters took place before the 1987 championship season. He was a well-respected coach and early indications seemed favourable. Alas, he was removed after a bare eight months, without being given the time to implement his good ideas for an improvement in standards and application.

Interference in team selection was a feature of these years with many high-ranking GAA men within the county, insisting on having their say in who wore the purple and gold jersey. Their enthusiasm for the task was matched only by their lack of knowledge in the finer points of the game.

Weak Defence

Another problem also developed. The age old dilemma of a lack of scoring forwards had now been worsened by a weakening in Wexford's traditional strongest area, the defence. Many of the close defeats in the period from 1980 onwards were caused by late scores against a shaky and badly organised defence.

Beating Kilkenny – Wexford's Real All-Ireland

Wexford beat Kilkenny in 1981 but failed to reproduce the same form in the Leinster final and was beaten by Offaly. Tony Doran suffered a serious head injury in the early stages of the game and heard the last few minutes on radio from his hospital bed. A bare two points separated the sides at the end. Christy Keogh, who had been an excellent Wexford player from 1969 to 1979 took over as manager in 1981.

In the Leinster semi-final of 1984 the Wexford men had a great win over Kilkenny, courtesy of a late goal from Tony Doran. The team was favoured to win the final against Offaly. Offaly, well on top in the first twenty minutes of the game, played intelligent and controlled hurling and went into an eight-point lead. In the second half Wexford fought back well but proceeded to hit wide after wide. It seemed that the Wexford men could not possibly continue to be so profligate. It was heartbreaking to watch.

Offaly somehow weathered the storm. Wexford still appeared eminently capable of winning, but despite incessantly attacking the Offaly goal, failed to get the necessary scores. Finally Billy Byrne scored a goal to leave a point between the teams. It was all Wexford in the last few minutes, as they swept down in hordes on the Offaly goal. With just under two minutes to full time, the referee, Paschal Long, blew the whistle to end the match. Wexford people were enraged, but to no avail. Offaly were Leinster Champions. Wexford had, once again, beaten Kilkenny in the earlier round and it began to look as if vanquishing their Noreside rivals was the extent of Wexford's ambition. The final score was Offaly 1-15 Wexford 2-11.

In the 1988 Leinster final against Offaly, Wexford shot seventeen wides to Offaly's nine and ended up losing by four points.

The Roscommon Debacle

An event took place in 1984 which brought an unwelcome rain of publicity down on players and management. The team had travelled to Athleague to face lowly Roscommon in The Centenary Cup. Many of the players were still suffering the after effects of a major defeat – that of the 1984 League final to Limerick, which had taken place on the previous Sunday. The hotel chosen for the overnight stay had the ideal distraction. A disco, called The Spider's Web was a temptation which the players found difficult to resist. They entered into the frivolities with abandon. On the following day, much the worse for wear, they faced up to Roscommon, and, in a result that shook the hurling world, were beaten. The media ferreted out the story of the late-night carousing at the disco. It made headlines on the sporting pages. 'Players Caught in Spider's Web', screamed one headline. The team became the butt of Roscommon jokes. John O'Connor has good reason to remember the occasion. With hindsight, he can now laugh at the events of that memorable weekend. He was very conscious that he was making his senior intercounty debut in the match and was determined to make a good impression on the team management. In what he thought was an act of great discipline, he unselfishly forsook the delights of the night, and declining the attractions of the disco, went to bed early. Much to his disgust he was substituted in the following day's match, while all round him his team mates struggled to determine which of the three sliotars in their line of vision was the correct one.

It was, to say the least, an inauspicious debut.

Martin Quigley Takes Over

In September 1989, Martin Quigley took the reins as team manager and brought a refreshing and more professional approach. His backroom team consisted of Dave Berney, who had won an All-Ireland at centre-field with Wexford in 1968 and Jimmy Furlong of Adamstown, a sub on that 1968 team. Berney was now a Dublin-based businessman and well aware that change was needed. Together they scoured the clubs of the county for new talent. A professional trainer was brought in and personal assessment charts, on fitness and performance, were computed and made available to each player. A concentrated effort was made to reduce the number of senseless frees which the Wexford back line had fallen into the unfortunate habit of conceding. All personnel of minor and under-21 teams of the previous ten years were examined for their potential contribution. In too many cases those players had given up the game. In the early 1980s the drop in standards which was reflected at senior level was even more stark at minor and under-21 level. This changed in 1986 and 1987 when the county had Leinster under-21 hurling triumphs. Galway however, put paid to All-Ireland hopes in the final of '86 and the semi-final of '87.

The Success of the Wexford GAA Supporters Club

In late 1989, shortly after Martin Quigley became manager of the Wexford hurling team it was decided to form a Wexford Hurling Supporters Club. The idea originated with Martin Quigley and the then County Board chairman, Joe O'Shaughnessy. The executive committee under chairman, Matt Browne oversaw two branches, one in Wexford, chaired by local builder, John Doyle and another in Dublin, chaired by Pat Quigley, ex PRO of the GAA and cousin of the hurling Quigleys of Rathnure. The idea was to provide financial backing for the senior hurling team. The success of the supporters club which had been formed in Tipperary was one of the main motivating forces, but unlike Tipperary, a conscious decision was made to remain distanced from the affairs of the team. At all times the Wexford club would be answerable to the County Board. The club was an immediate success. It took on tasks such as the promotion of the game amongst teenagers and the seeking out of sponsorship. Seamus Howlin contributed great work. It was instrumental in negotiating a major sponsorship deal with Wexford Creamery, which has been of immense benefit. Funds were raised by membership and various other ventures such as golf classics and race meetings at Wexford Race Course. Following a 1992 directive from Croke Park that all supporters clubs should be for the benefit of football as well as hurling, the club became the Wexford GAA Supporters Club. It raised £50,000 annually and between 1991 and 1995 invested £75,000 in the implementation of the hurling coaching scheme in primary schools. The present chairman of the Dublin branch is Tom Moriarity and a further branch in the midlands has Eugene Lacey in the chair. The WGSC is presently under the overall chairmanship of Martin Quigley.

The runaway success of WGSC showed the huge appetite for hurling success in the county. There was a growing feeling, however, that unless significant triumphs were soon achieved, they would run out of steam.

Defeats by Laois and Dublin

Even Dublin and Laois had the temerity to stand fast against Wexford and add to the decline. Laois beat Wexford, for the first time in ages, in the Leinster semi-final in 1985 and Dublin did likewise in 1990. Wexford's self-esteem was slipping to a level not encountered in hurling terms since prior to the 1950s.

Cyril Farrell's View

In the 1980s particularly, many a hurling follower from south of the Blackstairs swore that he would never again make the journey which caused him such anguish. Cyril Farrell in his excellent hurling book *The Right To Win* sums up the Wexford position as follows:

> *'It was all so very disappointing. It was as if they couldn't move on to higher peaks, once they conquered one mountain. Yet despite the annual disappointments, Wexford fans remain amongst the most loyal in the country. They travel in force everywhere, waiting and longing to have something to celebrate. Per head of population, and bearing in mind the number of disappointments they have endured, they are probably the most loyal fans in the country.*
>
> *Wexford acquired a reputation as being All-Ireland champions only in inconsistency. The problem with that is that once a team loses some games it felt should have been won, personal insecurity sets in. That, in turn, feeds off itself and players start looking over their shoulders, as if waiting for trouble, even when things are sailing along smoothly. That has often happened to Wexford.'*

Kevin Cashman's View

Corkonian Kevin Cashman, of the *Sunday Independent* is a knowledgeable hurling man. His weekly column is anticipated with relish by hurling people. His passionate prose and Joycean streams of hurling consciousness, sometimes with sentences longer than Wexford's run of defeats, is usually highly informative and often sensationally intuitive. His love for the game shines through everything that he writes. His views on hurling are not couched in diplomatic terms. He exploded myths with crushing regularity. The Wexford hurling team repeatedly figures in his outpourings. So does his respect for the hurling traditions of the county. (Kevin is a one time member of The Wexford GAA Supporters Club.) The losing sequence of the Wexford hurlers has occupied many column inches. His frustrations with them is clearly evident, as is his wish for a return to better times. He has often asserted, forcefully, that the team plays with hurls that are not engineered in the proper symmetrical fashion for good hurling. He reasons that Wexford's run of defeats is due to a number of contributing factors. Among these are gross neglect of under-age, mindless and bad tactical play and a propensity to shoot themselves in the foot by the apparent frequency of infighting at County Board and management level.

The League – The Same Story

Neither did fortune smile on Wexford in the League. The county hurlers lost the 1982 and 1990 League finals to Kilkenny; the 1983 semi-final and the 1984 League final to Limerick; the 1986 semi-final to Galway and the 1988 semi-final to Offaly. In short, the hurlers of County Wexford had forgotten how to win. They continued to do well in the League. The cynics would suggest that other counties were taking it easy in these games, with an eye to the greater glory of the championship. That may, sometimes, have been the case in the preliminary rounds, but it certainly was far from the truth for those counties who won through to the latter stages of this competition. In 1991, Wexford again reached the League final where their opponents were the team that was now generally seen as their bogey side – Offaly. Once again the Faithful County was victorious.

The 'Wexford' Jokes

It was at this point that the national press began to veer away from tipping Wexford to win any championship match against either Kilkenny or Offaly. The first of the Wexford Jokes began to circulate. Many of these stories were international in their source and had been previously heard when applied to other sports, and other happenings, in a different context. Nevertheless these apocryphal yarns struck a bitter note by the Slaneyside. The following represent a sample of the genre:

(1) *An Irishman, an Englishman and a Scotsman were travelling by boat in the Florida glades. The boat sank and each decided to swim for shore. The Scotsman struck out and had just made the shoreline when a large crocodile appeared and swallowed him in one gulp. The Englishman was next and a similar fate befell him. Then the Irishman struck out for shore and almost made dry land when the crocodile again appeared and opened his jaws. Suddenly the crocodile flinched, and without touching the Irishman, closed his jaws and slunk off into the undergrowth. The cause of his retreat was the T-shirt worn by the Irishman. It read 'Wexford for the All-Ireland'. Even a crocodile wouldn't swallow that!*

(2) *Another joke concerned a Wexford hurler who was visiting a Waterford doctor. In the waiting room he met a young man who told the hurler that he was here because of beatings that he was receiving, at home, in school and from his mates. It seemed that no matter where he went there was always someone waiting to hammer him. He asked the hurler where he was from. On being*

informed that it was Wexford, he expresses a wish to travel back with him on the grounds that 'Wexford never beat anybody'.

(3) *'Then there was the sign on the Wexford side of New Ross bridge (which separates counties Kilkenny and Wexford). It read 'You are now entering a Nuclear Free Zone'. On the Kilkenny side someone had erected another sign which read, 'You are now entering a Trophy Free Zone'.*

(4) *Nelson Mandela, on release from his long incarceration, was being filled in on some of the earth-shattering events that occurred during his confinement. He indicated that there was one thing in particular that he wished to know. 'Did Wexford get out of Leinster yet?'*

Not Funny to Hurling People

Hurling people within the county gritted their teeth and stayed silent. They found it very difficult to muster even the faintest smile when these stories were recounted in their presence. Non-hurling people thought them hilarious and laughed uproariously. To those who had experienced the death defying valour and seen the glory, the passion and the warrior-like demeanour of the great Wexford teams in former times, these yarns were tantamount to sacrilege. Some uninformed writers even began to question Wexford's commitment and to express reservations about the quality of the blood that coursed through the veins of the representatives of the county on the hurling fields.

It was all a long way from the glorious 1950s and 60s.

Youth Losing Interest

Within the county, hurling matters continued as normal. The county championships drew excellent crowd levels and GAA matters were debated with the same fervour. But other signs were ominous. The kids were forsaking the old warrior game of hurling for the images of Barnes and Bruno, Lewis and Lynagh and Rush and Robson. The constant TV images of these unreal heroes that flickered from the box in the corner of every living-room seemed highly attractive to young impressionable minds. No longer were the hurls gathered, after tea, for the innocent game in the field. The signs were unmistakable. Hurling was on the wane in the land of Rackard and Doran and a dropping off in Wexford's legendary support became apparent. This was particularly evident among young people. The general feeling on the approach of a championship clash against Kilkenny or Offaly was 'I can't see them beating the cats' or 'We've got no forwards, we can't score'.

1991 – D.J. Carey and the Infamous Goal

Things improved somewhat in the early 1990s. The 1991 season opened with the defeat of Laois by 2-19 to 2-14, to set up a semi-final meeting with Kilkenny. Much of the old fighting spirit was in evidence against Kilkenny and the team played very well. As full time approached Wexford led by a point. Even the neutrals accepted that Wexford looked odds on to reach the Leinster final, where, for a change, Dublin would be the other finalists, having disposed of Offaly in a major upset. The referee was preparing to end the game when Liam Dunne was pushed in the back. No free was awarded and D.J. Carey got delivery of a ball around the half-forward line. Although hemmed in by defenders he set off on a last ditch run for the Wexford goal. Despite blatantly over-carrying the ball he was allowed to proceed and his kicked shot went through a ruck of players in front of the Wexford goalkeeper and ended up in the net. The long whistle went on the restart.

Wexford people were stunned into incomprehensible silence. Large numbers of Wexford supporters sat frozen in their seats. They just could not take it in. This one was the most heart-breaking of all. In hindsight, Wexford engineered their own downfall. Hurling writers, while generally acknowledging that D.J. had got away with fouling the ball, were largely unsympathetic towards Wexford. And it was hard to blame them as, although Wexford had been the better team on the day, once again, they had failed to put away enough chances. Kilkenny is a dynamic hurling county and only a fool thinks that the cats are beaten until well after the final whistle sounds.

In the post match interviews it even appeared that some of the Kilkenny management team felt embarrassed about it all. Nevertheless, Kilkenny went on to beat Dublin narrowly in the Leinster final.

1992 and Cyril Farrell

In the Spring of 1992, Cyril Farrell of Galway, a man with a proven track record in coaching, was brought in to give some guidance. Laois was again seen off in the first round of the championship by 4-8 to 1-11. An unfortunate accident to Liam Dunne resulted in his unavailability for the first two matches. A vintage display by Billy Byrne and a highly impressive debut in goal by Kilkenny man, David 'Stoney' Burke, were the highlights of Wexford's display. For some time past, the Wexford team, had been experiencing problems filling the space between the posts. The rotund figure of Burke seemed to be the answer and his display was highly impressive. In the semi-final Dublin went under by 3-16 to 3-8, thus setting up a Leinster final meeting with Kilkenny. Martin Storey, George O'Connor, Larry O'Gorman and Stoney Burke were greatly to the fore against the Metropolitans. Although the team had not been overly impressive in these two matches, there were slight signs that a change was taking place in general play. They showed more inclination to hit low crosses and let the ball do the work. Despite the fact that the team had no proven record, unaccountably, there was a growing feeling in the county that 1992 was to be the year in which the hoodo would end. The presence of Cyril Farrell, and the accompanying hype, may have had much to do with this. This hype was not confined to Wexford people. Even the national newspapers seemed to think that this was to be Wexford's year. The supporters threw caution to the winds and journeyed, in their thousands, to Carlow and Croke Park, to see the team triumph over Laois and Dublin. There was a promise of a new approach by this Farrell-coached, Wexford team which, so often in the past, had squandered chances like a Saudi prince at the gaming tables.

A Crushing Reversal

The 1992 Leinster final was, once again, a huge disappointment for Wexford. All the old bad habits resurfaced. The team failed miserably to rise to the occasion and was well beaten in all sectors of the field. Despite the team being unimpressive against Laois and Dublin, the supporters had fooled themselves into thinking that the Wexford players were keeping their best form for Kilkenny. They should have realised that what they had witnessed, in the earlier rounds, was their best form. Eamonn Morrissey was given the freedom of Croke Park and destroyed Wexford. Three Wexford players were booked and two more, Larry O'Gorman and Dermot Prendergast were sent to the line. Only the recalled Eamonn Cleary hurled to form and gave Kilkenny centre-back, Pat O'Neill, his toughest game of the championship. Wexford hit 18 wides to Kilkenny's 11. This indeed was the same old story, with hardly a change in the script. It was like watching a movie which one had seen again and again. A few of the actors had changed but the script and the plot was so familiar. The final result was obvious to all, even before half-time. One could only sit back and admire the skill, the craft and the intelligence of the Noresiders, who won by 3-16 to 2-9. They were superior in almost every position on the field and the familiar Kilkenny characteristic of never losing possession except to a team-mate was very much in evidence. Cyril Farrell's presence in the Wexford camp was an extra motivating influence for Kilkenny. They had old scores to settle with the Galway man.

Kilkenny went on to win another glorious All-Ireland.

Christy Keogh Takes Over Again

Following the 1992 defeat Martin Quigley and his team resigned and were replaced by Christy Keogh as manager. Joining him were the outgoing duo of Dave Berney and Jimmy Furlong, along with Jimmy Prendergast and

Mick Butler. The team had a good run in the League and reached the final stages. In the semi-final Wexford beat Limerick. Newcomer Larry Murphy figured prominently in the side. The League final was fixed for Thurles and once again the Wexford supporters were astounding in their loyalty.

New Talent Filters Through

The long serving players like George O'Connor, Billy Byrne, Eamonn Cleary, Niall McDonald, Tomas Dunne, John O'Connor, Martin Storey and Tom Dempsey were still the backbone of the team.

However new talent had appeared. Liam Dunne made his Wexford debut in 1988 and won All-Star awards in 1990 and 1993. This trio of League finals was to confirm his place amongst the great hurlers of the current game. Sean Flood had first played for Wexford in 1987 and after some periods of uncertainty was now becoming an established member of the team. Ger Cushe of Gorey had come on to the team in 1990 and seemed to be the answer to the full-back position. The tearaway Faythe Harriers man, Larry O'Gorman, had been introduced in 1987 and was a spectacular and skilful wing-back. Larry Murphy of Cloughbawn and Eamonn Scallan of Liam Mellows had both come on to the team in 1993. The selectors were experimenting at centre-forward with James Bolger of Marshalstown. Bolger and Scallan had won All-Ireland Junior hurling honours with Wexford in 1992. It seemed that the dearth of talent evident in the 1980s was at an end. Wexford had a rare Leinster title win in the minor grade in 1985, when they accounted for Kilkenny, before going down to Cork in the All-Ireland decider.

The Real Find

The real find of 1993, however, was Damien Fitzhenry, a young goalkeeper of extraordinary ability and confidence. It was not as if he appeared out of nowhere, having been a star of the Wexford minor team and a brilliant player for his school, FCJ, Bunclody, during the previous few years. But not all under-age stars progress to senior level. Some are tempted by other attractions that present themselves to young men in their late teens, while others are incapable of the continued commitment necessary to make the grade at senior level. 'Fitz' however was of a different breed. He had a superb pedigree, as the youngest of the famed Fitzhenry Clan of Curraduff, near Kiltealy. Here, beneath the dark rolling Blackstairs ten boys and five girls were born to Nancy and Mark Fitzhenry. The girls were hugely involved in camogie. The boys formed the backbone of the Duffry Rovers senior football team that won an unprecedented seven county titles in a row and, having rested for a year, made it eight in 1994. When Wexford writer, Patrick Kennedy wrote his classical *Evenings at The Duffry*, in the early 1800s, with its simple and effective narrative of local heroes in an older and more gentle age, he could have been writing about the sporting Fitzhenry family from the slopes of Mount Leinster.

From an early age young Damien was always likely to do something spectacular on the GAA field. For many years, Wexford had watched their neighbours, Kilkenny, produce a veritable conveyor line of brilliant net minders. There always seemed to be two or three great Kilkenny goalkeepers competing for the position on their team. All seemed to be made from the same stuff. They were eagle-eyed, sure-footed, arrogant, brave and intelligent. Following the retirement of Pat Nolan, Wexford invariably had problems in finding similarly talented players for the key position between the posts. Immediately on his introduction to the team, in the Hurling League quarter-final against Laois, young Fitzhenry showed all the signs of solving an age-old problem. A great shot stopper, he was cool under pressure and a good enough hurler to plant doubts in the minds of Wexford selectors, as to whether he would be better employed playing outfield. Although not yet 19, it appeared that he was the man for the position, for as long as he wanted it.

1993 – Semple Stadium

The trio of matches against Cork in May 1993, at Semple Stadium, Thurles, proved that this Wexford team was on the verge of winning something big. But, unfortunately, on the verge is where they were to remain for another three heartbreaking years. The first game ended in a draw, Cork 2-11, Wexford 2-11. Cork had lost the 1992 All-Ireland final to Kilkenny and were hungry for success. Their team included the great Brian Corcoran, (Hurler of The Year in 1992), as well as Tom Mulcahy, Kevin Hennessy, Jim Cashman, Pat Hartnett and Teddy McCarthy. Liam Dunne was magnificent in all the games and a number of newspapers, following the series, referred to him as the finest hurler in the country. Larry Murphy, in his second game for the county, showed what he was capable of, with a dashing and fruitful display, in the first game. With 90 seconds to go, he fired over the equalising point. Martin Storey, now established as one of the finest forwards in the game, gave three brilliant displays. Deservedly he won an All-Star Award in 1993. Larry O'Gorman sparkled. Ger Manley gave a great display for Cork, scoring both goals and he was well backed up by Sean McCarthy and Barry Egan. Unfortunately Wexford continued to be profligate in shooting and in the first game, shot thirteen wides to Cork's six. With 45 seconds left in the first game, Wexford were awarded a forty metres free. John O'Connor took it but the ball went wide.

In the second game, played in a downpour, Wexford improved and shot only eleven wides to Cork's six. The scores were level at full time, Cork 0-11, Wexford 1-8, Martin Storey firing over the important point in the last seconds. Extra time failed to separate the teams as they finished Cork 0-18, Wexford 3-9. Wexford led by a point as the end of extra time approached, but Jim Cashman collected a poor clearance and struck for the equaliser.

Despite a great display by Tom Dempsey at centre-field, the third game was a disappointment for Wexford. The teams were level with five minutes to go but a John Fitzgibbon goal for Cork saw the Wexford challenge peter out as Cork went on to win by 3-11 to 1-12. This time Wexford shot fourteen wides to Cork's five. Barry Egan and Ger Manley were to the fore for the Munster men. Cork's sharp-shooter supreme and delicate hurling artist, Tony O'Sullivan, returned to his county colours in this game, having some time earlier announced his retirement.

Wexford Fans Out in Force

The numbers that made the long journey from Wexford to Thurles emphasised, if emphasis was needed, the hunger within the land of the Slaney for hurling prominence. The roads to the Premier County were alive with purple and gold. Despite the defeat, Wexford people took comfort in the fact that their hurlers could live with the best, and reasoned that with a little bit of luck, they could have been League Champions. They knew that this trio of top class matches would hasten the maturity of the young players on the team. In this summation they were probably correct. Among the Wexford substitutes for those games were three men whose names would be heard on future, glorious occasions. They were Billy Byrne of Gorey and the Guiney brothers of Rosslare.

1993 Championship

Thus, the 1993 championship campaign gave much reason for hope. Having disposed of Dublin in the first round by 1-14 to 0-10, an apparently easier than normal passage to the final seemed to be provided by Laois, whose fast-improving team shocked the Slaneysiders before going under by 0-15 to 1-9. Thus, another in the long running saga of Leinster finals against the old and well-respected Noreside neighbours loomed.

The Wexford men were generally unfancied by the national press to beat Kilkenny in 1993. On too many occasions, the national pundits had been let down by the inconsistent Slaneymen. The experience gained in the three match epic against Cork however, was a key element in the great display that the team gave in the Leinster final. Well coached by Christy Keogh and his colleagues, they came out full of passion and fire – elements that had been missing in some of their championship battles in recent years. Wexford were a revelation and for long periods they hurled the All-Ireland champions off the pitch. The match was a delight for neutrals and partisans alike. Supreme skills, lots of passion and death defying bravery from both teams resulted in the hurling match of the year. Although taken aback, Kilkenny, typically, never lost touch and were still in the game at half-time when the scores were Wexford 0-10 Kilkenny 1-3.

A Classic Point

Wexford continued to perform brilliantly and as the seconds ticked away it seemed, at long last, that the Wexford run of defeats was to end. In the Hogan Stand, the exuberant Wexford faithful waited impatiently for the long whistle, ready to invade the pitch and carry their heroes to the winners podium. Alas! they reckoned without the renowned resilience of the fabled cats. Kilkenny were not All-Ireland champions for nothing. What followed was one of the great scores of the game of hurling. Billy Byrne was bearing down on goal when he was hooked and lost the ball to Liam Simpson. The black-and-amber corner-back delivered it to Willie O'Connor. He transferred it quickly and cleverly down the wing to Adrian Ronan. With a Wexford defender breathing down his neck, Ronan looked up and spotted Eamonn Morrissey running out towards the centre-forward position. Expertly, he sent a shoulder-high ball towards Eamonn. Morrissey gathered and with Ger Cushe on top of him and barely a glance at the posts, he sent over the bar for the equaliser. It was a stupendous score, under the utmost pressure, and had all the hallmarks of the legendary craft, skill and brains for which Kilkenny hurlers are, rightly, celebrated. It rocked the Wexford team and followers. No Wexford player had touched the sliotar from the time it was collected by Simpson. The long whistle went on the puck out. Wexford, once again, had missed the boat. The frustration and bewilderment that was etched on the faces of the Wexford supporters as they trekked from Croke Park, was almost tragic. The final score was Kilkenny 2-14, Wexford 1-17.

The Replay

Wexford were well fancied, within the county, for the replay. The national hurling writers felt, however, that Wexford had missed their chance and that Kilkenny would not be caught napping a second time. Their views were only too prophetic. The replay, played in a downpour, featured a Wexford team whose display was unrecognisable from the first match. Wexford had fourteen wides to Kilkenny's three. The final score was Kilkenny 2-12 Wexford 0-11. It was a bad week for feline house pets in Wexford.

1994 – The Nadir

The frustration continued. A bad series of results in the 1993-94 League, with little indication of a change in fortunes, resulted in relegation to Division Two. The 1994 season was the nadir. In the first round Dublin were unlucky not to win as the game ended in a draw, Wexford 3-13 Dublin 2-16. A fracas resulted in the dismissal of George O'Connor and Tom Dempsey. Wexford improved in the replay, and courtesy of a memorable display from Billy Byrne, triumphed by 3-22 to 1-11. Billy had come out of retirement to strengthen the depleted team.

The extra game benefited the Slaneysiders and they played brilliantly against a Laois team that was fancied by many. The final score was 4-24 to 4-6, a couple of the midlanders goals coming as consolations in the last few minutes.

In the Leinster final, Offaly were, once again, the team to beat, having been victorious over All-Ireland champions Kilkenny. Despite the half-time introduction of George O'Connor and a highly effective Tom Dempsey who had been left off the original selection, the Wexford men were not at the races and Offaly won going away by 1-18 to 0-14. Donal Keenan writing in the *Irish Independent* summed it up as follows:

'Offaly, led by Martin Hanamy, bounced onto Croke Park as if it was their natural habitat. The stride was immediately purposeful and the aim was true...With the maximum effort but little fuss, Offaly scored 1-18 yesterday. Wexford matched the effort, but created a lot of fuss about their 14 points and numerous other squandered opportunities'....

Both full-backs Ger Cushe and Kevin Kinahan played superbly and John Troy hit a sublime pass to Billy Dooley for the Offaly goal. The stylish Johnny Dooley scored nine points for Offaly. A 19 year-old, Rory McCarthy, made his championship debut for Wexford in the last few minutes.

The Faithful County went on to win the All-Ireland, when hypnotising Limerick in the last five minutes.

Secondary Schools to the Fore

Hopeful signs were beginning to appear that the long neglect of under-age hurling in Wexford was coming to an end. Higher achievement levels in hurling were evident amongst the county's secondary schools. St Peter's College, the traditional stronghold, was showing signs of an ability to compete again at a high level. The exploits of Enniscorthy CBS and FCJ Bunclody were other hopeful signs. The real breakthrough, however, was made by Good Counsel College in New Ross. Although their team had a fair smattering of Kilkenny boys, the school reached the All-Ireland Colleges final in football and the semi-final in hurling in 1994.

Christy Keogh Resigns

Christy Keogh had given his all for Wexford hurling. Having retired as a player he took over the team management for the 1981 championship. He had further spells in 1984, 1988 and 1993-94. He resigned after the 1994 championship defeat to Offaly.

The queue of potential candidates for the position of manager of the perennial losers of hurling was short. Understandably, many viewed it as a poison chalice. Hard won coaching reputations were not about to be put on the line in the off chance that the continual 'nearly-men of hurling' would finally come good.

Wexford, the lemmings of the hurling world, were back in the doldrums.

Or so it seemed.

Appendix to Chapter 1

The long list of Wexford hurling defeats up to 1994, with only an occasional victory, makes depressing reading, but for the record, it is included below.

All-Ireland Championship

1969	Leinster semi-final	Offaly	5-10	**Wexford**	**3-11**
1970	Leinster final	**Wexford**	**4-16**	Kilkenny	3-14
1971	Leinster final	Kilkenny	6-16	**Wexford**	**3-16** *(had beaten Offaly)*
1972	Leinster final	Kilkenny	6-13	**Wexford**	**6-13**
	replay	Kilkenny	3-16	**Wexford**	**1-14**
1973	Leinster final	Kilkenny	4-22	**Wexford**	**3-15** *(had beaten Offaly)*
1974	Leinster final	Kilkenny	6-13	**Wexford**	**2-24**
1975	Leinster final	Kilkenny	2-20	**Wexford**	**2-14** *(had beaten Offaly)*
1976	Leinster final	**Wexford**	**2-20**	Kilkenny	1–6
1977	Leinster final	**Wexford**	**3-17**	Kilkenny	3-14
1978	Leinster final	Kilkenny	2-16	**Wexford**	**1-16**
1979	Leinster final	Kilkenny	2-21	**Wexford**	**2-17** *(had beaten Offaly)*
1980	Leinster semi-final	Kilkenny	4-18	**Wexford**	**3-16**
1981	Leinster final	Offaly	3-12	**Wexford**	**2-13** *(had beaten Kilkenny)*
1982	First Round	Offaly	2-16	**Wexford**	**3-12**
1983	Leinster semi-final	Kilkenny	5-13	**Wexford**	**3-15**
1984	Leinster final	Offaly	1-15	**Wexford**	**2-11** *(had beaten Kilkenny)*
1985	Leinster semi-final	Laois	1-18	**Wexford**	**2-13**
1986	First Round	Kilkenny	1-21	**Wexford**	**0-18**
1987	Leinster semi-final	Kilkenny	3-20	**Wexford**	**2-15**
1988	Leinster final	Offaly	3-12	**Wexford**	**1-14** *(had beaten Kilkenny)*
1989	Leinster semi-final	Kilkenny	4-15	**Wexford**	**2-18**
1990	Leinster semi-final	Dublin	2-16	**Wexford**	**1-17**
1991	Leinster semi-final	Kilkenny	2–9	**Wexford**	**0-13**
1992	Leinster final	Kilkenny	3-16	**Wexford**	**2–9**
1993	Leinster final	Kilkenny	2-14	**Wexford**	**1-17**
	replay	Kilkenny	2-12	**Wexford**	**0-11**
1994	Leinster final	Offaly	1-18	**Wexford**	**0-14**

League Finals and Semi-Finals

1973	League final	**Wexford**	**4-13**	Limerick	3-7
1982	League final	Kilkenny	2-14	**Wexford**	**1-11**
1983	League semi-final	Limerick	3-10	**Wexford**	**2–6**
1984	League final	Limerick	3-15	**Wexford**	**1-9**
1986	League semi-final	Galway	3-10	**Wexford**	**1-16**
	replay	Galway	3-11	**Wexford**	**2-5**
1988	League semi-final	Offaly	2-16	**Wexford**	**3-11**
1990	League final	Kilkenny	3-12	**Wexford**	**1-10**
1991	League final	Offaly	2–6	**Wexford**	**0-10**
1993	League final	Cork	2-11	**Wexford**	**2-11**
	replay	Cork	0-18	**Wexford**	**3-9**
	replay	Cork	3-11	**Wexford**	**1-12**

∞ CHAPTER 2 ∞

'WHAT THE HELL DOES HE KNOW ABOUT HURLING'?

The Under-Age Coach

As the long-suffering Wexford supporters trudged wearily from Croke Park following the 1994 defeat by Offaly, one man picked his way despondently among them. Unlike many of his fellow countrymen he had not removed the outward signs of his county allegiance. The cherished purple and gold colours were not about to be discarded in a Dublin gutter. The latest in the long procession of reversals for the county team, while utterly disappointing, did not diminish his enthusiasm for the game. The following Monday would see him continuing, resolutely, to impart his knowledge of hurling to the children of his area. Far from the hysteria and pomp of Croke Park the innocent enthusiasm of a small, but willing group of youngsters would help him to forget the latest in a lengthy and seemingly endless chapter of disappointments.

His romance for the game was not of recent vintage. It was not a flickering flame, rekindled once yearly, by the splendour of great All-Ireland occasions. And it was not likely to be extinguished, even by forty years of defeat at county senior level.

He was one of the small number of hurling men who coached at schoolboy level, purely for the love of the game. Almost to a man, they had played the game themselves, for as long as they were able. When the stiffening of limbs and the creaking of joints dissuaded them from continuing to participate at competitive level they continued their involvement by passing on the vast store of expertise to those who were willing to listen. There were others throughout the towns and villages of County Wexford. Mostly unheralded, they were remembered only by the boys who passed through their hands, accruing the basic skills, the proper grip, the correct stance, self protection under a dropping ball and all the little touches that are part of the make-up of a successful hurler. Their names do not figure in the build up to major championship matches.

Rarely are they asked for their opinions by the sports writers of the day. They seldom figure prominently in the pages of big match day programmes – except in the profiles of well known senior players. Their names regularly appear, hidden away in the small print, in answer to the question 'Who introduced you to the game of hurling?' The under-age coach is not involved in hurling for glory – or reward. At least not of a pecuniary kind. Their motivation is a stubborn belief that an upswing in the fortunes of the county's senior teams would only come about by a long term plan. The instilling, by proper coaching methods, of the basic skills. Without pomp or written agenda these men were implementing that plan.

One of them lived in Rosslare. His name was Liam Griffin.

His Family Background

He was born in Rosslare in 1946. His father Mick, one of a family of ten, was born in Carrowmere, near Maurices Mills, close to the town of Ennistymon in County Clare. A member of the Garda Siochana he had moved to Rosslare in the late 1930s. Mick Griffin was a big, warm, open man who wore his heart on his sleeve and invariably spoke his mind without regard to the consequences. Liam's mother Jenny, nee Hall, was born in Ballygarrett, but her family roots are in Boolavogue. The Halls owned and occupied the house in Boolavogue which incorporated part of an older room in which a young curate partook of daily breakfast in Wexford's cataclysmic year of 1798. His name was Fr John Murphy.

Liam Griffin is very proud of his pedigree and loves all things Wexford. Questions and doubts, raised by others, in relation to courage, lineage, or the quality of Wexford's bloodlines are apt to send the Rosslare man into a seething rage. He is related, through his mother, to many who have played notables parts on the hurling fields of Wexford. Among his cousins are the legendary Tony Doran and his brother Colm and Pat and John Nolan, all of them All-Ireland senior hurling medal holders with Wexford. Pat Nolan's three winners medals were won as a goalkeeper in 1968, 1960 and as a sub in 1956. John Nolan was the man whose name was on everybody's lips on the approach to the 1960 All-Ireland. Not only did he make his senior inter-county debut on All-Ireland final day, but he was picked at left half-back, thus given the onerous task of holding in check that prince of hurlers, the mercurial Jimmy Doyle. It was a sensational decision by the Wexford selectors and was the talk of the hurling world. Most pundits doubted if Nolan was up to the task. But then most pundits had never seen him hurling. As it turned out he was more than capable of the allotted marking job and was one of the star performers in a remarkable Wexford victory. Without ever employing foul tactics he outhurled the Tipperary man.

Formative Years

Growing up in Rosslare in the 1950s, at a time when his beloved Wexford was pre-eminent in hurling, it was natural for the young Liam to aspire to fame on the hurling fields. His days were invariably spent on endless games of hurling on any patch of grass or vacant site which he and his pals encountered. He was rarely to be seen without his hurl and his activities resulted in many a windfall for the local glaziers. When his primary schooling was completed, Liam went as a boarder to De La Salle College in Waterford. He remembers, on his first day at that school, strolling arrogantly through the gates with his hurl in a prominently contrived position. He felt that he could afford to be pretentious, as his county were the 'top dogs' in the hurling world in the 1950s and the day before he first entered boarding school, had beaten Tipperary in the 1960 All-Ireland.

He developed into a good athlete. He became a fine middle distance runner specialising in the 880 yards and the mile. His real love, naturally, was hurling. De La Salle, however, was more famous for its prominence in Gaelic football. Liam excelled here also and won two Munster Colleges medals in the mid 1960s. He captained and played right half-forward on the hurling team that lost the Harty Cup final to Limerick CBS, whose star player was Eamonn Grimes. Liam's leadership qualities were spotted by the school authorities and he was made school captain.

Career Training

Following a period training at Shannon College of Hotel Management he went to Switzerland to train with the famous Movenpick Group. While working in the shadows of the snow-capped Alps he continued to puck a ball, on any available patch of bare grass. The Swiss suspected that he was deranged. He travelled back to New York, on a few occasions, to play for the Clare club, in that city, at weekends. These trips have now become the stuff of legend. His departure through Zurich airport, armed with what security staff saw as a dangerous looking ash weapon, shaped suspiciously like a rifle, caused hilarious delays. The eloquent Griffin lectured the cosmopolitan personnel of the airport on the merits of this game of the Gods. When he returned, usually a day or two later, sometime showing the bloody effects of a tough New York club game, the security staff were convinced that he was some kind of eccentric international terrorist. His bloodied photo, complete with ash weaponry, is probably still buried somewhere deep within the files of Interpol.

Personality

Liam is outgoing, passionate, animated, emotional and supremely enthusiastic. He hates injustice and is good-natured. On occasion he can be as innocent as a child. He is forward thinking and inspires tremendous loyalty from his staff. He sees the potential in people and gives great leeway to his managers. He approaches every task with the same enthusiasm and the equally unbridled energy and single-mindedness. This quality can make him impatient with others who seem less committed to the job in hand. He can accept the individual who doesn't know and who says so, but abhors the type who doesn't know and thinks that he does. He makes little allowance for people with a laid back or casual attitude. A nonchalant or half-hearted approach is anathema to him. He sees no problems – only solutions. Those who verbalise their uncertainties are often steamrolled into submission.

His Verbosity

A conversation with the Rosslare man is likely to be one-sided. This has more to do with his quick brain and constant stream of sentences than to his inability to listen. Underlying this is a consistent ability to take on board the views of others, especially when he believes that those views are given from experience. His speaking prowess is of legendary proportions. Unlike Mark Twain, who claimed, 'It usually takes me more than three weeks to prepare a good impromptu speech', Liam rarely devises a script. He stands up and turns on a verbal tap. The key to understanding Griffin's wordiness is the realisation that the conduit to this tap leads straight to his heart. The results are always interesting and often extremely memorable. Words tumble from his lips like a river in spate. He can explode when his spirit is moved. To say that he can get carried away is like saying that it can be cold at the North Pole. When the torrents begin to flow he is often poetic, moving and inspiringly touching. At other times he seems to turn into the reincarnation of an old-fashioned preacher of the American deep south. On these occasions, his rhetoric can be excessive and occasionally, he is liable to antagonise. Neither does Liam always stick to the point. He can branch off suddenly into a tirade against South American military juntas, the bureaucracy and inefficiency of civil service mandarins or the scandal of the destruction of rain forests. If he decides to tongue-lash an unfortunate individual, it is an experience that his target is unlikely to come through without short-term damage. In GAA circles there are a few who have been subjected to these waterfalls of withering put-downs.

Returns to Ireland

Following a short period training in North Wales, he returned to Ireland, in the early 1970s and went to work for Intercontinental Hotels. In 1960, his family had bought the old Pier Hotel in Rosslare, which had been set up in 1906 to cater for the little groups that commenced to use the burgeoning new port in the village. In the 1920s Sean McBride and Eamon de Valera had been secreted away here, for a time, before their departure for England.

In 1974 Liam returned to Rosslare and set out to run the Pier Hotel.

Marriage and Family

In 1972 Liam married a Wexford girl, Mary Lambert. The couple have four sons. 23 year-old Michael is studying hotel management at Shannon, 19 year-old Niall is carving out a successful equestrian career, 16 year-old Liam Anthony is a secondary student in St Peter's, in Wexford and nine year-old Rory attends Kilrane National School.

Expansion of Hotel Business

Liam set about building up the business. He became involved in the local Rosslare Development Committee, which had been set up to assist in the creation of proper infrastructure for the fast growing 'Gateway To Europe'. The old Pier Hotel was revamped and turned into a modern hotel complex, renamed Hotel Rosslare. When Hotel Rosslare became well established he began to look further afield.

With a partner, Liam Curtin, he bought the old Rosehill Hotel in Kilkenny. Following a refurbishment job it was opened as Hotel Kilkenny. The Kilkenny people became familiar with Liam and his passion for hurling but they felt that his confidence in the renewal of Wexford hurling was misplaced. In the early days he had, in the hotel, a 'Sporting Bar' which was festooned with every kind of feline figure that could be found. Black and amber cats, white cats, green cats and now and again, a purple and gold cat. Images of Kilkenny hurling heroes of old stood side by side with their Wexford counterparts. Tributes to Lory Meagher and Ollie Walsh balanced others in honour of Nick Rackard or Christy Ring. Kilkenny people even took it in good part when Griffin unveiled his personal favourite. It was a dramatic photo of a Nick Rackard twenty-one yards free, against Kilkenny, taken from behind Ollie Walsh's goal. Six Kilkenny heads are turned, with expressions of horror and consternation captured for infinity, as they watch the ball hit the back of the net. Underneath is the caption 'The Only Way to Have Kilkenny Men'.

He showed his generosity when, in the Winter of 1995-96, the gym in Hotel Kilkenny was made available at no cost, to injured Kilkenny hurler Liam Simpson to help him recover from injury and be available to face Wexford in the first round of the 1996 championship.

Later, together with his good friend, Tom Noonan of Noonan Construction, with whom he already had a business relationship, Liam purchased an hotel on the banks of the Slaney, in a scenic area, just outside Wexford Town. Following a major refurbishment it now trades as Ferrycarrig Hotel.

Love of Sports

The GAA follower is among the most ecumenical of sporting types. The typical member of the genre attends rugby and soccer internationals at Lansdowne Road, is regularly seen at Fairyhouse, Leopardstown and Shelbourne Park and avidly follows all sports on TV. The same can not be said for other sporting followers who, almost exclusively, confine themselves to the attractions of their own sport. Within the GAA there are two types. Those who like 'the games' and those who love hurling. And never the twain shall meet. Hurling followers are a breed apart. The hurling man, while ecumenical in his sporting outlook, reserves his passion and his emotion for the game that he considers to be the greatest field game in the world. Griffin is of this ilk, while still capable of travelling vast distances to view other sports. Gaelic Football is grudgingly tolerated. Tom Humphries, writing in *The Irish Times*, admirably reflects this view:

'As spectacles, the qualitative differences between football and hurling are more than just illusory. Hurling is trailed as a joyful atavistic expression of our native culture. Football, well, roll up folks for live coverage of the pullers and draggers' big day out.'

Liam is as enthusiastic in Lansdowne Road at Ireland's rugby internationals as he is at Hickstead for the equine competitions. Wembley, Cardiff Arms Park and Stuttgart also figured on his sporting itinerary. That hurling was, and is, his real sporting passion, however, was never in doubt. This was borne out when he accosted another Wexford man, as they left the stadium in Stuggart, following the Euro '88 match in which Ray Houghton scored the dramatic winner against England. 'You didn't, by any chance, hear who won between Rosslare and the Harriers in the District Junior 'B' hurling match?' he asked his startled fellow countyman.

Sporting Prowess

Before his nineteenth birthday, Griffin had played all grades of hurling and football for Wexford, except senior. He played minor football for the county and then was part of the Wexford panel that brought an All-Ireland under-21 hurling title to Wexford in 1965. A fellow player on that team was Seamus Barron, who was later to be asked, by Liam, to assist with the senior hurlers.

Following his move to Clare he joined the Newmarket-On-Fergus club, with whom he won an under-21 Championship and two Clare senior hurling titles. He played in Munster under-21 hurling and football finals for Clare and was selected for the Clare senior hurling team. In the National Hurling League of 1967-68 a good Clare team reached the semi-final.

Griffin was one of their star performers. Kilkenny finally beat them after two drawn games in the semi-final. The great Kilkenny corner-back, Jim Treacy, was his direct opponent in some of these games. John D. Hickey of the *Irish Independent* testified that the young Rosslare man had the better of the encounters. In the first round of the 1968 Munster Championship, Clare met Waterford. Griffin contributed 1-2 as the Banner men advanced to the next round. It marked the end of Griffin's intercounty career. It was at this point that his hotel training took him to Switzerland. As he tells it 'I twinkled like a star, as an intercounty hurler, but I was finished by the time I reached 21'.

Unfulfilled Ambitions

He refers to this intensive training period spent preparing him for a life in the hotel and tourist industry as 'his lost hurling years'. These years are of major significance in understanding the intensity with which he approached the management and coaching of teams in later life. Many intercounty players have their hunger for the game well satiated by the time their active playing career comes to an end. A long and auspicious spell of intercounty exposure, dotted with the odd major win, or a brief career marked by All-Ireland success can combine to lessen the burning ambition and hunger for achievement that drive a sportsman. The feeling that there are no further peaks to conquer grows stronger. They have been fulfilled in a sporting sense. With Griffin, the opposite was the case. Not only was he finished at 21, but he had never experienced the highs, in real hurling terms. John Maughan, the Mayo manager, is another example. He retired from playing due to injury at 26, and readily admits that his unfulfilled ambitions as a senior footballer are what fuels his drive as a manager. Maughan, at least, had about six years as a senior player. Griffin had but one year. Therein lies the secret of Griffin's undiminished involvement in hurling. The combination of natural inborn drive and obsessional personality, allied to his deeply felt sense of deprivation for his 'lost hurling years' created, in Griffin, a hungry and formidable force.

Type of Hurler

As a hurler Liam was uncommonly fast and his skill level was well up to intercounty standard. At his peak he weighed a bare 60 kilos. As a schools player he was a phenomenon. As a young upstart, on the Clare senior hurling team, he gave clear evidence that he could be a powerful force at intercounty level. He believed, as a player, that skill should be fostered and was unhappy about the roughhouse tactics employed by some sides. He would be described by knowledgeable figures in the game as 'a dainty hurler' and 'a very good stick man'.

First Experience as a Team Manager

Years later, back in Rosslare, Liam was to resume his GAA career. It also marked his first managerial experience in sport. He trained and played, at centre-forward, on the Rosslare St. Mary's Junior football team that won the county title in 1975. As a result of this success he was asked to train the Wexford District senior football team in 1977. Naturally, they won the county title. His playing career was curtailed by a serious injury, when he lost a kidney following an incident in a football game in 1977. It failed to dim his ardour for hurling and seven years later he embarked on another county championship campaign

Stint in Charge of Wexford Senior Football Team

The position of team manager of the Wexford county senior footballers beckoned, as a result of his success with the Wexford District team. Griffin took the job and following a run of victories over Kilkenny, Carlow, Wicklow, Waterford and Meath were comprehensively beaten in the group semi-final.

A serious clash of personalities caused a rift between Griffin and some of the other selectors. They strongly disagreed with his training methods. They also took exception to his impetuousness during a crucial stage of the Meath game. He found himself incapable of waiting while his colleagues deliberated on some incisive changes that needed to be made on the field. Griffin made the changes himself. Some of his fellow selectors were not amused and he was called to task shortly afterwards. The matter was debated between them. The Rosslare man's legendary verbosity resulted in a lengthy meeting. Griffin wanted to add two players to the panel. At every waking hour he had explored the avenues that his team could take. One of these footballers was an experienced, hard, tough-as-teak performer, who was probably a few years past his best. The other was a dainty, accurate non-physical stylist, who was also a good free-taker. The percentage success rate from frees was low. Both were forwards and Griffin had concluded that one was needed to break the ball and feed the other. He readily admits that he thought that lowly Wexford could readily reach the National football league final. The other selectors probably thought that he was mad. Liam's involvement level, in whatever project he undertook, was so intense, so extreme, that their feelings were somewhat understandable. To be fair to the other selectors, they viewed the position of selector as a part-time occupation. The words 'part-time' are not in Griffin's vocabulary. Everything he does is undertaken with the same missionary zeal and burning intensity.

Griffin Resigns

In the event a very good Laois team won the next game. A second incident spelled the parting of the ways. He was informed by a fellow selector that they intended to approach the Football Board with a proposition to bring in Joe Lennon, the famous Down coach, to assist with preparations for the championship. Griffin strenuously objected, on the justifiable grounds that it would undermine his position. He told them that if they got it passed, he would resign. The Football Board were not made aware of his threat and passed the motion. When Griffin resigned, the football board attempted to rescind the motion, but it was too late. Griffin had had enough of interference and petty GAA politics and attempts to persuade him to reconsider his decision proved fruitless.

Aftermath of Resignation

Griffin had made a huge impression on the members of the Wexford football team. Tom Foley, a member of that team and now a doctor in Carlow, looks back on the era with nostalgia and a lasting appreciation of Griffin. 'They were a fine bunch of players who had come through the under-age game together. Liam Griffin inspired loyalty and he was innovative in his approach.' he said. 'Lasting friendships that continue to this day, were forged. Tactically, he was also excellent and the team appeared to be going places.'

Following his resignation, the players approached Griffin and told him that they were going to strike. Griffin was flattered but persuaded them to drop the idea. The resignation made the newspapers, but was forgotten within a few weeks. Although the footballers themselves were unhappy, the concept of player power had not yet appeared and the whole episode passed into history. Suggestions were aired by some, to the effect that Griffin was in it for the money and was now returning to his Rosslare hotel where the pickings were richer. The begrudgers had a field day. It was, for Liam, a lesson well learned. He promised himself that if he ever again got involved at county level, he would firstly make damn certain, that he would have absolute control over the selection of his management team.

Under-Age Involvement

Following a losing Leinster senior hurling championship outing to Kilkenny in the early 1980s, Liam returned to Rosslare and put up a sign which read 'Hurling in the field tomorrow evening. All are welcome'. He felt that too many were talking about the under-age neglect in County Wexford and not enough were taking action. A small group turned up. Among them were Dave and Rod Guiney. At this time there was no hurling, of any consequence, in Rosslare, despite the best efforts of local man, Bob Lambert, who was also doing good work with the local footballers.

Liam became heavily involved in under-age coaching in 1983. With other committed people like Tony Kehoe, Margaret Doyle, Jimmy Donoghue, Noel Hayes, Noel Goff, Jim Sweeney, Joe Murphy, Gerry Wickham and Jim Doyle, sessions were run for the children of the Rosslare district and surrounding areas. By 1984, Rosslare were good enough to win the county Junior B Hurling title, with Griffin playing centre-forward, at the age of 38 and minus a kidney. Griffin persuaded such notables as Noel Skeehan, Michael O'Grady, Mick Kinsella and Brendan O'Sullivan to attend coaching sessions in Rosslare.

Adult and under-age hurling was now established in a club and in a village where the game had previously been dormant for decades.

Liam, who was never backward in voicing his beliefs in relation to the problems that faced hurling in the county, undoubtedly ruffled some feathers.

Rejected as Manager of the Minor Hurlers

Liam was sounded out a few times about whether he would consider taking the position of manager of the Wexford senior hurlers, but always declined, feeling that the timing was not appropriate. He had always wanted to begin at county level, through an under-age involvement. This, he felt, would enable him to oversee the continuing development of individual young hurlers. He ran for the position of manager of the Wexford minor hurling team for the 1994 season. He indicated that he knew the capability of every minor hurler in Wexford. Few doubted him, but he failed to secure the position. It went instead to his friend, Willie Carley. The following morning Griffin warmly congratulated him.

The Search for a Manager

Meanwhile the search for a manager to take over from Christy Keogh began. Groups of County Board officials gathered, behind closed doors, debating the possible solutions to the dilemma. A sub-committee was appointed. Where, in former years, there would have been a parliament of candidates, now the volunteers were few. It was like asking someone to lead The Charge of The Light Brigade. Whoever took on the job would not have to face a battery of guns, but he would be subjected to the rant of the countless 'hurlers on the ditch', a breed which Wexford has in abundance. His credentials would be scrutinised more closely than a competitor in the Mr Universe contest. The length of time served on various committees would be measured against others and judgements would be made accordingly. His experience, expertise, leadership qualities and previous record would be put under the microscope. He would be inundated with crackpot suggestions, herbal remedies and secret solutions. Recommendations and proposals would flow from every quarter. Some of these would come from people who were so out of touch that they had not adjusted to the fact that hurling was no longer played as 21 aside. He would, from time to time, find himself in grave physical danger from sober but deranged blockheads.

The job of a county hurling manager is not for the fainthearted.

The job of managing the Wexford hurling team, as the Autumn of 1994 loomed, seemed designed strictly for the foolhardy and the reckless. Bungee jumping or skydiving seemed risk-free in comparison.

National Interest

In hurling circles, throughout the country there was great interest in Wexford's dilemma. Advice came from all quarters. Every amateur critic from Antrim to West Cork had his own solution to the Model County's hurling woes. Former Offaly manager, Dermot Healy, said that the whole approach in the county, from club level up, must be changed – and even refereeing had to be brought into it. 'Skill is not winning out in their club games – there's a lot of dirt', he commented perceptively. 'Players can't switch from one style to the other when they move up to intercounty.' 'They will have to draft in referees and show them how to referee,' he added. Healy's name was one of those that was being bandied about as a possible candidate. His comments were not well received in Wexford, where it was perceived that club hurling in Offaly was much tougher than its Wexford counterpart. The names of other prominent Wexford ex-intercounty men were also mentioned as probable candidates. None of these were ever approached officially and at least one of them was very annoyed that his name was being used.

Deliberations of the Subcommittee

The sub-committee that sat down to consider the difficult issue of finding a saviour for Wexford hurling was made up of committed hurling people. They had but one task. That task was performed well. So well, that the short-lived committee should be remembered as the most successful ever in the history of Wexford hurling. They did not stick with the usual formula. They did something very unexpected. Former county hurler and one time All-Star, John Quigley, was one of the members of that sub-committee. He and his colleagues felt that new blood had to be introduced at management level. All the usual formulae had been tried. It was time for something different. Dozens of names were put forward. Among them were many high profile hurling managers from other counties. Former players, club coaches, former intercounty managers, both hurling and football were all considered. All were rejected as being from the same hurling culture strain – an area that had failed for 28 years. A list was finalised. Then it was narrowed down.

It finally contained but one name.

The Approach to Liam Griffin

Some of the committee were adamant that the solution to Wexford hurling problems lay in the person of a hitherto unknown (in hurling circles) Rosslare hotelier, Liam Griffin. Although he had never coached at any grade above junior hurling level, he was known to them as a man of immense capability. After much debate the Rosslare man was asked to attend an interview. It was a decision that was to have the most profound effect on the fortunes of Wexford hurling.

From that moment on Griffin was a certainty to get the job – if he decided to take it.

Interviewing the Rosslare man is a singular experience. With the sartorial elegance of a Cary Grant and the enthusiasm of first night bridegroom, Griffin exploded into the room like a chattering cyclone. The committee hardly got a word in, as the loquacious hotelier outlined in detail his views on how to end the famine.

Any 'doubting Thomases' were immediately won over. No further candidates were interviewed. The committee queried him on issues like training techniques, discipline and tactics. His answers were all that they wanted to hear. Although no definite decisions were made on that evening, the Rosslare man became the favourite to succeed to the job. Firstly, he requested time to discuss the matter with his family. It was by no means definite that Liam himself wanted, or would accept, the position. He astounded the sub-committee, early on in the discussions, by advising them – 'If I were in your shoes, I would not appoint me. I'm a loose cannon. But I will help you to find somebody else'. He felt strongly that things should never have progressed to the stage where he was being offered the position. 'Where are all the fellows that have graced Croke Park? Where are they now when their county needs them? Why have they funked it?', he demanded. He said that it was a black day for hurling in Wexford when all those individuals stayed trembling in the background, traumatised into helplessness by the fear of more failure.

But he knew that the opportunity might never again come his way. He was also keenly aware that he could never again pontificate about the ills of Wexford hurling if he was seen to turn down the most influential hurling job in the county. For many years he had been an outspoken critic of the lack of input into coaching and under-age activities. He was the current chairman of the Wexford Coaching Committee. From podium and platform he had preached the gospel of resurrecting the fortunes of the senior team. 'We are only paying lip service to hurling', he had thundered.

He is also very strongly opposed to what he calls the 'mercenary managers'. These are the high profile hurling coaches, from outside Wexford, who in Griffin's estimation sell their services to the highest bidder. While he has no difficulty with fair expenses, he abhors the practice of paying large sums of money to these practioners. He believes in the pure amateur ethic and the voluntary character of the game, and is far from happy about the activities of these migratory hurling tutors. One could well be appointed to the Wexford job. He did not want this to happen.

It was time to put up or shut up.

He had also presented the sub-committee with other problems. If he decided to take the job he was insisting on a major input into the appointment of his backup team and the complete say in all matters pertaining to team affairs and selection.

The sub-committee waited for his answer in great anticipation. They knew that they also were putting their collective heads on the block. Some of the small minds which inhabit the corridors of power in GAA land would be less than enamoured with their choice. Griffin's appointment would not be received with anything approaching total acclaim in Wexford hurling circles. After all he was an unknown under-age coach. And he was from a mere, less than high profile, junior club. His installation in the exalted position of Wexford hurling team manager would not go down well among the elite backroom teams of the senior hurling clubs of the county.

The most likely reaction to the selection of Griffin would be, 'What the Hell does he know about hurling?'

Quite a bit, as it turned out.

Griffin Accepts the Post

Griffin hurried home to discuss the matter with his wife and family. He knew what they would be subjected to. He described what lay in store and they were taken aback. Insults, jealousy, questioning of his pedigree, hate mail and abusive phone calls were some of the hazards that he outlined. The family sat down together. Mary, his wife, and the older boys probably reasoned that he would be frustrated and very hard to live with, if someone else took the job and Wexford continued to get beaten. They felt that he had to get it out of his system, once and for all. They advised him to accept. He then had consultations with the staff in his hotels and found support and encouragement also coming from that area. A few days later Liam Griffin, happy in the knowledge that he had the support and encouragement of Mary, his family and his staff, indicated to the sub-committee, his willingness to accede to the top position in Wexford hurling. It was for a three-year term, subject to ratification every twelve months.

It was Monday the 12 September 1994.

His Backroom Team

As a successful businessman, Griffin knew that his backup team was highly important. He was not about to have one foisted upon him. He debated and argued the point tenaciously and eloquently. The sub-committee finally came around to his way of thinking. Although they would not have been the personal choices of some of the sub committee, the men proposed by Liam as his backup team were sanctioned. He selected two men from the under-age game. None had a high profile. Because of their unselfish involvement in this grade Griffin knew that they were completely genuine and not in it for the glory.

If Griffin was a surprise to the hurling cognoscenti of the county, then so was his backup team.

Rory Kinsella

Rory Kinsella was born in Gorey in 1954. His brothers, Sean and Mick are former intercounty hurlers. Mick is the current County Wexford GAA secretary. Rory attended secondary school at Gorey CBS and like his brother Sean, had immense skill as a hurler. He played for Wexford over a six or seven-year period and was part of the team that lost the crucial 1974 Leinster final to Kilkenny. He came on as a sub in the second half of that game, scoring 1-1 and his display posed questions as to why he was not on from the beginning. An early advocate of better training regimes he was uncommonly fast on the hurling field. Like Liam Griffin and Seamus Barron, Rory, in his playing career, was stylish and skilful and not an adherent of the 'up and at them' brand of hurling. He was no longer speedy when he won an Intermediate hurling title with Bunclody in 1993, but was still a vital part of that team, which included a young man named Colm Kehoe. After a spell teaching at St Aidan's in Dublin he moved to FCJ Bunclody, where he teaches history, geography and PE. He has been closely involved with the success of that school in camogie, hurling and football. 28 Leinster titles have come their way. Very highly regarded in GAA coaching circles, he is highly meticulous and studies opposing teams in great detail before games. A thinking man, the difficult skill of bringing a player to his peak on the important day is one which has occupied many of Rory's hours. He is married to Gerry, also a PE teacher in FCJ, and they have two sons, Ronan and Conor.

Seamus Barron

Seamus Barron is a garage proprietor in Rathnure. The same age as Griffin, he has been involved in hurling all his life. He won All-Ireland medals with Wexford as full-forward on the winning minor team in 1963, at left half-forward on the under-21 in 1965 and as a senior substitute in 1968. As a hurler he was very skilled but not overly aggressive. A bad knee injury curtailed his senior career. He had the misfortune to fall seriously ill in 1995. A heart by-pass followed but he returned to the fray in 1996. The late Syl Barron, who was a selector on the winning Leinster title sides of 1976 and 1977 was his brother. He is married to Anne and they have two sons, Barry and Shane, and one daughter, Mairead. He spent short spells in charge at senior hurling level, at his club, Rathnure, but his real love is coaching young hurlers. On the under-age sidelines of the county he frequently came into contact with Griffin.

The Rest of the Backroom Team

Sean Collier was born in Killiane, Drinagh in 1970 and went to school in Piercestown. He was never seriously into hurling or football, rather he took up boxing when he was 21. He boxed at intermediate level for four years before progressing on to become a full Irish international. Liam Griffin asked him to become the team's masseur in 1995 and he graduated from there to becoming central in the physical preparation of the side. He supervised much of the Winter work, conducted twice weekly, which the team undertook at Dominic Kiernan's gym in Wexford.

John O'Leary, who was to become the mysterious 'Shadowy Figure in The Stand' in the 1996 championship campaign is a native of Gorey. A Wexford town based solicitor, his passion is hurling. He played a large part by his astute summing up of on field activities from his 'crow's nest' in the stands, relaying the information constantly, by mobile phone, to the dugout. His contribution did not end there. Griffin credits O'Leary with 'keeping me sane by his balanced, neutral and optimistic outlook when things looked dark and unpromising'. 'A man like O'Leary would never have been allowed to make a contribution to Wexford hurling under any other regime'. John shuns publicity and remarkably, succeeded in keeping his name and his important contribution, out of the newspapers.

Dr Stephen Bowe looked after the medical needs of the team and has wide experience in dealing with on-field injuries.

Low Profile

Griffin's personality and expressive behaviour was in sharp contrast to the disposition of his backroom team. They were quiet and restrained. They were also knowledgeable in their own disciplines and at all times supportive of the manager. They had no wish to be quoted in the sports pages. Nor did they care to see their profiles appear. For a long time their wishes were granted.

They were not to know, however, that the events that were to unfold in the near future were to place them, in hurling terms, on the national stage.

∞ CHAPTER 3 ∞

A Tough Baptism

First Meeting with the Players

Anyone from the business world who gets heavily involved in active sports management runs the risk of having their motives questioned by the all too prevalent begrudgers of Irish life. There is an underlying suspicion, in the minds of a minority, that monetary gain is the spur. This minority see it as a way for the individual to increase his profile and his profits. This suspicion would rarely be voiced. Nevertheless, it would circulate, just below the surface, in the dressing rooms and social gatherings. A cursory examination of the reality would show that a personal voluntary involvement in sports management is a costly business for the individual. It certainly was in the case of Liam Griffin. As the managing director of a busy hotel group, time was money. He is not the first business man to have his motives questioned. Those who had first-hand experience of his under-age involvement knew that he was in it for the love of the game. These people were in the majority. A small minority, however, had suspicions and hinted as such when there were willing ears to listen. A few of the players, while realising that the new man had hardly built a hotel group on the back of the GAA, had heard this talk, but they wanted to make their own judgements and see the truth for themselves.

Liam invited the players to a meeting at Ferrycarrig Hotel in the Autumn of 1994. This was to be an introductory session. Some knew him already from under-age activities. Others, like George and John O'Connor, were well acquainted with him without any major exposure to his coaching or management techniques. For the majority, however, he was an unknown force. This was their first meeting with the man who was to shape their hurling lives for the foreseeable future. They were a dispirited bunch. A group of players lacking in confidence and well used to defeat. Griffin and his management team had invited every hurler whom they thought would be likely to make a contribution over the coming few years. There were about 62 individuals present.

Following handshakes and some chit-chat Griffin rose and walked towards a flip chart. Dramatically he wrote the word 'honesty'. The reaction he saw was one of general inertia. He outlined his views, gave vent to his hurling philosophy and spoke enthusiastically of his beliefs and the type of methods that he intended to employ to resurrect Wexford hurling from the doldrums. He told them the story of his sojourn in charge of the Wexford football team and highlighted the fact that the players got honest treatment. He named some of the those footballers and pleaded with his listeners to talk to them about their experience under his management. He did not set any targets initially, rather he tried to get to know them and indicated that they would be taking it match by match in the early months of his campaign. He made a strong plea for personal responsibility and asked the panel members to do some extra training on their own over the winter months. He gave them targets to reach while doing this training. He was endeavouring to discover the individual character strengths and weaknesses of each player.

He was slightly disappointed, but not surprised, to see that his charges were less than stimulated.

The Players' Initial Reaction

They had heard much of it before. They had listened to many similar intentions being outlined, at other initial meetings, by previous well meaning managers. All the plans, all the promises that this year would be different, had come to nought. Always it had ended in tears followed by an idle summer watching their May or June conquerors stride to fame and glory. Many of them had all but given up hope of ever experiencing the acclaim of a Leinster triumph or the even greater distinction of a September day in Croke Park. The recriminations that followed their annual exit from the championship were getting harder to take. The vituperative allegations of lack of spirit and fortitude were growing in direct proportion to the impatience of the Wexford followers. The new man was mildly interesting. He seemed more passionate and eloquent, but eloquence never won a hard championship match against Kilkenny or Offaly.

Nevertheless, some of Griffin's agenda had been welcomed by the listeners. Griffin had plans and handouts prepared and John O'Connor felt that he was probably well ahead of the players in his visualisation of the coming events. John also remembers that he talked of protecting the team. This was new. But could he deliver? Martin Storey expected him to be enthusiastic, from previous knowledge of his personality, but felt that the first night ran like most first nights, ebullience and lots of talk from Griffin. Martin remembers saying to one of his team mates, as they drove home to Oulart, 'Lads, this guy really has the gift of the gab and we're going to have very sore ears over the next couple of years'. George O'Connor detected, in the words spoken by Griffin, a welcome respect for the players and their talents. The new manager did not dwell on the past and the failures, but was positive in his assurances that Wexford hurling was equal to the best. With missionary-like zeal he told them that the road ahead could lead to success if desire and application, among the players, was strong enough. It was also obvious to all that he loved hurling, and Wexford hurling in particular, with a passion bordering on fanaticism. Others detected the same signals.

At first Storey and the others didn't know, or really believe that things would change, but within a couple of weeks it was obvious that the Rosslare man was working harder and longer than any previous incumbent of the job. Consequently, many of the panel began to feel obliged to increase their personal contribution to fitness. Others felt that 'The Three Wise Men of Wexford hurling' had succeeded in opening up the minds of many of the players, particularly later on, by their announcement that they were bringing in other successful sportsmen, to talk to them. Most of these people were from non-team disciplines. Swimming coach Ger Doyle; veteran athlete John Joe Doyle; cyclist Pat Whitney; and former Irish boxing champion Billy Walsh; all of whom had achieved success at solitary-type sports, were brought in to pass on their experience. It soon became obvious to the hurlers that they had underestimated the level of training and self-sacrifice that other sportsmen were putting into their game. It opened their eyes. They were impressed by Griffin's ability to take on board the achievements of these other sportsmen. But he seemed to want more than any previous manager in the way of dedication.

He never professed to know all the answers. 'I never want you to think that I know everything', he told the players. 'If I don't know, I'll ask someone who does. The man who knows everything is not born yet, and if he was he would be dangerous.'

John O'Connor noticed that Griffin, initially, spoke the language of business management. While the same values were retained, he detected a subtle change over the coming months. The manager's terminology changed and crystallised into firstly, a vernacular GAA-type expression and finally the language of the hurler.

Larry's Favourite Position

Larry O'Gorman is the 'Joker in the Pack' of the Wexford team. A hurler of scintillating skill and dexterity he had been among the finest exponents of the game in recent years. He has filled many different position with great distinction. Always the life and soul of any gathering of players, he came to play an important part in diffusing the tension in the build-up to big games. Seemingly nerveless, the comical Faythe Harriers man would sing, dance, tell yarns and do impersonations in the team bus on the way to important matches.

The management team, seeing the relaxed atmosphere that he created, encouraged his Chaplinesque activities. At one of the first meetings with the panel Griffin gave them a questionnaire to fill up. It contained queries like 'Where would you prefer to train? How many years have you played senior intercounty hurling? What grades have you played in?' At the bottom was a further query, 'What is your favourite position?' The players answered, 'full-back, centre half-back, wing-forward' as their preferences directed. Larry O'Gorman's answer was short and to the point.

'On Top!'

The management quickly realised that they would have to be much more specific with Larry.

First Interview

In a full page interview, with Alan Aherne, in *The Wexford People* Griffin called for a 'relaxed approach' and outlined his hurling philosophy –

> '*Wexford fans have to be more realistic about what the Senior hurlers can achieve in the short term. The weight of expectation is getting to the players. It's time to relax a little and take a logical look at things. We haven't won a Leinster Minor title since 1985 so we can't expect to be winning all round us at senior level. We need to lighten up and say that we're grafting hard and will get to the top eventually. I don't buy comments like "This is our last chance". We're starting to get much closer, and what the players and management need more than anything is plenty of encouragement from supporters...*
>
> *I've been at the coalface of under-age hurling for a long time, and I feel that this is important. It's very wrong to talk about Senior hurling without mentioning the Minor grade in the same breath... I feel that I can do a reasonable job, and I'm happy that we didn't have to go outside the county. Wexford people have always solved Wexford problems and I don't see why that can't continue... I'm totally opposed to the cult of manager. It's something I don't like, but it's been copied from the soccer scene overseas... If I said we're going to win all around us I would become part of the problem myself. I prefer to keep an open mind...We are in serious competition with other sports. I've no problem with other sports, but I want to see ours up there at the top and competing with our rivals.*'

He went on to comment on his fellow selectors;

> '*Seamus Barron comes from a very well-respected hurling family and we played together in our younger years. I've known him for many years and I respect his opinions on hurling.*

> *Rory Kinsella qualified from Thomond College as a PE teacher and like myself he has gone through a lot of hard graft with younger players... All of us have contributions of a different type to make.'*

Alluding to his predecessors, Michael O'Grady, Martin Quigley, Cyril Farrell and Christy Keogh, he added:

> *'All these people have done a very good job under difficult circumstances. I don't want to use the word "unlucky" but there has only been a stroke of the ball between success and failure on several occasions. They did it for Wexford and they should be respected for that.'*

Search for Players

Griffin and his backup team decided to undertake an exhaustive search for hurling talent in the county. An appeal was made to the hurling public to forward to the selectors the names of any players who showed the potential to make it at senior intercounty level. A very large panel was drawn up. This was the first of many panels that the selectors were to draw up over the next two years. They soon came to the realisation that quality strength in depth was sadly lacking among the hurling population of the county.

Initial Targets

Liam felt, with his good business training, that realistic and achievable targets had to be set for the team. Reaching the League play-offs was the initial goal. They felt very confident of beating teams like Kerry, Carlow, Meath and Down and also fancied their chances against the stronger opponents in their section, Waterford and Dublin. They knew that the last match, against bogey team, Offaly, would be the real test. Promotion to Division One was essential, where Wexford would be competing against the real forces of the hurling world in every match.

The real challenge however, was to remove the culture of defeat. It hung like a millstone around the necks of the players. The Wexford management team were convinced that it was almost 100 per cent psychological. During a trip to America, Griffin had gathered sheaves of material on this aspect of team preparation and was undergoing an intensive study course to increase his already considerable knowledge on the subject. He was well aware of the fundamental principle that a man with a little knowledge of a subject is a dangerous individual and was determined to become expert in matters relating to sporting psychology.

All through the winter campaign, the players were attempting to discover what Griffin and his colleagues wanted. Griffin was not being overly specific. A bit of mental trickery was being used. In order to get them to work on their own he had been purposely vague. Some of the players were now beginning to rise at 7 a.m. and do some running on their own. Further lone stints were being undertaken after work in the evening.

The 1994-95 League Campaign

Facing in to the winter of 1994-95, the new backroom team knew that many of their first choice players would be missing for the League matches. The club championships in the county, both in hurling and football would see to it that they would have to experiment. As usual, the Wexford local championships were behind schedule. The contingent from the county senior champions, Oulart-The-Ballagh, would miss most of the pre-Christmas games, owing to their participation in the All-Ireland club championship. A few of the long serving county hurlers had also made no secret of their dislike for winter hurling. The new management team did not see this as a major drawback, as they intended to give trials to a large variety of hurlers.

League v Kerry

The 1994-95 League campaign opened with a match against Kerry. Most people do not associate the Kingdom with hurling but it was not always so. In Wexford's second appearance in an All-Ireland final, in 1891, the team was beaten by Kerry. It was Kerry's one and only hurling title.

The 1994 Wexford Senior Hurling final was to be played on the following Sunday, thus limiting the selection. Initially it was decided that championship goalkeeper, Damien Fitzhenry was to be given an outfield position in this Winter campaign. This would allow other young goalkeepers to be tried. The 1994 league clash took place in New Ross. Kerry were managed by Wexford-born John Meyler. Although Wexford won by 6-14 to 2-10, the team appeared sluggish.

Carlow, Down and Waterford Matches

Wexford then met Waterford in an Oireachtas quarter-final at Portlaw and were victorious by 1-19 to 3-7. A 19 year-old from Glynn-Barntown, Garry Laffan, made his debut in this game.

This was followed by a second League victory, this time over lowly Carlow by 1-18 to 1-9. Wexford were bad and Carlow – even worse. Clare conceded a walk over in the Oireachtas semi-final and Wexford then faced Down in a League match in Wexford Park. Garry Laffan scored the decisive third goal as Wexford triumphed by 3-10 to 0-12. A new style was being implemented by the backroom team and the players were finding it difficult to adapt.

Wexford were now top of the League and two weeks later faced into their final pre-Christmas League game against Waterford at Dungarvan. This was their biggest test to date. The team did not pass it, going down by a point, 2-12 to 2-13. The pitch was a quagmire and the exchanges often resembled mud-wrestling. Wexford were two points ahead when Brian Greene, the Waterford wing forward, squeezed the ball past Wexford keeper, Archie Scallan, in the last attack of the game. Wexford were, once again, unimpressive and shot far too many wides. While being careful that his team did not see it as a form of excuse, the Wexford manager complained loudly about the heavy nature of the pitch.

Oireachtas Final 1994

Wexford teams have always had a great relationship with the Oireachtas tournament. In the 1950s and 60s it was a major date on the hurling calendar, but by the 1990s had been reduced to a minority competition. Cork were their opponents in the final. The match was played in early December and the Slaneysiders played honestly and effectively and triumphed by 2-7 to 1-8. Although they showed lots of heart, there was no improvement in their shooting, with fourteen wides in the second half alone. 'We made it hard for ourselves', was selector, Rory Kinsella's after-match comment.

So unfamiliar with the concept of winning were the Wexford men, that captain Sean Flood, almost forgot to collect the Oireachtas Cup in the stand after the game. As the newly-married Cloughbawn man left the ground with the handsome trophy, John O'Leary remarked, 'That will look very well on your sideboard, Sean'. 'It would', retorted the diminutive back, 'if I had a sideboard'. The win represented Wexford's first victory in any hurling competition since they last won the beautiful Oireachtas trophy in 1987. Tom Dempsey laughed, 'I've two medals now'. It was a scant haul for a long intercounty career. He had learned to be thankful for small mercies. Griffin had promised the team something if they won. True to his word he entered the winning dressing room after the match and proceeded to spray champagne on the delighted players. For most of them it was a new and exhilarating experience.

Austin Codd's Injury

During the game, Wexford player Austin Codd received a serious injury from a careless and dangerous pull by a Corkman. This Cork player had previously been involved in other incidents with high profile intercounty players. Austin sustained a fractured bone in the forehead with multiple hairline fractures to the skull. He was removed to Ardkeen Hospital and thence to Beaumont. County Secretary, Mick Kinsella was unhappy. 'It was a careless stroke and it shouldn't have happened', he said. Austin later made a complete recovery. Griffin and his colleagues were strongly of the opinion that the Cork player in question should not be allowed to play intercounty hurling again. They can see no place in the game for this kind of activity and feel that the Croke Park authorities have been less than thorough in their attempts to eradicate it. It was a clear indication to all that some of the 'old ways', sometimes adopted by Wexford in the 1980s, with disastrous results, were no longer acceptable to the new management.

Dublin in the Walsh Cup and the League

In February, Liam Dunne of the county champions, Oulart-The-Ballagh, was announced as the new captain of the senior hurling team to take over from Larry Murphy of Cloughbawn.

Dublin were beaten in Belfield, Dublin in the Walsh Cup quarter-final by 1-16 to 3-9. In a very experimental Wexford side, Damien Fitzhenry, at centre-field scored five points and Adrian Fenlon scored the winning point in injury time. A player who was soon to become established made his intercounty debut in this match and gave an outstanding display. He was 21-year-old Colm Kehoe of Bunclody. The Walsh Cup semi-final against Kilkenny followed a few weeks later. Played in Gorey, the game resulted in a draw 0-14 to 2-8. Much to the embarrassment of the Wexford officials and even more to Kilkenny's embarrassment, the Noresiders were disqualified from the Walsh Cup for fielding more than the regulated number of substitutes. The Kilkenny selectors had agreed with Wexford, before this match, that both teams could use more than the usual number of subs. Kilkenny used six and Wexford, fortunately used only three.

Wexford had won the Oireachtas trophy, were in the Walsh Cup final and were well placed in the League with three wins out of four matches. So there was some grounds for optimism. Griffin and his team were happy that winning habits were being formed.

Wexford now faced Dublin, in Swords in their fifth match of the League campaign. Wexford were going well until defensive slackness allowed Dublin to embark on a scoring burst which yielded 2-1 and the Metropolitans triumphed by 2-6 to 0-11. Griffin endeared himself to the players by pushing the blame for the defeat on to himself and his backroom team. 'I will take the responsibility for losing. I know that people will be looking for someone to blame, but the players did their very best. We made a calculated decision to blood new players and we don't regret it in the slightest. The scene is set for our crunch match against Offaly in Wexford Park.' Liam did not mention the forthcoming League game against Meath. Like the rest of the hurling world, he seemed to be taking a win from this outing for granted.

Defeat by Meath

Meath came to Enniscorthy as underdogs even though Offaly had been accounted for in their previous match. After twelve minutes Wexford led by 0-7 to 0-1. At half-time it was Wexford 0-13 Meath 1-6. Meath then began to show that they were no pushovers and grew in confidence. Railway Cup player, Pat Potterton, started to assert himself and with corner-forward, Benny Murray to the fore, Meath ran out winners by 0-16 to 1-16. On the morning of the match, Liam Dunne had travelled back from Kerry, where the Oulart-The-Ballagh players were on a club outing, and he showed the effects of the journey.

The Wexford fans were devastated and found it difficult to accept defeat by a team who had no championship aspirations and whose hurling horizons were significantly lower than Wexford's. Not only had Wexford been beaten, but The Royal County hurlers were clearly the better combination on the day. This defeat was the nadir for Griffin and his team. If Meath had been beaten, the team would have had four wins from six outings and would have been in with a very good chance of promotion to Division One. Now even that was in serious doubt.

Following this game an incident occurred which was to be referred to by Griffin on many occasions in the future. As the Wexford manager headed back to the dressing room he was accosted by group of irate supporters. One of them launched into a string of invective and finished off by spitting, directly into the face, of the Rosslare man.

Griffin later spoke to the press and commented that while he was disappointed for Wexford, he was very glad for Meath. 'They deserved to win and it should give hurling a great boost in The Royal County,' he said. This comment provoked further outrage among the die-hards of Wexford hurling.

The 1994-95 League Match v Offaly

This was a crucial match for Wexford. Because of other results, both Wexford and Offaly had to win this game to qualify for the play-off stages. Unrest was brewing, following the Meath defeat, with *The Wexford People* commenting on 'the loyal supporters growing impatient at the alarming loss of form'.

The game was played at Wexford Park. Offaly were short of their Birr contingent, but otherwise travelled with most of their championship team. Wexford had learned from the previous matches and Damien Fitzhenry reverted to goal. George O'Connor was placed at centre half-back and Diarmuid McDonald of Crossabeg at centre-forward. It was a close game and Offaly held on to win by 0-14 to 0-16. Paul Codd played exceptionally well for Wexford and although performing more as individuals than as a team, showed flashes of good play. Offaly as usual, were constructive and intelligent and deserved to win, with Johnny Dooley hitting ten points. The Wexford backroom team were happy that their lads had stayed with the All-Ireland champions and could have sneaked a win, in the last minute, when a goal was disallowed in questionable circumstances. After the game Griffin gave a TV interview in which he responded to the question, 'Is this a major setback for Wexford?' 'No it's not a major setback, the sun will shine tomorrow... it's not the end of the world', retorted the Wexford manager. A few days later he received a letter from an anonymous 'fan' berating him for 'daring to suggest that the sun will shine tomorrow when he had put the sun out forever on Wexford hurling'. Eamonn Cregan was forthright in his after-match comment to Griffin. 'I think you're mad to take this job. I wouldn't take it for all the tea in China', said the Offaly manger, indicating that he thought the expectations of the Wexford followers were far too high, based on their record.

A Lesson Learned

The Wexford backroom team learned a valuable lesson from this game, one of many that they were to absorb in the coming months. The depressed Wexford fans who trooped from the game were not to know that the infant Wexford management team had gained priceless experience.

The Wexford selectors noticed how the Offaly management team, particularly Eamonn Cregan and Andy Gallagher dominated the sideline. They were everywhere, urging on their players, actively jogging the length of the line to follow play and counteracting any tactical switches made by the Wexford mentors. The Wexford men, who greatly respected their Offaly counterparts, were also surprised to observe that the more active management style of the Offaly men seemed to have an effect that, on occasion, appeared to influence match officials. They felt that many of the referee's decision went against them. Particularly so in the case of Ger Cushe, who although sluggish, was often penalised for his attempts to stop Brendan Kelly, the Offaly full-forward.

They also thought that they detected weaknesses in the Offaly team. They noticed that when their charges followed instructions and followed the game plan, Offaly began to have problems.

It was to be a lesson well learned.

A Biting Comment

Vincent Hogan, in his column on Monday's *Irish Independent* made some biting comments about Wexford's performance:

'Wexford blunder like it is an art-form. Open the door and they'll

clamber towards a window... Something in their bloodlines.

Science doesn't cover the strange queasiness that infects these men in purple and gold. Logic can't define their capacity to tumble...

Hurling with zeal and rhythm they threatened to chase what remains of the All-Ireland champions out of town. But then Offaly stuck their chests out. Dammit, why did they have to do that?

Wexford needed to win, to feel good about themselves far more urgently than Eamonn Cregan's men needed promotion.

But midway through the second-half with danders up and timber flying, something started eating their defiance. Just two points adrift with a harsh wind buffeting them forward, they surrendered their coherence...

If only these men could hurl the full hour like they did the closing, tumultuous seconds. If only pigs had wings...

They battle on because they have to, not because they honestly believe.'

The Wexford selectors were hurt. They felt that Hogan was being unfair. After all, Offaly were the All-Ireland champions and Wexford had held them to two points and could, with luck, have won the game. The comment about bloodlines wounded Griffin deeply. How dare a commentator cast doubts on the valour and fighting spirit of his beloved Wexford! Griffin respects Hogan greatly and has a high regard for his perceptive writing. He also liked him, but was determined that he would make him eat his words.

An Unenviable Record

Historically, this was one of the worst League campaigns in which Wexford had ever been involved. They failed to reach the play-offs. They failed to get promoted. Thus they became the first Wexford hurling team, in the modern era, to fail at the first attempt, to gain promotion from Division Two. Nevertheless, Griffin and his selectors were reasonably happy. Many of their plans were slowly, coming to fruition. A few new players were showing promise and the long-term targets were still achievable.

The 1995 Championship – Westmeath

The Summer of 1995 and the first championship outing against Westmeath was now focusing the collective minds of Wexford's hard-working management team. Four newcomers, Colm Kehoe, Robert Hassey, Michael Jordan and Paul Codd were given their senior championship debut. Ger Cushe was dropped and John O'Connor slotted in at full-back. Adrian Fenlon was a midfield absentee, due to injury. George O'Connor at centre half-back was embarking on his seventeenth championship campaign.

'We are presently working with a panel of 34 players, 18 of whom are under 23 years of age. We are trying to build for the future and supporters will have to realize and accept that.....I am confident that we will beat Westmeath and we will take it from there. We have stepped up training to three nights a week and the lads are getting plenty of practice with the all-county leagues. They look sharp and are confident.'

The match witnessed a Westmeath collapse in the face of a much superior Wexford outfit. It illustrated, yet again, the growing gap between the haves and have-nots of hurling. It was pitiful to observe the enthusiastic but limited Westmeath players play second fiddle in every position of the field. The final score was 6-23 to 1-7. Many of the newcomers to the Wexford team played impressively but the management team were realistic enough to know that the contest did not reflect a fair test of their charges' capabilities.

The Lead up to the Offaly Game

Offaly, the 1994 All-Ireland Champions were the Model Country men's next opponents. The long-disillusioned Wexford supporters had no great expectations for the game. Griffin's enthusiasm and his way with words had won over a few, but many supporters were too prudent to fall into the trap of optimism in any match against the county's bogey team. The game was fixed for the unusual time of 6.15 p.m. at Croke Park, preceded by the clash of Kilkenny and Dublin. It was to be televised live. Wexford had absentees through injury of Adrian Fenlon and Larry O'Gorman and three further players carried minor impairments into the game. Sean Flood, omitted from the original panel, had been recalled and went straight into the team at right half-back. The team, given to the newspapers on the Tuesday before the match, was as follows: D. Fitzhenry, C. Kehoe, J. O'Connor, T. Dunne, S. Flood, G. O'Connor, R. Hassey, L. Dunne, P. Finn, M. Storey, T. Dempsey, R. McCarthy, P. Codd, B. Byrne and L. Murphy.

Griffin and his team were keeping a low profile. They had not had a good League campaign but thought that they had unearthed a few new players who would contribute well to Wexford hurling in the future. In the meantime, the spirit of the squad was good, a good camaraderie existed among the players, improvement was apparent and the long-term plan was still in position.

By Wednesday morning everything had changed.

The Oulart-The-Ballagh Incident

On the Tuesday night before the Offaly game, a senior hurling league match took place between Oulart-The-Ballagh and Crossabeg-Ballymurn. County Board regulations concerning these leagues specified that if the fixtures clashed with a competitive Wexford intercounty match, then the county team had priority. It had been seven weeks since Oulart had a complete panel together and they felt that their players needed preparation for the championship match against St Martin's, fixed for the week after the Offaly game. They had won the previous year's final by a bare point from St Martin's. The Oulart mentors played Liam Dunne, Tomas Dunne and Paul Finn against Crossabeg. Martin Storey did not play due to injury. The club claimed that there was no direction from the County Board that the county players should not participate. The view of the County Board and the Wexford backroom team, was that there was a clear understanding to this effect. No player likes to refuse to play for his club, or even to be put in a position where he has to make a choice. Accusations of 'being too big for the little village' would flow from all quarters. The players had been put in a very difficult position. They felt that the match should have been cancelled. Many of them blamed the County Board for fixing the match. Weeks earlier, Griffin had asked the County Board to have the fixture postponed, but they had refused. Other clubs however, who had Wexford senior players in their team, were also engaged in league fixtures, but did not play the Wexford panellists. The Dunne brothers, Martin Storey and Paul Finn knew instinctively that Griffin and his team would react. They probably underestimated his reaction. They knew that he had to be seen to give a decisive response, but probably hoped that it would be low-key and private.

The Wexford management team was shattered when they heard about the participation of the players in this match. They could not believe that the Oulart mentors, most of them former Wexford hurlers, could do such a thing. The Wexford selectors perceived the incident as a lack of faith in the county team's chances against Offaly. They thought that there was a reasonable chance of beating Offaly and this news, guaranteed to be detrimental to team spirit, was akin to being let down by a friend. Griffin, Barron and Kinsella viewed the matter as a serious breach of trust and discipline and knew that appropriate action had to be taken. They had a long meeting and discussed all the possible solutions. Suggestions had been made to them that they should say that it was too late to take any action, because the Wexford team had already been given to the newspapers. They rejected this as a cop out. They knew that if they did not respond, a loss of face with the other clubs and the other players would result, particularly as, the principal of retribution for misdemeanours had already been introduced and accepted by the players. Earlier in the year they had disciplined two other long-serving and prominent players for a similar breach. Thus, if they did not take action, and Wexford went down to Offaly, their authority would have been seen to be clearly undermined. They would be faced with no alternative but to resign in the aftermath of the match. They decided to strip the Oulart-The-Ballagh club of the captaincy for the Offaly game. They saw this as the least damaging action for the supporters of Wexford hurling. The club's representative, Liam Dunne was stripped of the captaincy and it was given to George O'Connor of St Martin's.

The Oulart club personnel were furious. It was the first time that the club had ever earned the right to nominate the Wexford senior captain. Following many years of bitter disappointment they had finally won the Wexford Senior Hurling championship the previous year. Now the honour of their nominee captaining Wexford in Croke Park, before the eyes of the hurling world, was being taken away from them. The Dunnes,

Finn and Storey, while not agreeing with the action, accepted the situation and said so publicly. While Storey is honest enough to admit that had he been 100 percent fit, then he too would have played in the league game, he felt, viewing the problem from his club's perspective, that Griffin was wrong and asked him to change his mind. As Martin himself did not play in the game, he felt that the problem could be solved by transferring the captaincy from Liam Dunne to himself. Griffin listened but refused, on the grounds that it was a club punishment. Oulart sought a meeting with the County Board. This took place on Friday. While assuring the Oulart representatives that the captaincy would be restored to the club after the Offaly match, the County Board supported the action of the Wexford management team. To further exacerbate matters, a spokesperson for the Oulart-The-Ballagh club read out a statement on South East Radio on Saturday evening. It gave the Oulart side of the story. The spokesperson was not subjected to questioning on the matter and no attempt was made to contact Griffin and his team for their views. Griffin and his team were incensed. They felt that they were entitled to balanced and fair comment on the local airwaves.

Phil Murphy in his 'Sporting Forum' column in *The Wexford People* made no bones about where he thought the blame lay:

'I feel the Oulart-The-Ballagh club was completely in the wrong in what it did, more so the club officials and senior team mentors than the players involved... To place at risk three of the county's players – in a club league match that turned out to be completely one-sided anyway- a mere five days before the most important hurling game of the year so far was simply scandalous, and based on totally selfish club considerations.... I'm told that Oulart wanted to field a full team in that now infamous league game against Crossabeg-Ballymurn because it would be their last game before putting their title on the line against St Martin's. But St. Martin's were in the same boat, and they lined out that very same night in the county league without George and John O'Connor and Rory McCarthy.'

The 1995 Championship Defeat to Offaly

In a live TV interview, before the game, Liam had been questioned about the Oulart incident. He played it down. There was little else he could do. He admits, however, that he and his management colleagues felt that 'the heart and soul had been taken out of the team and it badly effected the morale of the players'. They were pleased to see that most of the panel appeared to support the action taken. The atmosphere in the dressing room, prior to the game, was sombre. Nobody spoke about the Oulart incident but it hovered in the background and, in the view of many of the Wexford team, had a huge effect on their display.

Offaly were short of Billy Dooley and Hubert Rigney, through injury, and lined out as follows: David Hughes, Shane McGuckian, Kevin Kinahan, Martin Hanamy, Kevin Martin, Brian Whelehan, P.J. Martin, Johnny Pilkington, Daithi Regan, Johnny Dooley, John Troy, Joe Dooley, Michael Duignan, Brendan Kelly and Declan Pilkington. It was an unusually hot evening and water carriers were active throughout the match. Despite many of the old failings, Wexford matched Offaly everywhere except in the matter of putting away chances. In the first half they shot twelve wides to Offaly's four, six coming from Martin Storey and a further three from Paul Codd. Coming up to the break, Offaly hit a purple patch and had five unanswered points. The half-time score was Wexford 0-5 Offaly 0-12. Larry O'Gorman came on at left half-back and Liam Dunne and George O'Connor swapped positions. Adrian Fenlon came into midfield and Wexford started to look better. Fitzhenry began to find Wexford players with his puck outs. Early in the second half a mishit free by Tom Dempsey was cleared and resulted in a Joe Dooley goal for Offaly. The Wexford men then got a grip on the game, mostly through the influence of Liam Dunne and Adrian Fenlon. Billy Byrne, who gave Kevin Kinehan a very uncomfortable evening, hit a Wexford goal after ten minutes of the second half. Offaly were less cohesive in that second half and also hit too many wides. They went 23 minutes without scoring. Further Liam Dunne points from frees resulted in just four points between the team with six minutes left. Wexford's shooting remained atrocious and many good chances were wasted. The clinching score came in the last minute when John Troy, who had moved into the full-forward line, got possession of a loose ball and gave Fitzhenry no chance. It was a good comeback by Wexford but the second half improvement was not enough to repair the damage of the disastrous first period and a total of seventeen wides and hasty shooting in front of goal resulted in a another Offaly win. The midlanders were not overly impressive but were still too accurate for Wexford. Johnny Dooley looked the best player on view, closely followed by Liam Dunne. The final score was 2-14 to 1-10. In the Leinster final Offaly were awesome in their destruction of Kilkenny by 2-16 to 2-5.

Dan Quigley, captain of the Wexford team that beat Tipperary in the All-Ireland final of 1968, receives the McCarthy Cup from GAA president, Seamus Ó Riain, with the late Brendan Corish a face in the crowd between them.

A 28-year gap is bridged as Martin Storey holds aloft the McCarthy Cup in 1996, flanked by President Mary Robinson, GAA President Jack Boothman and Taoiseach John Bruton. *(Photo: Ray Flynn, People Newspapers).*

The Wexford Team that beat Tipperary to win the All-Ireland senior hurling title in 1968, a feat not repeated until 1996.
Back L–R: Dan Quigley (Capt.), Eddie Kelly, Willie Murphy, Jack Berry, Phil Wilson, Tom Neville, Tony Doran, Dave Bernie.
Front L–R: Pat Nolan, Seamus Whelan, Paul Lynch, Christy Jacob, Vincent Staples, Jimmy O'Brien and Ned Colfer.

The Wexford minor hurling team that beat Cork to make it an All-Ireland titles double in 1968. Wexford has not won the minor title since.
Back L–R: James Murphy, Pat Cox, Paddy Breen, Aidan Kerrigan, Jack Russell, Paddy O'Connor, Tom Byrne (Capt.), Tom 'Gawny' Walsh, Pat 'Kenny' Walsh, Denis Kinsella.
Front L–R: Martin Quigley, Larry Doyle, Mick Butler, Martin Casey, George O'Connor (Harriers), Larry Kinsella, Martin Byrne, Phil Kennedy, Larry Byrne, Peter O'Brien, Liam Bennett and Matt Wickham.

Tony Doran, Wexford captain, receives the Bob O'Keeffe Cup from Leinster Council chairman, Wexfordman Jimmy Roche, after the 1976 Leinster final, a scene that was repeated in 1977 when Wexford won again.

20 years later in 1996, Jim Berry is the first Wexfordman to be Leinster Council chairman since Jimmy Roche, and he hands the Bob O'Keeffe Cup over to a Wexfordman for the first time since 1977. Berry is on the right, and Rory McCarthy and Liam Dunne block out captain Martin Storey in their excitement.

(Photo: Adrian Melia).

ALL - IRELAND FINALISTS 1996

The Wexford team that beat Limerick in the All-Ireland final.

Back L–R: Dave Guiney, Paul Finn, Larry O'Gorman, Rod Guiney, George O'Connor, Garry Laffan, Adrian Fenlon, Larry Murphy, John O'Connor, Ger Cushe, Billy Byrne, Jim Byrne, Declan Ruth.

Front L–R: Paul Codd, Seamus Kavangh, Liam Dunne, Tom Dempsey, Martin Storey, Damien Fitzhenry, Sean Flood, Eamonn Scallan, Colm Kehoe, Rory McCarthy, Tommy Kehoe, Shane Carley.

The Limerick panel that lost to Wexford in the All-Ireland final.

Back L–R: Padraig Tobin, Shane O'Neill, Sean O'Neill, Owen O'Neill, Gary Kirby, John O'Brien, Mike Nash, Barry Foley, Frankie Carroll, Dave Clarke, Brian Tobin.

Front L–R: Turlough Herbert, John Flavin, Mike Galligan, T.J. Ryan, Mike Houlihan, Damien Quigley, Declan Nash, Ciaran Carey, Joe Quaid, Stephen McDonagh, Mark Foley, John Kiely and John Foley.

Sean Flood bursts clear with the ball in typical style, ahead of Charlie Carter and P.J. Delaney, in the first round victory over Kilkenny in 1996. *(Photo: Adrian Melia).*

Colm Kehoe, one of the 'finds' of the year, gets away from Limerick sub Turlough Herbert, with Frankie Carroll in the background, during the 1996 All-Ireland final.

(Photo: Paddy Murphy, People Newspapers).

Damien Fitzhenry, the Wexford goalie dives to block out this shot by Galway's Cathal Moore in the 1996 All-Ireland semi-final, while Liam Dunne and Ger Cushe run back to give support. *(Photo,Paddy Murphy, People Newspapers).*

Damien Fitzhenry in his other guise, ace penalty taker. He smashes the ball (arrowed) past Liam Coughlan and Brian Whelehan on the Offaly line for a goal in the Leinster final of 1996. He also scored one against Dublin in the provincial semi-final.
(Photo, Adrian Melia).

Tom Dempsey (on ground with arm raised), manages to poke the ball to the net in the Leinster final, although almost buried by a tangle of Offaly bodies, and Kevin Martin arrives too late.

(*Photo: Adrian Melia*).

Dempsey gets off the deck to celebrate while Offaly's Martin Hanamy is despondent.

Garry Laffan, whose original shot came back off the woodwork, also shows his delight while Shane McGuckin is dismayed.

(*Photos: Adrian Melia*).

Griffin lays his plans. Liam Griffin works out his strategies during a training session with George O'Connor, Eamonn Scallan and Rory McCarthy.

Billy Byrne, the master stickman and super sub, works hard at a training session.

Colm Kehoe, the first senior hurling All-Ireland medal winner from Bunclody.

AN EARLY END FOR JOHNNO

It's an early and unfortunate end to the 1996 All-Ireland semi-final for John O'Connor as he is led from the field by team doctor, Stephen Bowe and selector Rory Kinsella after being concussed. He was replaced by his brother, George.

(Photo: Adrian Melia)

A rare moment of quiet on a hectic 1996 All-Ireland final day as substitute Paul Finn (left) chats with panel member M.J. Reck in the Wexford dug-out.

(Photo: Ray Flynn, People Newspapers).

Liam Dunne is one of the key final confrontations with Limerick's Gary Kirby. Dunne got the RTE 'Man of the Match' award for his display.

(Photos: Adrian Melia).

Rory McCarthy, one of the young lions of the Wexford team, is first to this ball ahead of Offaly's Johnny Pilkington in the Leinster final.

Larry Murphy, RTE 'Man of the Match' in the Leinster final, gets in another shot despite the attentions of Offaly's Kevin Martin.

George O'Connor was a big influence on the squad, whether playing or on the line. Here he is on patrol during the Leinster final.

Damien Fitzhenry, the Wexford goalie, is all balance, concentration and power as he is beautifully 'frozen' in this shot. He is about to lash the ball downfield as Limerick's Damien Quigley comes in to challenge during the All-Ireland final of 1996.

Garry Laffan, the Wexford full forward gets in his shot against Offaly in the Leinster final of 1996.   *(Photos: Adrian Melia).*

Dancing at the crossroads. Psychologist Niamh Fitzpatrick and physiotherapist Pat Whitney celebrate.

Team doctor, Stephen Bowe, and County secretary, Mick Kinsella, survey the scene after the 1996 All-Ireland semi-final victory.

Seamus Barron, selector.

Rory Kinsella, selector.

Martin Quigley, chairman, and John O'Leary, of the supporters Club, key people in the background.

Sean Collier, international boxer and team trainer.

The Wild Swans, Paul Bell and Brendan Wade (who had two of the best ever All-Ireland songs Dancing at the Crossroads *and* The Purple and Gold*) are joined on stage at the victory banquet at the Grand Hotel, Malahide, by Sean Flood, who sings with his own group,* Running on Empty. *(Photo: Ray Flynn, People Newspapers)*

Billy Byrne and Ger Cushe, Gorey's first All-Ireland hurling medal winners, were astonished by the enormous turnout that welcomed them home after the final. (Photo: Pat O'Connor)

Rory McCarthy, one of the glamour boys of the squad who is a big hit with the girls of Wexford!

Anthony Storey, James Byrne and Ciara Storey proudly show off the McCarthy Cup as Martin Storey senior and junior lead the Wexford team onto the pitch at Wexford Park for the annual GOAL challenge which drew a crowd of almost 13,000 people. Members of the Rest of Ireland team applauding them onto the pitch include Tom Helebert, Ciarán Carey, Frankie Carroll, Frank Lohan and Niall Rigney.

(Photo: Pat O'Connor, People Newspapers).

Bill Peare, the Enniscorthy man associated with Wexford county teams as bagman and hurley carrier for more than half a century, proudly holds the All-Ireland cup as he is flanked by Enniscorthy men Declan Ruth and Adrian Fenlon.

(Photo: Paddy Murphy, People Newspapers).

Martin Storey, the Wexford captain, enjoys a special day when he brings home the Liam McCarthy cup to his native village, The Ballagh, followed through the crowd by sub goalie Seamus Kavanagh, Liam Dunne and selector Rory Kinsella.

Inset: A special moment as Martin holds the Cup with his proud dad, John.

(Photo: Paddy Murphy, People Newspapers)

An ecclesiastic welcome home for the heroes. Roman Catholic Bishop of Ferns, Dr Brendan Comiskey (left) and Church of Ireland Bishop of Ferns and Ossory, Dr. Noel Willoughby, share in the joy of victory in Wexford town on the Monday after the final with team captain Martin Storey, team manager Liam Griffin and County Board chairman, Paddy Wickham.

(Photo, Pat O'Connor, People Newspapers).

A winning team: two happy men after the post-match lunch in the Burlington Hotel on the Monday after the final. Manager Liam Griffin and captain Martin Storey have a firm grip on the Liam MacCarthy Cup before they start the triumphant journey home to Wexford. *(Photo: courtesy of The Star).*

In the wake of this defeat Griffin called for 'a think-tank to discuss the future of hurling in the county'.

Griffin Must Go!

Stirrings of unrest among some followers became apparent in September 1995. A meeting was called for Murphy-Flood's hotel on Monday 4 September 1995. About 20 unhappy hurling men turned up and the issues of Wexford's apparent slide into hurling oblivion were discussed at length. Under the headline 'Hurling Supporters voice their concern', *The Wexford People* reported as follows:

> *'GRIFFIN MUST GO was the theme behind a meeting of disgruntled Wexford hurling fans held in Enniscorthy on Monday night... The Chairman made no bones about the timing of the meeting. It was deliberately staged just before the ratification of the current senior hurling selectors comes up before the county board.*

> *'If Liam Griffin and Seamus Barron are left there for another three years, then Wexford hurling really will be in the doldrums,' he said. 'I wanted to highlight the unrest that there is in the county before the boys are ratified'.*

> *And he promised that there would be another such gathering in coming weeks to allow more people to have their say on the matter. He has now set up contacts in all four districts in the hope of bringing more people to the next meeting, at a date to be arranged. There were many empty seats in the hotel ballroom on Monday evening but no shortage of ideas on where the sport has taken its wrong turnings...'*

The chairman summed up as follows:

> *'We are at an all-time low with no prospect of an improvement.'*

It was the first public utterance of criticism, but it seemed that there was not yet a large enough caucus group to carry the sense of disenchantment further. It seemed to the management that confidence in them was now lower than when they first took on the most difficult job in hurling.

A week later the management team was ratified by the County Board for a further term. A huge show of support was apparent and only four dissenting voices were heard. A proposal that their services be dispensed with and an outside manager appointed was roundly rejected. To his credit, County Chairman, Paddy Wickham, made an emotional, hard-hitting speech in their defence. At least, Griffin and his colleagues appeared to be making a favourable impression in the corridors of power. They were gratified that the support from the County Chairman and the Wexford County Board was so strong and it offered them great encouragement for the coming year.

Clare's Homecoming

Like the All-Ireland football championship, there is only a very small number of teams who have a real chance of gaining All-Ireland honours in hurling. These are Cork, Tipperary, Galway, Kilkenny, and Offaly as favourites, and Wexford, Clare and Limerick as possibilities. Antrim, Laois, Dublin, Down and Waterford are apt to have the odd unexpected victory but, in terms of the ultimate prize, rank as complete outsiders. An unexpected and exhilarating shift in these rankings occurred in 1995 as a result of Clare's breakthrough. The memorable triumph was welcomed enthusiastically across the land. Liam travelled to Clare in September to be present at the glorious celebrations. The combination of a Clare father and a memorable 18 months in the Clare senior jersey had sown deep feelings of nostalgia for the Banner county. He loved the people and felt that he was among kindred spirits. In Newmarket-On-Fergus, Liam's old club, all former Clare players had been invited to sit on the victory platform. Griffin, well-known in the town, was called up and given a seat. The Wexford manager felt embarrassed and retreated quietly to the back of the platform. He was soon spotted by Ger Loughnane who approached him. 'It might be Wexford next year, Liam'.

Liam took great heart from Clare's victory. At the beginning of the year, no one was tipping them to win the ultimate prize, but dedication, a shrewd manager and a refusal to be beaten enabled them to record one of the great All-Ireland triumphs. He had gone to Clare's matches and studied the team closely. All the time he was matching his own charges against them. He saw a team with a great full-back, a highly impressive half-back line and a set of forwards, that were not world-beaters, win through. He began to feel that Wexford could match them in many positions and could field six better forwards. We are as good as these fellows, he thought. Maybe an All-Ireland really is possible.

A grain of optimism began to sprout.

∞ CHAPTER 4 ∞

A THURLES WATERSHED

Request to George and Billy

Wexford played an All-Star selection in Enniscorthy in August 1995. This game was a fund-raiser for the celebrations in connection with the approaching bicentenary of 1798. George O'Connor of St Martin's and Billy Byrne of Gorey were in the panel but both were well into the twilight of their careers. Both were three years past their best, although their application and fitness levels belied the fact. Both men embodied the old Olympian spirit and their love for hurling was profound. They were like old prospectors scratching away at the dirt for one last glint of the golden metal and one last shining hour before retreating into the vacuum of hurling memories. Those memories would always be of countless days rowing manfully against the strong tide of a superior force and few recollections of a place on the winning rostrum on big days.

George was 36 and had made his Wexford debut in the Oireachtas final of 1979 against Offaly. It was his only medal from seventeen years of high class hurling. Possessed of great athletic physique, he had excelled, as a young man, at high jump, long jump and 100 and 200 metres. He became a recognisable national sporting figure as a result of his participation in the RTE Superstars competitions in 1983-84. A legend in Wexford, his surname is hardly ever heard. He is simply 'George'. He readily admits that he never really bothered learning how to protect his hand as he soared like an eagle for the sliotar. He acknowledges that that was a mistake. But he has no regrets. George disliked winter hurling and many times, voiced his opinions on the matter. He loved the big stage and graced it with performances of panache and swashbuckling splendour that were cheered by friend and foe alike. Lithe and deeply tanned he was the embodiment of the old buccaneering hurlers like Mick Mackey. Oblivious to the ash that bounced across his frame, his towering catches and all-round athleticism have thrilled thousands on the hurling fields of Ireland. His left hand is a testimony to the countless battles in which he has engaged. The bones in all the fingers and those on the back of the hand have been broken more than once. Ankle and knee troubles add to the list of injuries. Most of his front teeth lie buried deep in the green sod of Croke Park. Seven Leinster final appearances and seven League finals, without once being on the winning side, have failed to dim his ardour for the game. He had seriously considered retirement following the 1994 Leinster final defeat to Offaly. Then rumours began to circulate. Rumours that were music to his ears. They concerned the possibility of the appointment of Liam Griffin as Wexford team manager. George had always held Griffin in the highest regard. It was the passion and commitment of the man that excited him. And his knowledge of the game. Many times he had left Griffin's company after talking hurling for hours, renewed and refreshed in spirit and ready for another campaign. He made up his mind to wait until the new manager was appointed. If that man was not Liam Griffin, he would quietly fade back into club hurling.

Billy Byrne was 35-years of age, having made his Wexford senior debut in 1983. He is a very talented footballer and has played senior football with his county. Indeed, football connoisseurs who have watched Billy in action, rate him extremely highly. As a hurler, he is a remarkably skilled stickman and possesses a fine hurling brain. He has played for his county in every position from centre-field to corner-forward. Popular and soft-spoken he had been Wexford's best goal scorer for a long time. Once before, he had retired from intercounty activity but had been persuaded to return when his services were badly needed. To his surprise, he had played some of the best hurling of his career following his comeback. He was the Supporters Club choice as Wexford Hurler of The Year in 1995.

Conscious of the number of young and inexperienced hurlers in the Wexford panel, Liam Griffin approached George and asked him to consider staying on for another year. Griffin bluntly told him that he was unlikely to figure on the first choice selection, but would appreciate his presence on the panel as a morale-booster for the younger players. 'Whether it is number five, number twenty or number twenty-five, I'll be there', was George's answer. Griffin outlined the same scenario to the Gorey man. 'We need experience in the dressing room.' Griffin said. He got a similar reply. 'I'll carry the oranges, if you ask me', said Billy.

The selectors now felt that they had, in the Wexford dressing room, two men whose dedication and example would be an inspiration to the younger players.

Congratulations!

The Wexford GAA Supporters Club, for the first time, held an annual function at which the players of the year, in both hurling and football, were announced and presented with mementoes. This event was run on a very professional basis. Exhibitions of GAA paraphernalia, guest speakers and videos of matches all formed part of the occasion. In Wexford, support for the efforts of the senior hurlers comes from all aspects of life and from all social classes. The younger players were awakened to the intense longing for success among the supporters. They were surprised at the extent and variety of the crowd. Some of the fringe events for this initial occasion were organised by a man whose support for the team was matched only by the size of the cultural gap between himself and the majority of the supporters. He decided to hire a string quartet to play while the festivities were in progress. Brahms and Beethoven echoed soothingly across the function room. Beautiful renditions of Schubert and Mozart intermingled with the recollections of the GAA year. Griffin arrived late and as he made his way to the function room was accosted by a genteel lady who had been enthralled by the string quartet. She was forthright in her compliments to the Wexford manager about the highbrow musical tone of the evening:

'Congratulations, Mr Griffin', she gushed, 'It's super that you have succeeded in taking the GAA out of the bog'.

Griffin, oblivious to the presence of the string quartet, and surprised that he and his team had already been perceived as putting the fine old game of hurling on to a new cerebral plateau, was quite chuffed. He assumed that he was in the presence of a rare female hurling connoisseur. Preening with delight, he flicked an imaginary piece of fluff from his immaculate lapel and retorted, 'Well thank you, madam, we're doing our very best.'

Doubts About Tactical Ability

Those who had welcomed Griffin's appointment as Wexford supremo did so in the knowledge that he would bring a thorough and innovative approach. They knew that he saw solutions – not problems and that his motivational powers would extract the maximum effort from all concerned. There was one area however, that concerned them. His lack of tactical experience, at the highest level, was seen, by some, as a weakness. Other coaches, like Cyril Farrell and Babs Keating had taken a few years before they made a real mark. Neither Liam nor his colleagues Rory and Seamus had first-hand experience of the big time occasion. The ability to read a game, to ascertain what was happening and to take effective counteraction in the heat of a major All-Ireland championship encounter was something that they had never before been exposed to. The under-age sidelines are a long way from Croke Park. Could they bridge the gap? And how long would it take? More importantly, how long would it take to gain the confidence of the players? Similar doubts were in the minds of the team. He talked a good game – but could he deliver?

A New Atmosphere

When the team had their first meeting in the Ferrycarrig Hotel, following the long summer break, there was a whole new mood in the camp. The effect of the Oulart incident and the action taken by the management team in the lead up to the 1995 Leinster semi-final, had been an important rallying point. The players now knew that these three men were not about to capitulate to anyone in their goal to put Wexford hurling back to the forefront. Griffin and his colleagues had not planned it this way, but the Oulart incident became a major turning point.

The meeting was held on the Tuesday night after the 1995 All-Ireland final. Martin Storey suddenly began to realise that things had changed. Until then he did not think that everyone had realised just what single-mindedness was necessary to succeed. What level of intensity of training it took to win an All-Ireland, what personal sacrifices had to be made, and what disruption of family life had to occur. Griffin and his team had finally got the message home. Although previous managers had pointed out similar messages, it had not really got through to the players. Maybe they had lacked the communication powers of the present team. Maybe Griffin was one of the all-time great nagging machines. But Storey acknowledges that there was more to it than just nagging. Griffin and his team had become very professional. They had begun during the previous September by getting every player to fill out a sheet outlining his feelings about everything connected with Wexford hurling. Then he had proceeded to drown them in sporting literature. Printouts on all aspects of preparation had been handed out. John O'Connor admits that initially, he put them in his kit bag and never read them. In the early Spring of 1995 he began to get interested. He saw that they were very applicable and began to devour them. The physical and mental sides were covered in great depth. Rules were outlined and strict adherence was insisted upon.

A Professional Fitness Programme

'They left nothing to chance', says Storey. Diet sheets, a commitment to avoid alcohol, strict supervision of weight and muscle tone, an adherence to drinking large quantities (minimum – four pints!) of water on a daily basis, regular reports on sprinting prowess and recovery powers, advanced schedules of downhill running to build up speed, endurance training of a highly professional nature – all were part of an exacting agenda of discipline drawn up for panellists.

Following the 1995 campaign, Griffin had recognised that there was a great disparity between the present day Wexford team and the legends of the Nick Rackard-led men of the 1950s in the matter of upper body strength. Together with Rory Kinsella, they decided that this area needed extensive improvement. Griffin succeeded in obtaining advice, indirectly, from the British Hockey Federation. The UK team had won the Olympic final in 1988 and had continued to play at the top level ever since. He recognised that hockey was close to hurling in the context of the use of particular muscles. He got all the data and together with Sean Collier and Rory Kinsella, discussed it in great detail. Much of this technique was then applied to the hurlers, in their weight-training programme during the winter of 1995-96 in Dominic Kiernan's gym. He wanted to be certain that all the fitness work was undertaken on a purely scientific basis and that guesswork was eliminated. The axiom 'a little knowledge is a dangerous thing' was forever in his mind. Players who were known to be good hurlers but slow in turning, or moderate in reaction time, came under the microscope. Griffin was not prepared to discard a good hurler unless he failed to respond to the latest improvement techniques. The dangers of over emphasis on certain fitness aspects, to the detriment of others, was always at the front of their minds. The key element was balance. Great attention was paid to this factor.

Canada became another important source for Griffin's endless search for access to the latest fitness regimes. He read extensively and became familiar with the latest concepts. He recognised that Canada was one of the world leaders in all areas of physical and psychological preparation. The previous October he had contacted The Coaching Association of Canada and requested literature. Much of what he received was in the form of academic papers. Together with Rory, a qualified PE instructor, these were studied and appropriate portions translated into everyday language. A language that the players understood.

The training reached an intensity few of the players had ever experienced. Griffin borrowed tackling bags from Wexford Wanderers Rugby Club and the forwards used them to take on the backs in training.

Griffin and his colleagues knew that the real results of the austere physical and mental training would not pay real dividends until the later stages of the League. Those games, and the beginning of the championship they began to anticipate with relish.

Dave Goes Over The Top

Dave Guiney had a burning ambition to make the Wexford hurling panel. When his twin brother, Rod, secured his place on the team it increased his determination. Whatever Rod could do, he could do. Single-mindedly, he entered into a torturous training regime. He approached George for advice. 'How much training should I be doing on my own, George?' he asked. 'Well Dave, if you're serious about this and you really want to get fit enough to be considered for the Wexford panel, you have to be doing at least 1,000 press-ups per day' answered George, without a hint of a smile. Dave never suspected that he was being taken for a ride and commenced the incredible routine. George was astonished to receive a phone call from Dave a few days later: 'George, do your arms not get sore after a few days?'

The Meetings

Then there were the meetings. These occurred after almost every training session. Storey says, 'I tried making excuses – to avoid them. I wanted to hurl, not talk. We all had pains in our heads listening to him. He persuaded me to stay- for five minutes. Two hours later I was still there, and damn it – it was getting interesting. Despite myself, I began to enjoy these get-togethers. I began to see that they were very constructive – with little bullshit. The management team took players into consideration, they kept asking us for comments. At first it was the same people who did all the talking. Then the more reticent began to be dragged in by Griffin. Then the majority began to join in. Then everybody. Now I could sit and listen to him talk about hurling for ever – because of his love for the game'.

Changing Old Habits

The production of reports on each player's on-field performance was initially treated as a joke by the players. These were computed after every match by John O'Leary, an important member of the backroom team, and reached Griffin's desk on the following Monday morning. The tables contained the most detailed statistics ever compiled for the game of hurling. They were astonishing in depth and showed every minute detail of how each player fared in relation to an infinite variety of on-field activities. Reams of tabulations and figures were computed and their review and interpretation became paramount to the elimination of bad habits and the reinforcement of new methods. Running totals and percentage success rates were applied to each panellist. At first the players hated O'Leary and his infernal tabulations. It felt like an invasion of privacy. But statistics continued to be strictly logged and posted on the dressing-room wall. In the beginning, Griffin rarely commented on them. He wanted self-motivation. He was a great believer in parables 'Give a man a fish', he would say, 'and you've fed him for a day'. Teach him to fish, and you've fed him forever.' Some of the players wondered what all this had to do with hurling. Still Griffin persevered. 'These may interest you', he'd say, nonchalantly, as he pasted another batch of O'Leary's immaculate records on the notice board. Then he began to highlight certain aspects of a particular player's figures. Notes like 'well done', 'excellent', or 'a very good improvement over last week' began to arouse scraps of interest. The commendations were sometimes related to players whom, in the opinion of the other team members, had under-performed in that particular match. And often a player who was satisfied with his performance was shattered to discover that he was the subject of a pithy written censure.

Slowly things began to change. The lists began to arouse the players' interest. They began to examine their personal success or failure ratios. Their levels of application to these hitherto ignored aspects of the game became meaningful. Backs became as inquisitive about their fouling ratios as about scores conceded. Forwards began to examine the number of clearances by their marker. On the rare occasions when the figures were not ready there was great disappointment shown by the panellists.

The Mental Approach

Gradually, he was persuading them to think about their game. To play a certain way. Many of them did not want to think too deeply. They were not used to this approach and, at first, resisted it. Some were convinced that if they thought about it too much, they would lose their flexibility and natural flow. They would end up as restrained and inelegant purveyors of the game. Griffin demanded mental as well as physical fitness and told them that one of the most difficult things to do in life is to think. He used axioms and maxims to illustrate his points. Sometimes these were well-trusted philosophies or extracts from the writings of famous individuals. Sometimes he made them up or altered them to suit his purposes. 'There is little difference in people, but that little difference makes a big difference. The little difference is attitude. The big difference is whether it is positive or negative.'

'Anything that the mind of man can conceive and believe, it can achieve.'

'Doubt your doubts...not your beliefs.'

'Many of life's failures are people who did not realise how close they were to success when they gave up.'

'The man who wins may have been counted out several times, but he didn't hear the referee.'

He told them that being a great hurler was not necessarily going to win them anything. That attitude was the most important thing.

Concession of Frees

Another significant change was a gradual lessening in the number of frees conceded. Initially the players had problems with this concept. They found themselves holding back when going in to win a ball. The management insisted that they give 100 per cent in the tackle – without fouling.

Skill – the Real Priority

The greatest significance of all was placed on skill. They felt that the PE man alone could achieve much in football, but not in hurling. PE, without an inside knowledge of hurling, was ineffectual. Griffin is strongly of the opinion that hurling fitness is a particular science. The over-emphasis on fitness levels to the detriment of the skill factor, in Gaelic football, was always at the back of their minds. They were determined that this would not happen to their hurlers. Ball skills were practised again and again. Roughhouse tactics were discouraged. Dispossession by flick and hooks was routinely practised. Great emphasis was placed on the skills of blocking, hooking and tackling. Griffin referred to this as 'hassling'. He pointed out that the great Christy Ring was a superb 'hooker' and that no player could consider himself a complete hurler unless he was proficient in this aspect of the game. Particularly so in the case of forwards, whose attempts to stop opposing backs from clearing had often been pathetically inefficient. It was pointed out that when a forward loses possession, he becomes a defender. Now they were to tackle back and make life difficult for the opposing defence. Tough intercounty backs do not expect a skilled, nifty, wing-forward to be an adept tackler. They do not expect him to be proficient in the art of defence. This became a major part of the on-field training over the winter months.

Something else was also different. There was no abuse from the sideline. Agitated remonstration by off-field mentors is a part of every GAA match. Often contradictory in nature, these distraught overtures often upset players and cause a loss of concentration. Griffin's game plans were explained clearly and succinctly before the game and only the calmest reminders were issued from the sidelines during matches. These were nearly always encouraging by nature. The players liked this.

Emphasis on Ground Hurling

The large panel assembled by the selectors enabled full scale practice matches to be played. Griffin took charge of all the outdoor training. Ground hurling practice was introduced. The traditional Wexford hurler is not noted for his first time hurling. High fetching and picking was his game. The fact that this often slowed down an attack and enabled opposing backs to find time to cover more effectively was never really taken into consideration. Requesting him to play the ball on the ground was akin to asking a politician to be specific. It wasn't in his nature. Adrian Fenlon was one of the few who had the required ground skills in abundance. The management team set about changing this. Half of each match was given over to ground hurling. Anyone who picked up a ball was penalised. At first, mutterings of discontent were heard. These petered out as obvious improvement in the arts of overhead hurling, ground striking and quick deliveries became apparent. Forwards began to register scores from first time pulls as these skills were honed.

Growing Confidence

Griffin and his colleagues began to feel that 1996 could be their year. They were not yet thinking in terms of an All-Ireland win, but had a feeling that they could reach the final stages of the League and then, who knows? Griffin himself was growing more confident in his own tactical awareness. He realised that he had made mistakes in the first year and viewed it as a necessary learning process. He began to study opposing teams in even greater detail. Strengths and weaknesses were discerned and tactical counter actions planned. He spent hours discussing the tactical nature of the game with his co-selectors and even, from time to time with other intercounty hurling and football managers of his acquaintance, such as Michael McNamara of Clare, Canon O'Brien of Cork, Eugene McKenna of Tyrone, and on one occasion, Babs Keating. He never shied from seeking their opinions and they invariably encouraged his efforts.

The management and team were in a positive frame of mind as they entered into the League campaign of 1995-96.

The 1995-96 League v Laois

Seamus Barron warned that the Babs Keating-trained Laois were going to be no pushovers in their forthcoming League match in O'Moore Park, Portlaoise. He was proved correct when Wexford scraped through by 0-14 to 1-9. The team showed great spirit and commitment. Wexford began to experiment tactically in this game. Niall Rigney, a fine hurler, dominated from centre-field, in the first half. Wexford began to play an unusual tactical formation, with constant interchange between midfield, half-forward and corner-forward. They introduced George to this sector late in the first-half and he proceeded to win the game for his team with a power-packed display. Tommy Kehoe, Tomas Codd and George formed a three-man midfield. It worked a treat. John O'Connor had an outstanding game at full-back while young Rory McCarthy looked good at left half-back. Laois were well fired up and Babs Keating's influence was very apparent, although he seemed unable to counteract the unusual tactical formation of the Wexford men. At one stage an umpire hesitated over the validity of a point. Babs ran around to remonstrate with him. It was noticed that Griffin ran to 'mark' him. Observers saw a verbal altercation between the managers. Griffin, as usual, did not hold back and Babs appeared to come off second best in the frank exchange of views that followed. The players began to see that the new tactics and game plan were beginning to work. They also saw that their manager was not prepared to back down to anyone.

Westmeath in the League

Wexford now went through a series of matches which were to prove beneficial to players and selectors alike. The backroom team had recognised that successful hurlers from other counties engaged in far more hurling than their Wexford counterparts. In an attempt to put this right they were determined to get in as much match practice as possible, at a high level. Wexford first faced up to Westmeath in the League. The panel was decimated by injuries and inter-club games. Anyone who thought that the runaway win of the previous championship would be repeated was in for a shock. With only seven of their first choice players in the team Wexford managed a win by 0-18 to 1-9 with the accurate Tommy Kehoe accounting for 0-9.

Next came Kilkenny, in New Ross, on Saturday 28 October 1995 in the Oireachtas. Wexford beat the Noresiders by 1-17 to 2-10, after extra time. Tommy Kehoe again hit nine points and Ger Cushe was majestic at centre-back. Wexford had seven first choices on board, but Kilkenny fielded a team without any of their 'names' on the selection. It was a hollow victory.

On the following Monday, Wexford played Offaly in the 1995 Walsh Cup final in Wexford Park. Once again they were victorious by 2-11 to 1-12. Once again they fielded seven first team men and Offaly showed their disinterest by fielding an entire second team. After the game, Wexford's stand-in captain Tommy Kehoe was presented with the Walsh Cup by fellow Wexford man and Leinster Council vice-chairman, Jim Berry. For a Wexford hurler, winning a final – any final, did no harm for morale.

An away League game against Dublin now beckoned and, anxious to remain on top of the table, Wexford selected a team containing nine first choices. They triumphed by 0-11 to 0-7. Ger Cushe again looked impressive at centre-back as the team showed good teamwork and application.

In the Oireachtas semi-final, Clare were accounted for by 2-18 to 1-13 in Ennis. The Clare team had no resemblance to the one that the won the McCarthy Cup the previous September.

Further experimentation by the Wexford selectors saw Declan Ruth picked for the League game against Antrim. The team began to take on a more settled look, but many players were still unavailable due to injury. John O'Connor was now the first choice full-back with Ger Cushe continuing in the middle of the half-back line. Antrim were accounted for, in impressive fashion, by 2-14 to 1-10. Many of the young players were now responding well and showed that they were in the running for places. Ruth, Garry Laffan, Shane Carley and Jim Byrne all looked like they could develop into useful intercounty players. Damien Fitzhenry was excellent at centre-forward.

Oireachtas Final 1995

Next came the 1995 Oireachtas final against Offaly, who, this time fielded about eleven of their championship side, while Wexford had only six of what they then considered to be their best fifteen. The manager was very unhappy over the fixtures foul-up which caused him to play such a weakened team. A round of applause, in the Wexford dressing room, greeted selector Seamus Barron, on his return after his recent serious illness. It was to be the only joy of the day for the Wexford men. The run of seven successive victories was brought to a firm halt and the realities of playing a necessarily experimental side against such a strong Offaly selection were brought home in no uncertain fashion. Offaly won by 2-13 to 0-9. Wexford lacked the first touch to threaten Offaly and were well beaten, but learned further lessons from the defeat.

A Significant Win in Birr

The new year opened with a win over Dublin in the Walsh Cup by 0-22 to 3-10 followed by a meeting with Offaly in the semi-final of that competition. A near full-strength Offaly were beaten by 3-9 to 3-5 in atrocious conditions at Birr on 11 February 1996. This insignificant match has been cited by Griffin and many of his players as an important turning point in the fortunes of the team. Offaly were keyed up for the game and wanted to win it. Griffin saw a greater desire reflected in Wexford's performance. The results of the team's winter gym work was also clearly evident as they overpowered Offaly in the physical exchanges. Adrian Fenlon, in particular, was now beginning to realise his great potential. Garry Laffan ran marathons across the full-forward line and Tom Dempsey and Larry Murphy picked off good opportunist scores, Murphy's being a magnificent effort. Seven points down approaching half-time, the team rallied with two well struck goals. An impressive defence, well marshalled by Ger Cushe and Declan Stamp held Offaly to a single score from play in the second half. Unusual tactics were implemented and worked well, with Larry Murphy as a marauding rover. The Wexford forwards saw a rare panic develop in Offaly's full-back line.

This victory made it two wins in the last three meetings with the Offaly men and the players gained enormous confidence from the game. Wexford had only nine first choice players in operation. The players' belief in the new tactics, first apparent against Laois, was copper-fastened in Birr.

The League Loss to Limerick

Top of the table, Wexford travelled to Kilmallock in February to take on Limerick in the League. Limerick had thirteen first choices and Wexford had nine. The Shannonsiders won easily by 1-13 to 0-8 in a rain-lashed contest. Limerick dominated the first half, thanks to a brilliant half-back line of Dave Clarke, Ciaran Carey and Sean O'Neill and led at the interval by 1-10 to 0-2. There was little for the Wexford management team to enthuse about, although All-Star Gary Kirby, who scored 0-5 from frees, was held scoreless from play by Wexford centre-back, Ger Cushe. Griffin would like to have played the match in better weather conditions. No one could have guessed that, seven months hence, this encounter would take on a far greater significance. National sports reporters would pour over their notes and base widely read conclusions on the rain-lashed events of this bleak February day in Kilmallock.

After the game, Griffin admitted that his decision to play against the gale force wind in the first half was the wrong option. Rory and Liam felt that Tommy Kehoe had been 'put through the wars' by Limerick and had suffered badly at the hands of one Limerick player, in particular. Liam made a huge play on this and accepted responsibility for it. He promised the players that it would never happen to one of the team again. The players took careful note.

Down in the League

The Down match took place in Wexford Park and the home team had a runaway win by 2-19 to 1-2. While it was worrying that they hit 17 wides, the team looked impressive with Larry Murphy and Garry Laffan playing superbly. Martin Storey returned after a three month lay-off, during which he had an operation for his long standing hernia problem.

Revenge on Meath

Wexford's surprise conquerors in the previous year's League were the next opponents in Trim. The Slaneysiders took the Meath game very seriously and lined out with eleven of their strongest fifteen. A meeting in a Dublin hotel before the game had but one item of the agenda. That item was revenge for the previous year and to firmly lay the ghost that had haunted Griffin's management since that day. Meath should have been forewarned when the Wexford team were seen to arrive a half an hour early for the game. The men from the Royal County probably never met a more fired-up intercounty hurling team. Griffin admits that his team treated the game as seriously as an All-Ireland final. There was an obvious intensity about the approach of the Slaneysiders, who were fit, extremely confident and determined to wipe them out. Meath never knew what hit them, as an exhibition of razor sharp hurling obliterated their efforts. The final score was 2-20 to 1-5. This win ensured that Wexford finished as Division Two champions, on scoring difference from Laois. It also guaranteed promotion to Division One and set up an attractive quarter-final clash with Offaly. Storey was fast regaining fitness and hit four good points, with the Rory McCarthy/Adrian Fenlon partnership very impressive at centre-field.

Larry Is Taken to Task

Rory Kinsella and Seamus Barron had not been happy with Larry O'Gorman's general play in the Birr match against Offaly. He was warned about adherence to the game plan before the Meath match. He played his usual unrestrained, loose and spectacular game. One-handed pick-ups and hand-passing across the half-back line dotted his efforts. At half-time, Rory and Seamus wanted to take him off. He was spoken to once more, by the Wexford manager, who felt that he could cajole Larry into changing and adhering to the game plan in the second half. Griffin did not succeed and when Larry continued to play his own type of game the selectors substituted him after five minutes of the second half. An important signal had been given, not just to Larry, but to the team as a whole. This was a key incident in changing Larry O'Gorman from a free-spirited player of narrow focus into a team hurler of vision, control and purpose. From that point on, the old Larry was gone, replaced by a new model whose adherence to team-work and game plan would offer Wexford a priceless contribution in the coming months.

A Thurles Watershed

The quarter-final League clash with Offaly at Semple Stadium, in mid-April '96, was an important watershed for the Wexford hurlers. Although they had won two of the last three encounters between the sides, these victories had not occurred in important competitions. Two were in the Walsh Cup and the other was an Oireachtas outing. The Church & General Hurling League, however is different. And particularly the lucrative final stages. Large sums of money accrue to the County Boards of the competing teams and many a financial nightmare has been solved by a county reaching the League semi-final or final. Nobody would disagree that the League is second in importance only to the All-Ireland championship. Despite Wexford's growing confidence in their ability to match Offaly, the reality was that the last important match between the sides, the 1995 championship encounter, had been won, as usual, by Offaly. The midlanders were determined that their long run of victories over the Wexford men would continue. Eamonn Cregan was treating the game very seriously. Although the Wexford management cited the Walsh Cup win over Offaly as proof to their young players that the Offaly hoodo had been broken, secretly they knew that his was a sterner and a more realistic test. They admitted as much. 'We're looking forward to the challenge ourselves because it will tell us how well we're doing.'

Offaly lined out with a team that contained many of the best-respected hurlers in the game. Brian Whelehan, Johnny Dooley (introduced as a sub), Daithi Regan and the Martins were absentees. Wexford had tried a few goalkeepers but had now settled on Seamus Kavanagh, with first choice net-minder Damien Fitzhenry being played at left half-back. Ger Cushe was beginning to look trimmer and was still being played at centre-back. He had enough pure hurling ability to control this vital position, at least on the heavy grounds of the winter months. Larry O'Gorman, following his escapades against Meath, was dropped and Colm Kehoe was injured. Eamonn Scallan, George O'Connor and Billy Byrne were among the subs. The teams were as follows:

OFFALY

David Hughes

| Shane McGuckian | Kevin Kinahan | Martin Hanamy |
| Gary Cahill | Hubert Rigney | John Ryan |

Johnny Pilkington   Conor McGlone

| Joe Dooley | John Troy | Declan Pilkington |
| Billy Dooley | Joe Erritty | Pat O'Connor |

WEXFORD

Seamus Kavanagh

| Declan Stamp | John O'Connor | Shane Carley |
| Liam Dunne | Ger Cushe | Damien Fitzhenry |

Adrian Fenlon   Rory McCarthy

| Tommy Kehoe | Martin Storey | Larry Murphy |
| Paul Codd | Garry Laffan | Tom Dempsey |

The match had a very dreary first half. The second half saw Wexford play sparkling hurling. From a Wexford view point, the game represented a very important step on the road to rehabilitation from the ranks of the nearly-men. Offaly began well and had 1-2 on the board after eight minutes. Wexford then took over and ran up 1-4 before a soft goal allowed Offaly back into it. The Wexford full-back line seemed unsettled. The score at the interval was Wexford 1-4 Offaly 2-2. The unusual three man midfield tactic began to work in the second half, with Paul Codd revelling in the open space. With 19 minutes left it was 1-6 to 2-3. Then, to the surprise of the 15,573 spectators, Offaly were blown apart. Wexford were a revelation and all the hard training undertaken during the winter culminated in a display of power and precision, as they put ten points on the score board against Offaly's solitary point. The final score was 1-14 to 2-3. Ger Cushe gave a powerful performance, at centre half-back, and curtailed the skilful John Troy. Larry Murphy was brilliant and Rory McCarthy, not far behind. Tom Dempsey hit four good points. Martin Storey had assumed the Wexford's captaincy in succession to his clubmate, Liam Dunne and he recalls that second half with relish:

'When we hurled Offaly in the quarter-final of the league in Thurles, I suddenly realised that we were going to win something soon. I knew, with five minutes to go, that we had them beaten. On previous occasions I had thought we had them beaten. This time I knew it. And God, was it a great feeling. That match was a real turning point.'

In this game, Martin really began to deliver low, well-directed, quality ball to his inside colleagues. The results were self-evident.

Griffin talked about 'having broken a major barrier'. He used words like 'hunger' and 'belief' and seemed relieved and well satisfied. Eamonn Cregan commented after the match: 'Wexford came out in the second half and they just tore us asunder. We just weren't able to match them and it is as simple as that.' *The Enniscorthy Echo's* discerning hurling columnist, Enda McEvoy, however issued a note of warning:

'Before supporters fall over themselves hailing the return of Lazarus...two warning signs must be borne in mind. They are: (a) This Church & General NHL quarter-final was a truly awful game, its first half in particular surely being a contender for the title of the worst first half ever played... (b) Offaly gave up trying after ten minutes... Had Offaly been a horse, Eamonn Cregan would have been yanked before the stewards for running a non-trier.'

Griffin and his selectors felt that the press got it wrong about this match. They felt that the team had given a powerful performance, in the second half, which had gone undetected by the hurling journalists. The Cinderella story served up by Laois and Kilkenny, with Laois, for the first time in years, accounting for the black and amber brigade, served to overshadow the Wexford/Offaly encounter. They were far from unhappy about the under-emphasis placed on Wexford's excellent performance. It suited them well. It enabled them to remain undercover for a while longer. Stirrings of interest among the hurling cognoscenti in the possibility of a Wexford hurling renaissance would not, at this particular time, have helped the further development of the team.

The Final Lesson

Galway were Wexford's opponents in the Church & General 1996 League semi-final. To the disgust of Wexford supporters the match was fixed for Limerick. Having already travelled to Thurles for the quarter-final, the Wexford supporters felt that it was unfair that they should again be asked to travel such a long distance. The decision clearly indicated that the fixture had been made before the quarter-finals. Lowly Laois and humble Wexford had unaccountably come through against Kilkenny and Offaly. It appeared that these results did not represent the anticipated outcome, among the fixture makers at Croke Park. Now Laois was pitted against

Tipperary to play in Kilkenny; and Wexford unbelievably, had to play Galway in Limerick. As a result, apart from the major inconvenience caused to travelling supporters, none of the four semi-finalists now had the opportunity to see their final opponents in action. It seemed to be an anti-hurling decision and indicated that the establishment was not working to the benefit of the game and had little sympathy with the supporters. It was difficult to understand why remedial action was not taken, following the quarter-final results, in relation to the fixture.

Galway would have a few preliminary matches, before their meeting with the Leinster Champions in the All-Ireland series of 1996. These matches were against lowly rated opposition and were not considered to be real championship tests. Consequently, the Church & General League was being treated very seriously and the men from west of the Shannon had come through 80 hard training sessions.

The teams lined out as follows:

WEXFORD

Seamus Kavanagh

Declan Stamp   John O'Connor   Larry O'Gorman

Liam Dunne   Ger Cushe   Damien Fitzhenry

Adrian Fenlon   Rory McCarthy

Tommy Kehoe   Martin Storey   Larry Murphy

Paul Codd   Garry Laffan   Tom Dempsey

GALWAY

Morgan Darcy

Tom Helebert   P. Cooney   Gerry McInerney

Conor O'Donovan   Nigel Shaughnessy   Michael Donoghue

Michael Coleman   Brendan Keogh

Joe Rabbitte   Cathal Moore   Liam Burke

Kevin Broderick   Joe Cooney   Francis Forde

The first half was evenly contested with Wexford in encouraging form. Galway had a narrow escape when a Martin Storey goal attempt was saved at point blank range and rebounded to Paul Codd who hit the crossbar. Joe Rabbitte was menacing and picked off two good points for Galway. At half-time it was Wexford 0-6 Galway 0-7. After ten minutes of the second-half, Galway proceeded to take over. They shot four points, with two coming from Wexford's chief tormentor, Rabbitte, who was outhurling Damien Fitzhenry. With ten minutes remaining, an unsteadiness became apparent in Wexford's last line of defence resulting in a Galway goal from Peter Kelly, who had replaced Burke. Francis Forde had another Galway goal before John O'Connor converted a penalty to put a more respectable look on the score board. The final score was Wexford 1-10 Galway 2-15. The reality of competing against a division one team became clear. With due respect to Offaly, whose display was below par, Galway were a more potent force than the midlanders and served to illustrated that there was more work to be done in the Wexford camp. When things started going against Wexford in the second half, some of the players began ignoring the game plan and reverting to type. Keogh, Dempsey and Fitzhenry were taken off and replaced by Eamonn Scallan, Billy Byrne and Sean Flood respectively. The rehabilitated Larry O'Gorman was Wexford's best player but even he found it impossible to curtail the explosive Rabbitte, when he changed places with Fitzhenry. Rory McCarthy and Fenlon made a good impression at midfield. Griffin was blunt in his after match comment to Tom Humphries of *The Irish Times*:

> 'We were beaten fair and square by a team that played better. We over-carried when we had opportunities. We weren't taking long range scores. We have work to do, but in spots it was really close to what we wanted. We were doing some ground hurling and holding it together, but up against a good team like that it is hard to keep the plans going. Players get panicky.'

Asked if it was demoralising to lose in the League like this he answered:

> 'Ask Clare, Ask Clare'.

Aftermath of League Semi-Final

When a closer examination of the statistics of the Galway game was undertaken the picture began to look much brighter. Griffin dismissed the comments of many of the national hurling correspondents, by insisting that these were superficial reports. It is one thing for a beaten manager to rant on about the 'could have beens' the 'if onlys' and the claims of 'we could have won', in the aftermath of a defeat, in order to raise the morale of his players. It is quite another to prove the point with hard facts. In Wexford's case these facts were to hand. The volume of statistics tabulated by John O'Leary, represented a much clearer and more concise picture of the day's events. It turned out that the Wexford defence had cleared more ball than their Galway counterparts and that the Wexford attack had more of the play than Galway. But the Galway forwards scored, and Wexford's did not, at least not often enough. The players, by now, had become accustomed to in-depth analysis of their matches. Their aptitude for thinking had improved to a remarkable degree. Dissection of statistics took place, in a scientific manner, after every match, even in the case of a runaway victory. Players who appeared to put in star performances were often roundly criticised for undisciplined hurling or glory seeking exploits. The team now fully believed in the accuracy of the after-match statistics and took great heart from the tabulations of the League semi-final. Griffin hammered home the message and emphasised the good points from the display. 'You stuck to the game plan in the first half', Griffin told them. 'In the second half you did not. Please examine your performance. Think about it. I bear some of the responsibility. I erred in the case of Joe Rabbitte's curtailment, but I can assure you that it will not happen again. We are well able to play Galway'. The players took great heart from this inquest. George remembers something that forcibly hit him at this time. Griffin never made the same mistake twice.

It was to be Wexford's last defeat.

Some other events in this game had long term effects on Wexford's hurling future. One was Joe Rabbitte's eclipse of Damien Fitzhenry, coupled with the unsteadiness of Seamus Kavanagh in goal. To be fair to Kavanagh, he was coming back from a very bad leg break and it became obvious in this game that he had not regained his former speed. These dark clouds may have been a blessing in disguise for the Wexford management team. Although Fitzhenry is an outfield hurler of sufficient class to get his place on most county teams, he is undoubtedly a much more brilliant goalkeeper. Griffin admits to being in a state of turmoil during the second half of the Galway game. He was seeing Seamus Kavanagh, his goalkeeper playing badly. He was also looking at the eclipse of Damien Fitzhenry by Joe Rabbitte. The words of Noel Skeehan came back to haunt him. 'Always put your best player on goal,' the famed Kilkenny man had always preached. The primal importance of the number one position was forcibly driven home and Griffin changed his mind about who was to man the position on the Wexford team. It was to be Damien's last game outfield. The other significant event was an altercation between John O'Connor and Joe Rabbitte towards the end of the game. John broke a bone in his ring finger when it momentarily became trapped in Rabbitte's helmet. The injury caused him to be out of action for some time, resulting in Ger Cushe's restoration to the full-back position. A leaner and more confident Cushe, having hurled well all winter in the centre-back position, was now in his favourite position, with a measure of speed which he had never previously possessed. This speed was further increased by sprint training and downhill running undertaken after this match. Bunclody, near the foothills of the Blackstairs mountains became the favoured venues for this last important aspect of the Wexford fitness programme. In the coming months the new-found alacrity and fast reactions of the Gorey giant would cause many commentators to eat their words.

An Indicator of Things to Come

Early in May, Wexford continuing their blueprint for regular and sustained competitive hurling, played two matches in preparation for the forthcoming championship clash with Kilkenny. Cork were the opponents in the semi-final of the St. Patrick's Hospital tournament at Walsh Park, Waterford. Anxious to quickly get back to winning ways, Griffin appealed to the players before the game. 'You stuck to the game plan only for the first half of the Galway match. This match is not of great significance and I am now appealing to you to sustain our game plan for the whole hour. Try and concentrate. Do it for the whole game, just this once and let us see the result. And please, please do not go all out to create opportunities, because if you follow the game plan these opportunities will present themselves.' The players focused, and adhered to the planned pattern. Wexford won by 2-17 to 0-10 and were hugely impressive. Jimmy Barry Murphy was fascinated by Wexford's display and attitude. The final of the tournament was surprisingly, against Kilkenny. It is unusual for two teams to clash so near to a championship meeting. Both sets of mentors were wary, with each fielding only nine of those who would participate in the first round Leinster championship outing. Cushe played at full-back in both games. Wexford won by 1-15 to 1-11. Griffin, whose craft and tactical awareness was growing by the day, removed two of Wexford's best players, Larry Murphy and Sean Flood, at half-time. He was confident that Kilkenny could be beaten without them. It was a calculated risk, but it paid off and gave an important psychological boost to his team. 'Kilkenny', he hinted to his players, 'are not world-beaters – we have defeated them even without two of our best players.'

The players, the manager and the backroom team had, by now, gelled into a force of remarkable unity, confidence and purpose. It represented a formidable combination and, best of all, very few people in the hurling world realised that a new and utterly rejuvenated power was waiting to explode into the hurling consciousness of the nation.

After the game Fan Larkin told a very happy Liam Griffin that this year, Wexford would get out of Leinster. Not many in Wexford would have agreed with the legendary Fan.

The 1996 Walsh Cup Final

Laois were the opponents in the 1996 Walsh Cup final. The match, played at Wexford Park was Wexford's last outing before facing Kilkenny in the championship. Wexford had now settled on their best 15 and fielded the team that was to play Kilkenny with the exception of Paul Finn, on for Martin Storey and Paul Codd, on for Tom Dempsey. Laois had beaten Kilkenny in the Church & General League quarter-final and had run Tipperary close in the semi-final. The national hurling correspondents were impressed with the Babs Keating-inspired improvement in their play and they were seen as a coming force in hurling. Wexford won easily by 1-13 to 0-6. Only two of the Laois points came from play and all of the six forwards were held scoreless by the Wexford back line. The well practised hassling techniques were honed to perfection in this game with Sean Flood, in particular, revelling in the exchanges. It was a strong indication of things to come. The team was beginning to enjoy the experience of winning.

Mary Griffin's Illness

On the Monday before Christmas 1995 Mary Griffin, Liam's wife had just finished icing a cake when the doorbell rang. As she arose to answer it, she was disconcerted to find that her leg would not respond. Liam immediately came home from the Ferrycarrig Hotel and proceeded to massage it, but to no avail. They decided to call in their local family doctor, Frank Hogan. Frank reacted compassionately and speedily sent Mary to Wexford General Hospital. Later she went for assessment to Blackrock Clinic. A few days after their return to Wexford, consultant physician, Dr Paddy McKiernan, asked Liam to call to see him, at his home. It was Christmas Eve. With great sensitivity Paddy informed Liam that Mary had Multiple Sclerosis. Paddy offered comforting reassurances but, naturally, Liam was devastated. He decided to keep the news to himself until after Christmas. He did not want to spoil the festive season for Mary and the family. The news was finally broken to Mary early in the New Year. They then travelled to Dublin for a second opinion. The diagnosis was confirmed. Liam immediately decided to resign the job of Wexford hurling manager. Initially, he had every intention of seeing out his three- year term, but now felt that it would be extremely immoral to continue. While Mary has no intense interest in hurling, she naturally, followed the fortunes of her husband's Wexford team. She had been strongly supportive of her husband's efforts to put Wexford back on the hurling map. She coped extraordinarily well with the great disruption of family life in the Griffin household and her contribution to the great events of 1996 can never be overestimated. She was aware of the progress made with the team, and knew, from her husband's positive attitude, that he expected good things to happen in 1996. She pointed out that his resignation would not be fair on him or on his team. Mary was also aware that lots of publicity would ensue if her husband walked away from the job at this crucial time – and so asked him to postpone his resignation. He was opposed to this but as the days went by and medication began to have a positive effect on Mary's condition he began to reassess. Finally, after they had discussed the matter over a period, it was decided that Liam would remain as team manager until after the championship. No matter what resulted, Liam would resign when Wexford's participation in the 1996 championship ended. Both were happy with the decision. They told no one for a period of time, while Mary tried to come to terms with the unexpected trauma in her life.

Consequently, when Liam embarked on the restart of the League, in early 1996, he was aware that win or lose, this was his last campaign as

Wexford hurling manager. It was a difficult time. Many a journey to training sessions was tear-stained and full of heart-searching. On reaching the training venue he had, of necessity, to put on a good face. This was often excruciatingly difficult and required the complete subjugation of his inner feelings. The predicament of his wife's illness and his own inner turmoil could not be allowed to interfere with the spirit of the team. A few close confidants were made aware of the facts. Rory Kinsella and Seamus Barron were also apprised. In order that his eventual resignation could not be misconstrued, a small number of national GAA journalists were informed, but asked not to publish the information. To their eternal credit they kept the information to themselves.

Over the coming months the facts of Mary Griffin's illness became known to a few people in Wexford. The majority, however, including the avalanche of supporters of the Wexford hurlers that exploded across the country, were blissfully unaware of the trauma and turmoil that formed a melancholy backdrop to the public achievements of Liam Griffin, throughout the memorable events of 1996.

∞ CHAPTER 5 ∞

THE OLD ENEMY

Billy's Torture

Hotel Rosslare stands on a cliff top overlooking the modern port of Rosslare. The sweeping vista encompasses the village of Rosslare Strand and the bay of Wexford to the north, while southward Ptolemy's 'Sacred Cape', Carnesore marks the extreme south-eastern corner of the country. A short distance offshore stands Tuskar Rock, an imposing and silent sentinel to the regular movements of the huge ferries that now frequent these waters.

The Wexford hurlers grew to know the area well. They camped, in army tents, on the cliffs of Ballytrent and often trained on the broad deserted beaches of the area. They rose at 6 a.m. and following a short run, breakfast was cooked in the open air, usually by Griffin himself. Some nights they sat around a blazing fire, talking, singing and weaving dreams. The weekends usually ended with Sean Flood, a talented musician, leading everyone in a camp fire sing-a-long. Great camaraderie developed between the members of the team and management and a lasting bond was formed. Tactics and plans were discussed and opinions exchanged in a relaxed and memorable atmosphere. Griffin was always present and the man who had heard some impatient and irate Wexford supporters shouting 'stick to frying rashers ya long-nosed hoor,' did indeed fry the rashers and cook the sausages at the weekend barbecues. The Wexford manager once arrived wearing an unusual T-shirt. On the front was a very unflattering likeness of himself with the caption 'The Long-nosed Hoor'. On the back of the T-shirt was the comment which Griffin often made when he was asked how he reacted to such abuse. 'Rashers and small potatoes.'

The players will always remember these times and look back on them with fondness. They will also recall the torture as they pushed their aching limbs to the limits of endurance.

A few yards from Hotel Rosslare, 106 stone steps of severe gradient lead down the cliff face to the port below. Griffin took the players there and ordered them to run around a circuit which included these steps. It consisted of a downhill run, along the beach, up the steps at full pace and then a descending run for recovery across the bottom and back up the steps again. It was a carefully measured programme and needed endurance of a high order. 40 minutes was the running time allotted. Even the fittest found it breathtakingly difficult. There were still about fifteen minutes left after they had done five laps of the circuit. Their muscles ached and they were ready to drop from exhaustion as they completed the torture for the sixth time. To their horror, they were told that the required 40 minutes had not yet been attained. They set out on the seventh lap. Billy Byrne remembers the pain. 'My stomach heaved and my joints ached with pain. I thought I wouldn't make it. I remember really struggling as I tried to climb the last five steps. I had never gone through such torture before. It was then that it suddenly hit me. This is going to be our year. I could sense it. I knew no one could go through all this and fail.'

Sharpness

Griffin and the Wexford selectors were reasonably happy with the display against Galway in the Church & General National League semi-final because they knew that an important constituent of Wexford's preparation had still to be worked on. Liam had always had a great interest in physical fitness. He had acquired considerable experience in conditioning routines throughout his coaching career and had read extensively on the subject. All through his managerial term he had kept closely in touch with his brother, Pat Griffin, a professional swimming coach in Britain. The brothers had spent many hours on the phone discussing and analysing in minute detail the Wexford fitness programme. Together with Rory Kinsella and Sean Collier, they now began to execute the final part of the equation. This equation was particularly geared to hurling fitness and some of the components were distinct and innovative. Part of the final preparations involved easing down on strength training and increasing the emphasis on speed, power and sharpness. The intensive training engaged in all winter had been geared to increasing strength, endurance and power. On the dark winter evenings, hurling, through necessity, was often ignored, and strength endurance training was foremost. Following the League semi-final against Galway the emphasis on speed work and sharpness was increased. Further prominence was also given to skill work. For some time, Rory Kinsella had been on the National Coaching Council of the GAA and his knowledge of this aspect of the game was immense. Innovative skill training was intensified.

They also appreciated that a team could not sustain a fitness peak from March to September and they did not want the players to peak too early. They further realised that a sustained series of peaks was achievable, much as professional athletes like Michael Johnson and the Kenyan middle-distance runners regularly accomplish.

The Sports Psychologist

The use of sports psychologists is becoming recognised by forward-thinking managers as an important aspect of team preparation. Their first involvement in GAA was seen in the successful Ulster football teams. Later some Leinster teams availed of their expertise. Certain sports commentators continue to question their efforts and an element of derogatory comment can be seen to underlie reports of their activities. As a result, many counties are afraid to avail of such services for their players. They are afraid of being laughed at. But things are changing rapidly. Those who attempt to restrict the use of sports psychologists might as well be attempting to emulate King Canute. They are here to stay. They help a player to concentrate, to deal with the pressures of big-time competition, to set realistic goals and to reach optimal performance.

Liam Griffin wanted to ensure that the team could never be in danger of reaching a boredom threshold, while training. He was constantly looking for new ways to capture the players interest and keep their minds active and alert. Since he had taken over as Wexford manager, Liam had worked hard to familiarise the players with the concept of psychological preparation. They were now well acquainted with the idea and had a high acceptance level of its significance. He asked the players for their views on the introduction of a qualified professional sports psychologist. The players discussed the matter and felt that anything that would help their chances was welcome. Niamh Fitzpatrick was brought in before the Kilkenny game. She is a 28-year-old Dublin girl, and in Griffin's opinion, someone that he felt the team could relate to. Liam wanted someone who was active in the playing side of sport and had worked with athletes of a high calibre and who, consequently, was familiar with the hassles and pressures that could surround a player in the limelight. He also wanted someone who was in the same age group as his players. Niamh had all these attributes. Her personality, her logic and her common sense endeared her to the players and she made an important contribution to the team. She was made aware of the long list of defeats suffered by many panellists and her approach strongly recognised this fact. Niamh Fitzpatrick and Liam Griffin developed an excellent working relationship and became good friends. Their ideas on psychological preparation gelled to a remarkable degree. Niamh contributed some very worthwhile suggestions and Griffin and the team developed great respect for her capabilities.

While Griffin feels that sports psychologists have a part to play he is strongly of the opinion that their activities are subject to far too much media attention. He feels that it should be recognised by commentators and public alike that they represent just one facet of team preparation. There are many other factors and many other individuals, who make important contributions to the readiness of players, and whose activities are not highlighted by the press, who seem to liken psychologists to a type of witch doctor. This often makes a good story but is hardly ever in keeping with the reality. While their presence can have a very positive effect, they should at all times remain firmly in the background and should never be allowed to usurp the manager's responsibility in taking the hard and weighty decisions.

The First Big Test

Wexford was now facing up to the first stern examination of their new-found confidence. The team had been drawn to play Kilkenny in the quarter-final of the Leinster senior hurling championship. The match, fixed for 2 June 1996, was to be televised live from Croke Park. The other quarter-final between Offaly and Meath preceded it. Defeat for Griffin's team would spell the end of any hallucinations about removing the culture of defeat. It would be seen as a step on the slippery slope to abject failure. This was the crucial cross-roads. A gallant defeat would not satisfy. Anything other than victory would fuel the caucus groups which waited in the wings to ambush the outspoken Wexford manager and his fellow selectors. The manager knew it, the selectors knew it and the team knew it. This was the OK Corral and the Little Big Horn for Wexford hurling. And it could be Griffin's Last Stand.

K day had arrived.

Regard for Kilkenny Hurling

Among Wexford's real hurling fraternity there is a great admiration for Kilkenny hurling. They are seen as the game's true aristocrats and although Wexford have so often fallen to their neighbours, the respect for their skill and expertise is pre-eminent. The contribution made to Wexford sport and to hurling, in particular, by Kilkenny men is not forgotten by the Slaney. Paddy Mackey, an outstanding sportsman, won an All-Ireland with the Wexford hurlers in 1910. He then proceeded to set a record that is unlikely ever to be equalled. He won six Leinster senior football medals from 1913-1918 and he was part of the team that went on to win the four-in-a-row All-Ireland series from 1915-1918. Paddy was a Kilkenny man, a native of The Rower, who worked in New Ross. To qualify to play for Wexford he had to sleep in the county. Sean O'Kennedy ensured that everything was in order by supplying him with a bed at his home at Quay St., New Ross. The hurling skill and technique of Nick Rackard was honed and brought to perfection in a Kilkenny environment. Wexford All-Ireland winners, Nick

O'Donnell, Tom Ryan and Oliver Gough are natives of Kilkenny. Mick Heffernan of Glenmore (a relation of Christy Heffernan's) and Henry Doolan in the 1940s and John 'Hocks' Wall in the 1940s and 50s were other Kilkenny hurlers who turned out for Wexford. Ned Wheeler, although born in Laois, moved to Kilkenny at age five. He learned his hurling in Slieverue and settled in Wexford as a 15-year-old. In more recent times, a Kilkenny man, David 'Stoney' Burke wore the purple and gold colours and another Kilkenny man, Ned Power, a teacher at St Peter's College, made a seminal contribution to Wexford hurling and under-age hurling, in particular.

The Old Enemy

Although the debt is unlikely to be forgotten, it had done nothing to decrease the rivalry. In matches between the counties, no quarter is asked or given. Nothing is guaranteed to bring a Wexford hurler's blood to boiling point more readily than the sight of the black and amber jersey of the old enemy. From the first whistle, it is hell for leather with the skill, brain, artful dexterity and masterly first touch of the Kilkenny game pitted against the high catching, swashbuckling, fighting spirit and Herculean attitude of the Wexford men.

The 1908 Incident

In 1908, an incident occurred which illustrates that, even in those early years, there was a mutual respect and sporting attitude between the two neighbouring counties. In the Leinster senior hurling championship of that year, Wexford beat Kilkenny. One of the Wexford team, Sim Donoghue, had played in the junior curtain raiser and surprisingly turned out again in the senior match. Not unnaturally, Kilkenny lodged an objection. They were awarded the match but requested that it be replayed. The provincial authorities rejected this suggestion and Kilkenny refused to continue in the championship and awarded a walk-over to Dublin, who were thus crowned Leinster champions. On the too few occasions when Kilkenny was overcome by Wexford, the authentic hurling follower by the Nore was happy to see the men from east of the Barrow go on to win the All-Ireland. It also helped to motivate their hurlers to put the purple and gold-clad men in their place the following year.

An Old Insult

The confrontations and rivalries between the counties are written across the pages of history. The ancient kingdoms of Ossory and Ui Cinsealaigh roughly correspond to the present day county outlines. They were continually at war over lands and possessions. Nor did their religious counterparts see eye to eye. Church historians have written of the jealousy and antagonism that existed between the Diocese of Ferns and that of

Ossory. Much like the hurlers of Tipperary and Cork, or the footballers of Dublin and Meath, the clashes of Kilkenny and Wexford represent an explosion of rivalry that has the authentic fervour of all local derby matches. Abuse and banter are exchanged in the stands and on the terraces of Croke Park, like sympathy at an undertakers' convention.

One insult, however, is reserved by Wexford people as their most effective slur. In the torrid heat of a championship hurling encounter between the sides, one inevitably hears shouts and muttered comments about 'pissing on the powder'. This refers to an incident that dates back to 1798, when a group of miners from the village of Doonane, near Castlecomer, are said to have abandoned the hard-pressed Wexford insurgents, near Kilcumney, under the cover of darkness. They are supposed to have taken much of the insurgents' slim supply of arms with them and to have urinated on the remaining powder to render it useless to the Wexford men:

> *... the reneging treachery of the coal-men*
> *Who deserted in shame and*
> *Empty in spirit and bladder*
> *Slithered back to Castlecomer*
> *To enduring infamy.*

> *Summer of '98*

The incident is buried deep in the subconscious of many Wexford people. The fact that Doonane isn't even in Kilkenny, but in County Laois, is irrelevant. The Wexford supporters strafe the Kilkenny contingent with the age old insult, which is delivered with delectation and glee.

Wexford Team Selection

The Wexford selectors dropped Tom Dempsey for the Kilkenny game. They felt that he was not playing well enough and was not adhering closely enough to the all-important game plan. Tom, a man of unquestionable belief in his own abilities, was not happy about it and felt that he was being unfairly treated. He vowed that he would make the selectors eat their words. He began to feel that Griffin had written him off. He phoned the manager at one of his hotels and tried to put his case. An hour into the call he realised that he had not yet spoken. Hard as he tried, he could not manage to stem the flow from the Wexford manager. Exasperated, he finally blurted, 'Liam do you mind if I phone you back? Maybe then you will allow me to get a word in edge-ways'.

The Wexford selection included ten of the team that went down to Offaly in the 1995 championship. 19- year-old Paul Codd of Rathnure was given the right corner-forward berth. Garry Laffan, at 21 years of age, was making his championship debut at full-forward. To the surprise of many,

Rod Guiney was given the right half-back position. He had made his Wexford debut as far back as 1991 and although still only 26 years of age, had been on and off the team ever since. This was to be his make-or-break season. George was selected at centre-forward and given instructions to keep the forward line flowing. He was to be the mover and shaker of the team. Pat O'Neill, his direct Kilkenny opponent, was held in high regard in Wexford and it was essential that he be restrained from making the booming clearances that he thrived on. Pat has immense physical strength, but few can match George in close exchanges. John O'Connor was an absentee through injury, thus allowing Ger Cushe to regain the full-back berth.

An interesting situation presented itself on the edge of the Wexford square. Damien Fitzhenry, the Wexford goalkeeper, would be faced by his employer, D.J. Carey in the black and amber jersey. 'Fitz' was determined to show no undue reverence to the man who signed his wages cheque.

The Game Plan

Griffin had kept a close eye on Kilkenny throughout the spring and early summer and was well aware of the team's progress. The Wexford management outlined their game plan. Apart from the reduction in frees conceded, they wanted low and strategic delivery to the forwards and above all, they requested fast movement of the sliotar. They also wanted passion, but they stressed that passion alone was insufficient for victory. The Wexford players were not, as yet, totally convinced of Griffin's ability to produce a winning game plan. Confidence in his tactical awareness, however, was increasing rapidly among them. A few of the more sceptical kept their doubts to themselves.

Kilkenny Team Selection

There is little dispute in Wexford over the identity of the best hurling forward in the game today. D.J. Carey reigns supreme. Speed, dazzling ball-control, an astute hurling brain and the ability to do the unexpected, all combine to make him the prince of modern day forwards. Wexford were well aware of the threat of D.J. and made plans accordingly. They did not believe the reports from the Kilkenny camp concerning his injury problems. Kilkenny are the best bluffers in hurling and from the time of Paddy Grace have often conned opposing teams and lulled them into a false sense of well-being. Chairman of the Kilkenny County Board, John Healy, was worried about injuries to Liam Keoghan, Willie O'Connor, Michael Phelan and Adrian Ronan. In the event all except Ronan lined out. Rumours of discontent in the Kilkenny camp were disregarded in Wexford. Eamonn Morrissey, to the great relief of Wexford, was an absentee, having transferred to the Dublin colours. John Power, a flu' victim, was in the subs and the mercurial Eddie O'Connor was indisposed, for reasons not readily apparent.

Kilkenny – The Favourites

While Wexford had won just five All-Ireland titles, the Kilkenny men had 25, second only to Cork's total of 27. Wexford had not beaten Kilkenny in a championship encounter since 1988. The counties had clashed four times in the interim and Kilkenny had been victorious on all these occasions. They had last won All-Irelands in 1992 and 1993, but many members of those teams were now getting to the veteran stage and attempts to blood new players were not meeting with notable success. The Noresiders were beginning to feel that they were in the midst of a lean spell. A lean spell in Kilkenny is a year in which they do not win Leinster or All-Ireland honours. Offaly had won the Leinster titles of 1994 and 1995 and Kilkenny felt that it was time to assert their superiority once more. This superiority was never in doubt by the banks of the Nore. Within Kilkenny there were rumours that Wexford had improved dramatically under the new managerial regime. Hurling men like Fan Larkin knew this to be very true, but nevertheless, it was felt that when the chips were down, Kilkenny could always beat Wexford. Hadn't one of their renowned former players claimed that, in championship clashes between the counties, he could always see the fear lurking in the eyes of his Wexford opponents?

Despite the apparent problems with injuries and age, the national pundits were tipping Kilkenny to go through. It was hard to blame them, considering Wexford's dismal record. The odds being offered to win the All-Ireland at this stage were, 7/2 Tipperary; 4/1 Galway; 5/1 Offaly and Kilkenny; 6/1 Cork and Clare; 14/1 Limerick and Wexford; 16/1 Laois; 20/1 Antrim, Waterford and Down. To win out Leinster, 8/1 or 9/1 could be had on the no-hopers from the banks of the Slaney.

In the eyes of the hurling cognoscenti of the country at large, Wexford's line-out appeared to have one hurler who was past his best, seven who were merely callow youths and four more who had yet to prove that they had what it takes to compete effectively in the torrid heat of a championship battle. That left three trump cards, Liam Dunne, Martin Storey and Larry O'Gorman. Larry was likely to 'lose the head' and Liam Dunne, apart from his tendency to foul, was much too small in stature for a centre half-back. That left Storey, not always the most accurate of marksmen, and anyhow, one man could not carry a forward line. Kilkenny, as usual, would advance to the next round.

Within County Wexford there were two diverse groups. One consisted of the hurling followers, who felt a sense of apprehension and foreboding at the approach of the Kilkenny clash. Within this group there was an understandable lack of confidence in Wexford hurling. Too many false dawns had eaten away at any sense of conviction. The other group was made up partly of lapsed hurling fans and partly of those, mostly in the younger age groups, whose allegiance was to the artificial delights beamed in nightly by the magic Sky. Among this group there was a resounding sense of indifference.

The Mental Block

The Wexford backroom team was under no illusions about the spectre that haunted the Wexford players in relation to Kilkenny. They knew that Kilkenny's invincibility was an illusion. But it was a dangerous illusion and one that had to be removed. That their attitude to Kilkenny was a mental one was aptly illustrated by Niamh when she told them the story of what followed in the wake of Roger Bannister's achievement. Dozens of athletes had failed to crack the four-minute-mile barrier in the years before the legendary English miler accomplished the feat in May 1954. Within four years, the hitherto insurmountable barrier had been broken a further thirty-four times. This clearly illustrated that a significant element in the failure rate prior to Bannister's breakthrough was due to doubt, lack of belief and the perception in the minds of the athletes that the barrier was impassable. The Wexford players must believe. They had to decide that they could defeat the Noresiders. That decision must come from within. 'Just because the pattern is there does not mean that we have to follow it', she told them. The players were extremely receptive and their fertile minds readily embraced these new attitudes. Yes! They could and would beat the old enemy.

An article in the *Evening Herald* written by sportswriter, Paddy Hickey in the lead up to the Kilkenny game supplied further motivation. The feature tipped Kilkenny to win but it was the headline that supplied the real incentive to the Wexford players. It read 'So Sorry, Wexford'. Liam and Niamh rammed it down the throats of the team. Its sentiments greatly upset them. It was just the tonic to ignite the fires of resolve.

Attention to Detail

The performance of the Wexford management team was distinguished by their fantastic attention to detail. Everything that could impinge on the team's chances of success was examined. Nothing was left to chance. They even had the new Croke Park dressing rooms mapped out so that the players could visualise the layout. Consequently, when they arrived for the Kilkenny game there were no surprises. The surroundings were already familiar.

The First Half

Offaly beat Meath, unimpressively by 2-18 to 2-12 in the earlier game. The attendance of 21,000 was a poor turn out. It reflected the combination of fear and apathy which was prevalent in Wexford, a county which, in its glory years, had set every attendance record in hurling. Wexford County Secretary, Mick Kinsella, estimates the Wexford contingent at no higher than 6,000.

The Kilkenny manager, Nicky Brennan, was taking part in his first campaign. In a sideline TV interview before the game, he highlighted the well-publicised injury problems of his team and regretted that he was forced to field 'a team of crocks'. The opposing manager, Liam Griffin, retorted that 'Kilkenny never produced such a team'. TV pundits Babs Keating and Cyril Farrell were cagey, with Keating stressing that 'Wexford's defeat to Galway in the League semi-final was not as one-sided as everyone thought'. To the surprise of many, he appeared to favour Wexford's chances.

The conditions were humid with a very slight breeze. Wexford played very well in the first half and a dominant full-back line of Colm Kehoe, Ger Cushe and Sean Flood were more than equal to anything that Kilkenny could throw at them. Within a minute, Paul Codd had the distinction of scoring the first point. Immediately, it became obvious that the Wexford men had a game plan and were sticking to it. Nearly every ball delivered into the forwards was fast, low and effective. Towards the end of the first half with the scores standing 0-5 to 0-3 in Wexford's favour, 'The Galloping Nurse' took off. Martin Storey, the Wexford captain, shot three unanswered points from play in a scintillating bout of hurling. He was picking up plenty of ball and also shot four wides. Philip Larkin, a son of the great Fan, was having immense difficulty keeping him under control and Liam Keoghan was moved across to try to curtail Storey late in the first half. D.J. got delivery of a dangerous ball in the 31st minute, but Ger Cushe brilliantly blocked down his scoring attempt. Michael Phelan closed the gap near the interval. Amazingly, the entire Wexford back line conceded only one free in the first half.

At half-time the score read Wexford 0-9 Kilkenny 0-4. Rory Kinsella appeared worried when he told a TV interviewer that Wexford should have turned their greater possession into more scores. In the Wexford dressing room, George, with the experience of many false dawns against Kilkenny, warned the Wexford manager, 'They'll come back at us early in the second half. We've got to be ready'. On TV, Babs Keating commented that Wexford were completely on top and 'Kilkenny look a sick team'.

The Second Half

Kilkenny had the wind in the second half. John Power was introduced and immediately unsettled the Wexford half back-line. With his first touch he sent over the bar. Martin Storey was inches wide with a goal attempt, but in a tremendous Kilkenny spell of hurling they shot three points from Canice Brennan, Michael Phelan and P.J. Delaney. Philip Larkin was now hurling well for Kilkenny who were now only a point behind, 0-9 to 0-8. Eight minutes into the second came an incident which showed the effect of the new found Wexford adherence to 'hassling'. Sean Ryan, a Kilkenny sub for Derek Gaffney, found himself in an unmarked position in front of goal as a result of a Delaney hand pass. He was in the clear, eight yards out, with only Fitzhenry to beat, when Sean Flood came from nowhere and hooked him. It was a vital interception and the first of two crucial incidents that were to decide the outcome of the game. The Wexford contingent breathed easily again.

At this point in the game, Kilkenny had the upper hand and the game was slipping away from Wexford. The Wexford selectors now made the first in a series of clever tactical moves that were to distinguish their exceptional reading of the game throughout the 1996 season. Storey and Fenlon swapped positions and immediately, both began to prosper. The trend of the match was altered and the Slaneysiders regained the initiative. Liam Dunne began to get to grips with John Power. Larry O'Gorman had a great point followed by another from Storey before John Power hit another for Kilkenny. Scallan, from a free, and Fenlon added two more for Wexford to leave it 0-13 to 0-9 with fourteen minutes left. Guiney was now hurling like an express train and nothing could stop his irresistible surges. Where had this red-headed windmill of an all-action wing-back come from? Repeatedly, he burst through platoons of black and amber to clear his lines. It appeared that Wexford had the better hurlers and the winning of the game was readily within their grasp but, disquietingly, the gap between the sides was too close for comfort. The nervous Wexford followers thought of 1991 and 1993 and a half a dozen other occasions in matches against Kilkenny, when the wily Cats had wrestled victory from the jaws of defeat. The Kilkenny cat is different from the normal variety in the matter of survival. It has nineteen lives, not nine. The fat lady hadn't yet cleared her throat.

The Crucial Score of the Match

The judicious use of Billy Byrne's talents was the factor that made the difference in the end. Garry Laffan had great difficulty coping with Kilkenny's full-back Pat Dwyer. Pat's talents are highly regarded in Wexford, where it is felt that he is among the most underrated of the Kilkenny players. When the Kilkenny man cleared a few balls in the middle of the second half it seemed to the Wexford selectors that Pat Dwyer had reached a comfort zone. They decided to send on Billy Byrne. Although now at the veteran stage, the Gorey man could still produce the goods for short spells. It was the move that won the match.

Billy Byrne can be effective under any type of delivery. The players, together with management, had previously analysed the lead up to the scores achieved by Billy in competitive matches and in practice games. Not all were ground attacks. They knew that Billy could also produce under a high ball and they began to vary their game to allow for the arrival of the Gorey man to the pivotal position in attack. The Wexford midfield and half-backs mixed their deliveries. Some were low, others were high. In the 59th minute, a Damien Fitzhenry clearance was well caught by Adrian Fenlon, who delivered intelligently towards the full-back position. Billy Byrne and Pat Dwyer ran back together under the dropping ball. Dwyer was facing the sliotar but Billy was facing the goal. At the last second Billy turned and caught the ball in his left hand, a split second before the Kilkenny man could react. He stepped away from his marker and sent an unstoppable shot beyond Michael Walsh's reach. It was the crucial score of the match and left the teams at 1-13 to 0-9. Kilkenny fought on and had three unanswered points before Fenlon hit another. Sean Ryan and Lawlor hit further points before the long whistle sounded.

The last few minutes witnessed a dazzling rearguard action by Wexford's defence in which Colm Kehoe was defiantly solid. Kilkenny threw everything at their opponents, but there was no retreat. Towards the end of the game something very unusual occurred. It is doubtful if the Wexford fans had ever before seen it happen. Martin Storey was seen near his own full-back line, diving in to make a great block down. Kilkenny forwards were hooked, blocked and hassled as ball after ball was cleared by the magnificent Wexford defence. Sean Flood, Ger Cushe, Liam Dunne and Larry O'Gorman were everywhere and the final whistle brought a just reward and left the scores, Wexford 1-14 Kilkenny 0-14. Philip Larkin, John Power (both in the second half), Willie O'Connor, 'Tich' Phelan and Canice Brennan were Kilkenny's best performers. Martin Storey's five point contribution earned him the RTE Man of the Match award but Wexford's best player appeared to be Rod Guiney who gave a flawless display and cleared every ball that came his way. It was undoubtedly his best ever showing in a Wexford jersey. Colm Kehoe was the epitome of a great corner-back and was never once outwitted in the close exchanges. Liam Dunne was controlled and effective and Ger Cushe formed an impressive bulwark. The entire Wexford defence once again showed their new found discipline by conceding only three frees in the second half. Behind them stood the vigilant Fitzhenry, who played confidently and faultlessly throughout. Only 'Tich' Phelan with 0-2 and Delaney with 0-1 had scored from the original Kilkenny forward formation. Apart from Storey whose points proved invaluable, George did his job well, as did Adrian Fenlon and Paul Codd. The Gorey super-sub, Billy Byrne made the definitive contribution. Larry Murphy got a lot of possession and created a few scores, but did not finish well.

Larry Uses the Head

At one stage near the end of the game, Kilkenny were awarded a free near the Wexford goal. John Power tried to take a quick free, but Larry O'Gorman anticipated it and bravely, used his body to frustrate the attempt. John Power's hurl made contact with Larry's head and the Wexford man went to ground. Following some medical attention he resumed. After the match, in the Wexford dressing room, a groggy but ecstatic Larry, who in previous years had often been accused of not using his head at crucial moments, blurted, 'Nobody can ever again say that I didn't use my head for Wexford hurling!'.

Summaries

It was not a great game, but the tension-filled closing stages were memorable. In the first half Kilkenny were truly awful. The second half saw an improvement but really Wexford should have had the game sewn up much earlier. Cyril Farrell expressed delight at Fitzhenry's return to goal and said that for Wexford 'It was a lesson well-learned'. Babs Keating commented that 'the game went exactly as I predicted, but Wexford should have won by more'.

A Breakdown in Communications

John O'Leary, from the Wexford backroom team, had been dispatched to the stand before the game armed with a walkie-talkie. He was given strict instructions by Rory Kinsella to watch D.J. Carey and report on what position he took up from the start of the game. D.J. had been selected to play at left half-forward on the official team sheet but Rory suspected, rightly as it turned out, that the Kilkenny ace would line out at full-forward. When O'Leary saw D.J. going in to take up his position beside Ger Cushe, he immediately grabbed the walkie-talkie and tried to communicate with Rory in the dugout. He could not get through. For the next 15 minutes he frantically, continued to try to contact the Wexford selector. In the process, he became extremely agitated. Meanwhile, back in the dugout, Rory noticed that his walkie-talkie had been inadvertently switched off and proceeded to re-activate it. At once, the frenzied voice of a highly excited O'Leary screamed the message, 'He's moved in, he's moved in. Carey's gone in full-forward'. Rory who had spotted the move even before the match started replied, 'For Christ's sake, sure we knew that 15 minutes ago!'. Even the most electrifying court room drama had never reduced the

Wexford solicitor to such a state of apoplexy. When a TV interviewer asked Rory, at half-time, if the walkie-talkie system was working well, he replied, 'Yes, it's working quite well, thank you'. From that point on O'Leary insisted on a mobile phone as well as a walkie-talkie.

Aftermath

At the final whistle Paddy Wickham, the County Chairman, broke down and wept on the shoulder of the exhilarated Griffin. The atmosphere in the dressing room was euphoric. It was a great victory and everyone felt elevated. Liam, Rory and Seamus congratulated their players. John Healy, the Kilkenny County Chairman, was loud in his praise. He told them that it was Kilkenny's wish that the team go on to win Leinster, at least. He encouraged Wexford to get this win into perspective quickly and realise that nothing had yet been won. It was a sobering reminder. The Wexford selectors quickly worked to diffuse the dreaded 'We-have-beaten-Kilkennyitis' that had, on so many previous occasions, afflicted the team. They were determined that it would not reoccur this year. The players began to experience mixed feelings. Kilkenny had been beaten. Rejoice! Rejoice! Many of the older hands, however, had encountered the sensation before. While that memory did not lessen the enjoyment of this occasion, it brought back the recollection of the awful anti-climax of defeat at the next Leinster hurdle. They knew that the 'We've-beaten-Kilkenny-so-our-season-is-complete' syndrome was fatal. Quickly, they began to focus on the next hurdle. Griffin was delighted, but kept thinking about the pattern of the game. He knew that Wexford had, for long spells, appeared comfortable enough, but yet had allowed Kilkenny to get too near them coming towards the finish. It was a near fatal flaw that had to be ironed out before the next game. There was one thing that pleased him however. In his short term as Wexford manager he had three victories from three outings against Kilkenny.

Braveheart

A great sense of togetherness had been fostered in the Wexford camp. A specially commissioned team coach took them to the matches and sing-songs and tapes were part of the occasion. A video of the recent smash-hit film *Braveheart*, had been shown in the team bus on the way to the Church & General National League quarter-final against Offaly. The players loved it and felt that it produced a good spirit among them. It was not shown on the way to the losing semi-final against Galway but was reintroduced for the rest of the campaign. *Braveheart* thus became an important pre-match ritual. The players never saw the end of the video, as the arrival at Croke Park always coincided with the climatic rallying speech given by Mel Gibson, playing the part of Scottish hero, William Wallace. He is exhorting the troops from horseback while delivering his celebrated pre-battle oration. The voice of Gibson was joined by a dozen Wexford hurlers, who by now knew the lines off by heart, as the words echoed around the team bus:

> *'Sons of Scotland, I see a whole army of my countrymen here in defiance of tyranny. You have come to fight as free men and free men you are. What will you do with that freedom? Will you fight?'*
>
> *'No, we'll run and live.'*
>
> *'Fight and you may die. Run and you will live at least awhile. And dying in your beds, many years from now would you be willing to trade all the days from this day to that for one chance, just one chance to come back here and tell our enemies that you can take our lives but you will never take our freedom.'*

An eruption of cheering echoed around the bus as it turned the corner of Jones's Road and the portals of the old stadium came in sight. A fired-up, fit and confident group of sportsmen exploded from the bus and, carried on waves of adrenaline, entered the dressing rooms deep in the bowels of Croke Park. There, they attired themselves for battle. Quietly, Griffin and his selectors went over the game plan, for the last time. Wexford captain, Martin Storey, spoke a few short words to reinforce conviction. Then management and players went down on one knee to offer a silent player before the voice of an official summoned the Wexford hurlers of 1996 to the coliseum of their hurling destiny. Further motivation was unnecessary.

Braveheart had seen to that.

LEINSTER SENIOR HURLING QUARTER-FINAL
Croke Park, 2/6/1996

Referee: Aodain Mac Suibhne (Dublin)

WEXFORD

Damien Fitzhenry
(Duffry Rovers)

Colm Kehoe
(H.W.H. Bunclody)

Ger Cushe
(Naomh Eanna)

Sean Flood
(Cloughbawn)

Rod Guiney
(Rathnure)

Liam Dunne (0-1f)
(Oulart-The-Ballagh)

Larry O'Gorman (0-1)
(Faythe Harriers)

Adrian Fenlon(0-2)
(Rapparees)

Rory McCarthy (0-1)
(St Martin's)

Martin Storey(Capt.)(0-5)
(Oulart-The-Ballagh)

George O'Connor
(St Martin's)

Larry Murphy
(Cloughbawn)

Paul Codd (0-1)
(Rathnure)

Garry Laffan
(Glynn-Barntown)

Eamonn Scallan(0-3,0-2f)
(Liam Mellows)

SUBS: Billy Byrne (1-0) *(Naomh Eanna)* for Garry Laffan; Tom Dempsey *(Buffers Alley)* for Rory McCarthy; Paul Finn *(Oulart-The-Ballagh)* for Paul Codd.

KILKENNY

Michael Walsh
(Dicksboro)

John Costelloe
(St Lachtain's)

Pat Dwyer
(Carrickshock)

Willie O'Connor
(Glenmore)

Liam Keoghan
(Tullaroan)

Pat O'Neill
(Young Irelands)

Philip Larkin(0-1)
(James Stephens)

Aidan Lawlor (0-3)
(St Martin's)

Canice Brennan (0-3)
(Conahy Shamrocks)

Michael Phelan (Capt)(0-2)
(Glenmore)

Brian Ryan
(Fenians)

Derek Gaffney
(Tullaroan)

Charlie Carter
(Young Irelands)

D.J. Carey (0-1f)
(Young Irelands)

P.J. Delaney (0-1)
(Fenians)

SUBS: Sean Ryan(0-1) *(Dunnamaggan)* for Derek Gaffney; John Power(0-2) *(John Lockes)* for Brian Ryan; Damien Cleere *(Graigue-Ballycallan)* for D.J. Carey

∞ CHAPTER 6 ∞

A LACK LUSTRE DISPLAY

The Hurling Survey

During the summer of 1995 an in-depth survey was carried out among secondary schools students in County Wexford on their attitudes to hurling generally and under-age hurling in particular. The initiative for the survey came from the Wexford GAA Supporters Club and the Wexford Hurling Coaching Committee and was prompted largely by a desire to improve the standard of under-age hurling within the county.

Nothing as detailed as this was ever before attempted and in excess of 3,100 students from 15 schools completed the questionnaires. Every facet of the game was covered and the results were professionally tabulated into columns and graphs. Conclusions were drawn and recommendations set out. Prior to the survey there had been a feeling within the county that the future of hurling represented a gloomy picture. But, until the results of the survey became known, it remained just a feeling, with no scientific evidence available on the authentic standing of the game.

The findings were bleak and proved emphatically that the great old game was rapidly slipping in popularity among the young. There was no room for argument. A crisis was looming for hurling in Wexford. Among the students surveyed, 52 per cent did not play hurling. This was the average figure for all the schools, but in the case of Wexford CBS and Wexford VS those not playing the game represented 69 per cent and 62 per cent respectively. The number who played in sixth year was smaller than in first year. Hurling was listed as the most popular sport in only two of the fifteen schools surveyed. Overall, soccer was easily the top sport with hurling second and football third. Eric Cantona of Manchester United headed the poll as the most popular sports person, with 8 of the 14 schools listing him as their favourite. This, despite the fact that his recent kung-fu activities and his subsequent court appearance had been so well-publicised. In addition, the Frenchman's suspension had possibly cost his team the Premier League title. Encouragingly, D.J. Carey was in second spot and Martin Storey in third. The list of the top 25 favourite sports persons had 17 soccer players, 5 hurlers, 1 boxer, 1 basketball player and 1 from motor racing. Those who followed the fortunes of the Wexford hurling team came to a disappointing 57 per cent. This figure would have been slightly higher but for the large number of Kilkenny boys attending Good Counsel College in New Ross whose allegiance, naturally, lay across the Nore. The results also clearly indicated that hurling was losing out in urban areas while retaining a measure of support in the rural districts. The survey focused on the reasons for the decline and contained a detailed batch of proposed remedies, such as recruitment of more hurling coaches, the establishment of schools of excellence and extra financing.

Wexford is not the only county experiencing difficulty in maintaining an interest in hurling among the youth, as GAA Director General, Liam Mulvihill, outlined at the 1996 Annual GAA Congress:

'A combination of relentless television exposure, international appeal, high quality publications and professionalism of soccer and rugby are posing a huge challenge for us... Our dependency on schools, which was one of our great strengths in years gone by, could now become a weakness if we don't develop alternative recruiting policies, as the number of schools promoting (our) games declines.'

Those who were involved in the initiative of the hurling survey breathed a sigh of relief at 5.25 p.m. on Sunday 2 June when the referee blew the long whistle to signal Wexford's quarter-final Leinster Championship victory over Kilkenny. A defeat would have made their task of reviving hurling even more difficult. The win would, at least, maintain a modicum of interest in the forthcoming launch of the hurling survey. Another defeat however, either in the Leinster semi-final or in the Leinster final would hasten the impending demise of what for many years was a sporting way of life in the county.

The Wexford Schools Hurling Survey, a well-laid out 36-page booklet, was launched by The Wexford GAA Supporters Club on Friday 14 June 1996, by GAA President-elect, Joe McDonagh of Galway who addressed a very interested audience in the Talbot Hotel, Wexford. Its publication was an act of bravery by the WGSC. It would have been much easier to leave it on a shelf somewhere to gather dust. It takes a brave organisation to publicly highlight their own failures. A stunned silence greeted the figures. Joe McDonagh spoke eloquently and he was followed by others, including Martin Quigley, John O'Leary, Liam Griffin and Paddy Wickham. They hammered home the message. More time had to be devoted to regaining the interest of the young people in the game. Extra emphasis must be placed on under-age coaching. Minor and under-21 hurlers will have to be nurtured and fostered. The fundamental reason for the gloomy predicament in which under-age hurling in Wexford now found itself, however, was obvious to all. Wexford hurlers had stopped winning. At any level in any grade. A Leinster minor hurling title or an under-21 win would help the revival. A Leinster senior hurling title would be an even greater boost and an All-Ireland senior title, well, that was probably too much to hope for, just yet. Win an under-age title and possibly, just possibly, a senior title might follow at some indefinable future date.

Those present sagely nodded their agreement.

Effect of Win over Kilkenny

Committed hurling people, within Wexford, were very happy with the win over Kilkenny. It bridged an eight-year gap and showed that, when properly focused and prepared, the senior hurlers of the county could still be more than a match for the aristocrats of hurling. It was off-putting to hear commentators saying that it was one of the worst Kilkenny teams in living memory. Nevertheless, a win is a win. The bookies showed no great enthusiasm but, just in case, adjusted Wexford's odds for the All-Ireland down to 10/1.

Griffin and his co-selectors had not yet achieved any perceptible increase in their acceptance level. Wexford teams had beaten Kilkenny before, only to crash with a thud at the final Leinster hurdle. No one was about to get carried away. Neither were the faces of the Wexford management team recognisable in the county at large, except among committed supporters. Members of the Wexford general public were barely aware of their existence. They had yet to do anything remarkable. No eulogies were waiting to be printed. No autographs were being requested. The youth of the county could name the managers and players of every Premier League side in England, but few could name the manager or the selectors of the Wexford senior hurling team. This was illustrated admirably when Griffin was travelling from Wexford to visit Hotel Kilkenny in late 1994. Wexford had just had their first outing under his management and had defeated Kerry overwhelmingly, at New Ross, by 6-14 to 2-10. He stopped for petrol at a garage near New Ross. A teenager, who was operating the petrol pump engaged him in conversation. He turned out to be a keen hurling follower.

'Were you in the park on Sunday?' he enquired of Griffin.

'I was.' replied the Wexford manager, delighted to see a member of the younger generation so interested in Wexford hurling.

'That new Wexford manager must be some gobshite'.

'They won and won well, didn't they', said a peeved Griffin, as it dawned on him that he had not been recognised.

'Any manager that allows a team like Kerry to score two goals must be some eejit!'

A chastened Wexford manager resumed his journey.

20 months later, a championship win over Kilkenny notwithstanding, nothing much had changed.

The Next Hurdle

Wexford now faced Dublin in the Leinster semi-final. The match was to be played at Croke Park on 23 June. The game would be followed by the headline clash of 1995 All-Ireland finalists and current Leinster champions, Offaly and the fast improving Babs Keating-trained Laois.

Dublin in the League and Dublin in the championship are two different propositions. Wexford had gone down to the Dublin hurlers in the 1990 Leinster semi-final and it had taken a replay, before Wexford went through in the 1994 quarter-final. Wexford fielded eight of their 1994 side (ten if the suspended Tom Dempsey and George had played in 1994) while Dublin had five survivors. The Metropolitans, managed by Jimmy Grey, had been greatly strengthened by the arrival of two fine Kilkenny hurlers. Eamonn Morrissey and Jamesy 'Shiner' Brennan had transferred their allegiance from Kilkenny owing to their employment in the capital city. Morrissey, while in the black and amber, had so often been the scourge of Wexford. Immensely strong, fast, skilful and accurate he is, when he decides that it is his day, among the top five forwards in the country. 'Shiner' Brennan would get his place on any county team and offered the Dublin team great options at centre-field. John Twomey and Kevin Flynn were other members of the Dublin attack who could not be allowed any leeway. Sean Power at full-back was a fine hurler, and he was ably assisted by John Finnegan and Andy O'Callaghan. Nevertheless, the majority of hurling followers felt that the game would result in an easy win for Wexford.

The Wexford Selection

Wexford announced a team with two positions unfilled. The versatile A.N.Other figured at full-back and at right corner-forward. It was expected that Ger Cushe would recover from injury in time to man the space in front of the goalkeeper. John O'Connor was still an absentee, through injury. The corner-forward position was more complicated. Paul Codd was out, due to a fractured knee sustained in an under-21 match. That left three players, Tom Dempsey, Paul Finn and Billy Byrne, in the running for the position. Tom had suffered a family bereavement on the Tuesday before the game. His brother-in-law, Niall Glynn, had died as a result of a tragic accident. No one was sure whether he would be in the correct state of mind to participate in a championship hurling game so soon after such a traumatic experience.

The First Half

The attendance of 30,000 included about 6,000 from Wexford. They saw Dublin and Eamonn Morrissey, in particular, frighten Wexford in the early exchanges. The former Kilkenny man narrowly failed to connect with a McCann cross and then, within a minute, he rounded Sean Flood with a clever manoeuvre only to slip at the vital moment. Wexford then took over and for about 15 minutes played like champions. Fenlon, Scallan and Laffan hit points before Scallan converted two frees to leave it 0-5 to 0-0 for Wexford. John Twomey subsequently had a Dublin point before Morrissey again outwitted Sean Flood and saw his shot well saved by Fitzhenry. McCann collected the rebound but was held and Dublin had a penalty awarded. Morrissey fluffed the pick-up but Cushe missed the ground stroke and the ball ended high in the corner of the Wexford net. A Kevin Flynn point in the 19th minute brought the sides level. The Wexford selectors acted quickly to counter the Morrissey threat. He was coming off better in the physical exchanges with the much smaller Flood and his ability to hold off the Wexford man was causing danger to Wexford's defence. Larry O'Gorman and Flood swapped positions. O'Gorman had been a star minor corner-back and had recently figured in the position for Wexford against Galway in the League semi-final.

The small panel of top class experienced players in Wexford had prompted the backroom team to ensure that those in the first 15 were capable of playing in more than one position. This was to be the first example of this new found Wexford adaptability. O'Gorman was the most adaptable of them all, having figured in up to 12 positions in his intercounty career. Corner-back was no problem and he proceeded to snuff out the Morrissey threat and give a display that earned him man-of-the-match. Martin Storey had another point before the score of the game was registered. Storey sent a ball down the right wing where Dempsey created a diversion for Laffan to gain possession. There was no apparent danger to the Dublin goal as the Glynn-Barntown man grabbed the sliotar. Suddenly he dropped the shoulder, rounded Dublin full-back Sean Power and cut in towards the posts. He then released a good left-handed shot to register a fine individual goal. Laffan was now like a man possessed and two minutes later he grabbed the ball again, only to be illegally held by Power and a penalty awarded. 'Fitz' set off on a sprint from the Wexford goal and took up a menacing position over the ball. Those who questioned the wisdom of using a goalkeeper to take the penalties had their doubts laid to rest, as the slightly built son of Curraduff sent a blistering shot to the back of the Dublin net. It was now 2-6 to 1-2. A John Twomey point and two more from Storey and Larry Murphy made it 2-8 to 1-3 at the interval.

The Second Half

The second half was a total anti-climax. The Wexford forwards scored only four more points, while playing quite unimpressively and allowing Dublin the initiative for long spells. Nine wides were registered by Wexford while the paucity of Dublin's attack resulted in a second half yield of only six points. As the minutes ticked by and both sets of players huffed and puffed, the game became disjointed and uninspiring. If Rip Van Winkle had been in the Hogan Stand he would have remained undisturbed. An excellent Fitzhenry save from Kevin Flynn in the 68th minute did something to enliven the proceedings. Wexford's surprise packet, the excellent Garry Laffan, closed the scoring with a point. The final score was Wexford 2-12 Dublin 1-9.

How They Played

It was a tough physical encounter with plenty of timber wielded. Shiner Brennan had a magnificent game for Dublin, who refused to lie down and fought hard right to the end. Dublin had a good set of backs and made life very difficult for the Wexford attack. Forwards are needed and if they can be found, then Dublin will not be very far from a major breakthrough. O'Gorman was easily the best player on the pitch, with Laffan having a terrific game. Sean Power is one of hurling's better full-backs but he had no answer to Garry's pace and determination. The under-21 player showed, in this encounter, that he could become a potent force on the intercounty scene. Laffan's display was a great encouragement and justified the selectors' faith in the young Glynn-Barntown man. Adrian Fenlon displayed great consistency while Sean Flood, after his move to wing-back, together with Rory McCarthy, Liam Dunne, Ger Cushe and Fitzhenry all played well. Colm Kehoe, at times, had problems with Dublin's excellent corner-forward Kevin Flynn and was forced to concede some frees. However, he showed that he was turning into a very effective and close-marking corner-back. Rory Kinsella also felt that he was fast becoming an excellent reader of the game. Anticipation of a high order and the ability to read a game suggested that young Colm, as a defensive hurler, had many of the qualities that distinguished the displays of the great Franz Beckenbaur on the soccer field. Apart from Laffan, the Wexford forward line disappointed. Tom Dempsey had, after all, lined out at corner-forward and Rory Kinsella commented on the nine players used over the 70 minutes.'We simply didn't think we were threatening enough. Now everybody will be fighting for their place the next day.'

Reaction

The game was greatly overshadowed by the headline clash between Offaly and Laois. Another awesome Offaly performance saw them toy with Laois before despatching them with contemptuous ease. John Troy was irrepressible as he caressed the sliotar with scintillating skill, scoring 2-2 in a display of great virtuosity. The national press, justifiably, raved about Offaly's display. They were generally dismissive of Wexford. Neither Griffin or his colleagues were happy with the lack lustre second-half performance, but took consolation from the fact that the Wexford training programme had been designed to ensure that the real sharpness came for the crucial Leinster final. At this point in the season, the Wexford management team was taking risks. Unlike Offaly, whose players appeared to be at peak levels of sharpness for their clash with Laois, the Wexford team's build up had been designed to reach maximum potential for the Leinster final. It was high-wire management and indicated a certain amount of cockiness in the approach to the Dublin game. It was dangerous and it could have backfired, but the team did enough to beat Dublin, albeit unimpressively. This policy decision by management indicated their innermost thoughts. They were anticipating a long hot summer.

As the days passed they came to the realisation that the result was much more important than the display. An exhibition of hurling by Wexford would have been highly satisfying to Griffin and the management team. It would have copperfastened their decisions on team placings. It would have quelled doubts about forward accuracy. But it would also have brought rave reviews in the national press and served to forewarn Offaly that this year's Wexford model was different from that of other years. Thus the Wexford men did not have to bear the weight of great expectations. It was a burden that they were happy to side-step. Cregan and his well-proven team were welcome to it. Wexford's lack lustre display was a blessing in disguise. The omens for the Leinster final were not in Wexford's favour.

The pressure was on Offaly.

LEINSTER SENIOR HURLING SEMI-FINAL
Croke Park, 23/6/1996

Referee: Pat Horan (Offaly)

WEXFORD

Damien Fitzhenry(1-0f)
(Duffry Rovers)

| Colm Kehoe | Ger Cushe | Sean Flood(0-1) |
| *(H.W.H. Bunclody)* | *(Naomh Eanna)* | *(Cloughbawn)* |

Rod Guiney
(Rathnure)
Liam Dunne
(Oulart-The-Ballagh)
Larry O'Gorman
(Faythe Harriers)

Adrian Fenlon (0-1)
(Rapparees)
Rory McCarthy
(St Martin's)

Martin Storey (Capt)(0-2)
(Oulart-The-Ballagh)
George O'Connor
(St Martin's)
Larry Murphy (0-1)
(Cloughbawn)

Tom Dempsey (0-1)
(Buffers Alley)
Garry Laffan (1-2)
(Glynn-Barntown)
Eamonn Scallan (0-4,0-3f)
(Liam Mellows)

SUBS: Dave Guiney *(Rathnure)* for Eamonn Scallan; Billy Byrne *(Naomh Eanna)* for Larry Murphy; Paul Finn *(Oulart-The-Ballagh)* for George O'Connor.

DUBLIN

Eamonn Burke
(St Vincent's)

Derek McCormack
(Trinity Gaels)
Sean Power
(Commercials)
John Finnegan
(Commercials)

Sean Deignan
(St Brigid's)
Paddy Brady
(St Vincent's)
Andy O'Callaghan
(St Brigid's)

James Brennan(0-1)
(O'Toole's)
Liam Walsh
(Faughs)

John Twomey (Capt)(0-5)
(Erin's Isle)
Stephen Perkins
(Good Counsel)
Gerry Ennis
(Commercials)

Eamonn Morrissey (1-0)
(O'Toole's)
Conor McCann (0-1)
(Faughs)
Kevin Flynn (0-2)
(O'Toole's)

SUBS: Shane Cooke *(Commercials)* for Stephen Perkins; Brian McMahon *(Crumlin)* for Gerry Ennis.

∞ CHAPTER 7 ∞

THE RIVERDANCE OF SPORT

The Brotherhood

Larry O'Gorman is known as 'Scorcher'. He inherited the nickname from his father and no one is quite sure of its origin. Larry spent a week in Santa Ponsa in 1995 with a few of his mates. While not sticking religiously to the Griffin training regime he was determined that he would, at least, continue to eat plenty of fruit. He bought his daily ration of apples and coconuts from a coloured vendor on the beach, who got to know, and like the wise-cracking 'Scorcher'. He invariably greeted Larry with 'Brother, what can ah git you today?' Larry liked the fraternal greeting and used it on his mates. They took up the salutation. When Larry resumed with the Wexford team for the League campaign of 1995-96 he introduced the greeting to his team mates. They also began to take it up. It was 'Brother this' and 'Brother that'. Soon it became the normal form of address between members of the panel. Around the time of the Kilkenny game, Griffin picked it up and made a great play on it. The bond between players and management was growing daily and Griffin proclaimed that they were all brothers in hurling. Training sessions became like conventions of a socialist party as shouts of 'Pass it here brother' or 'Leave it to me brother' echoed around Wexford Park. At work or at play it was the same. Panel members greeted one another across a crowded hall with the familiar shout. The Brotherhood had been born.

Tom's Fatal Error

While the winter gym work was in progress, it was decided that each player would get in the ring with Sean Collier, another member of the backroom team, and don boxing gloves. This was intended to help increase upper body strength, improve footwork and introduce a bit of fun into the training routines. Collier, a boxer of no mean ability, commenced to spar with some of the more adventurous of the players. Tom Dempsey, nimble on his feet, fancied his chances of landing one on Collier. He succeeded, but regretted the foolhardiness of his action a moment later when he found himself flying through the air, as a result of a lightening right cross from the Irish international light-heavyweight. Tom ended up in a crumpled heap in the corner of the ring with blood oozing from a badly split lip. 'I didn't realise that he was allowed to hit me back', complained Tom, to the shrieks of laughter from his team mates. It was a fatal misinterpretation of the rules of the exercise.

The Hype of the Munster Final

The legendary glory of the Munster hurling final owes much to the hype of writers such as John D. Hickey, 'Carberry' and Raymond Smith. While no one would deny that the occasion witnessed epics from time to time, the majority of the finals were never as great, from a pure hurling viewpoint, never as exciting and never as sporting as the picture that was painted. Many of the early GAA journalists were Munster men and their hurling vision, in the view of Leinster people, was limited by their upbringing. They helped, in no small manner, to create a deceptively romantic and sometimes inaccurate picture of the glory of Munster final day. It seemed that it did not suit their purposes, or the purposes of the GAA authorities to whom they were beholden, to report the reality of these hurling clashes – usually between Cork and Tipperary, with occasional participation from the likes of Limerick, Clare and Waterford. Thus, the reader was fed a diet of legendary 'ham teas', 'saving the hay and beating Cork', momentous after-match gatherings in Hayes's Hotel, Thurles and similar dewy-eyed propaganda until the hurling people of Leinster and Connaught wondered whether they were playing a different game. The atmosphere in Thurles, a special place and a special stadium, may have been a contributory factor. While it was never possible to fill the much larger Croke Park venue for a Leinster final, Thurles was invariably packed to capacity for Munster finals and the excitement undoubtedly created a unique ambience.

The illusion was not confined to the commentators, for if one thumbs through the pages of Brendan Fullam's excellent hurling books *The Clash of The Ash* or *Hurling Giants*, one is left somewhat stunned by the insular view of some Munster hurlers when they sit down to name their greatest-ever 15. In many cases, the renowned hurlers whom they acclaim are exclusively confined to their own province.

Munster representatives did dominate the All-Ireland series prior to 1950, while winning 40 of the 63 titles on offer. Since then the power has shifted. Since 1950, Kilkenny has won more All-Ireland crowns than any other county. The same statistic applies if one counts from 1960. Since that year, Munster counties have won 17 times while non-Munster representatives have triumphed on 19 occasions. Yet, at times, we are led to believe that the borders of hurling correspond with those of the province of Munster.

When Charles Kickham wrote *Knocknagow* he was not to know that the hero of that great novel, *Matt The Thresher* would be used in such a metaphorically illusory manner. I doubt if he would have been happy had he seen some of the antics in Thurles or Limerick during the so-called glorious struggles for supremacy between counties in Munster hurling finals. While the game of hurling is not for ballet dancers, what passed for sportsmanship in some of these encounters and what was later assigned to the annals of hurling lore, was often petulant and bad-tempered. The 'hard' man was king and the writers of the day encouraged his behaviour by refraining from condemning his conduct. The artistry and skill of Christy Ring, Jimmy Barry Murphy, Tom Cashman, Tony O'Sullivan, Frankie Walsh, Paddy Kelly, Colm Honan, Jimmy Doyle, and Nicky English were often nullified by the hatchet men, who sadly for hurling, frequently occupied positions in the defensive lines of the competing counties. Some of these blood-and-guts characters, to whom good sportsmanship was anathema, became legends, largely because of the blinkered attitude of certain sports journalists. These individuals, more often than not, were exposed in the final matches of the All-Ireland series on the broad open spaces of Croke Park

The Leinster hurling final on the other hand, somehow never drew the same free-flowing cascades of adulatory prose from the pens of these writers. Their heart strings were never plucked, to the same extent, by the encounters in Croke Park on Leinster final day. Indeed, the Munster winners were arrogantly expected to win the All-Ireland, having, as we were emphatically told, already beaten Ireland's top teams.

This of course was wishful thinking, and delight was registered in Leinster, and often in Connaught, when the Munster final winners found that things were not quite as they were supposed to be in the All-Ireland semi-final or final.

It was always difficult for Kilkenny, Wexford, Galway and Offaly people to understand this Munster bias. Especially so, having visited these Munster coliseums of Cuchulainn, and witnessed the scrappy and one-sided contests which too often marked the occasion. The fact is that, despite the hype, the Leinster final has been, over the past 25 years, a contest of higher skill, a closer and more dramatic encounter and an epic of far greater sportsmanship than its Munster counterpart.

The advent of television and the highlighting of some of the rough tactics began to open viewers eyes to the reality. Thankfully, it also influenced team selections to the point where many of the hatchet men are now left in the hurling deserts of the junior grade.

When Kilkenny, to counter intimidation, adopted a more physical approach, with undoubted success, in the All-Ireland finals of the early 1980s, the team was condemned by the critics. This criticism did not go down well by the Nore, and one can understand their feelings. Too many times in the past their skill and artistry had been neutralised by the more physical and more robust type of game of the Munster final winners. That Kilkenny did not let it happen in those years is to their eternal credit.

It must also be said that some Leinster counties were noted, at one time, for an over-physical approach to the game. None who used that brand of hurling ever made the breakthrough. Wexford went through a spell in the years since their last All-Ireland win, when players who were unfamiliar with the tenets of good sportsmanship were sometimes picked on the senior hurling team. During this era, no titles came their way. Griffin and his co-selectors were adamant that this type of game would not be tolerated. In the early months of the new managerial reign close to 70 hurlers were assessed. Some were discarded because they were unable to accommodate the new discipline. It was made very clear to all panel members that sportsmanship and adherence to a strict disciplinary code was essential if the long-awaited breakthrough was to follow.

The old disreputable methods had no part in the Wexford hurling renaissance.

Clash with Munster Final

All the leading hurling correspondents wound their way to Pairc Ui Chaoimh for the Munster hurling final replay between Tipperary and Limerick. Having clearly written off Wexford's chances against Offaly the result was gross underexposure for the Leinster final and the best hurling game of the year. Indeed, in the view of many commentators, it was fit to be rated among the great Leinster finals. Both games were televised live and those who watched, enjoyed an afternoon of high drama beginning with the clash of Tipperary and Limerick. Ger Canning, RTE's first choice commentator, was assigned to the Munster Final. The betting on Wexford had now come down to 7/1 for the All-Ireland title. The shortening of the odds was more a reflection on the smaller number of teams left in the series than on any real hope that the Slaneysiders would succeed.

Wexford Tactics

The big question in the minds of the Wexford selectors was, would Wexford reproduce the sparkle of the second half of the League quarter-final, when they proved, once and for all, that they could beat Offaly. Or would they revert to their old ways when the bullets started to whiz and Offaly started to put on the pressure. The newspapers already knew the answer and were tipping Offaly for another Leinster crown. Offaly had been brilliant in obliterating the quietly fancied Laois in the semi-final. Wexford had beaten a poor Kilkenny side and struggled before overcoming Dublin. Offaly had contested the last two All-Ireland finals, winning one and going down very narrowly to Clare in the other. Wexford had contested their last All-Ireland final in 1977 and had not won since 1968. Offaly had won eight Leinster titles since 1980. Wexford had won none. Offaly had been very successful at underage; Wexford had not. Offaly had a team of winners. Wexford – well, they were the chokers, the 'nearly-men', the perennial losers. Sports reporters are human. They have no wish to be ridiculed. To assert that Wexford would beat Offaly was like hinting that the Rev. Ian Paisley would captain Young Irelands in next year's Kilkenny senior hurling championship.

Griffin was adamant that Wexford would not beat Offaly by playing their game of previous years. The new methods had to be adhered to and special moves had to be implemented to counteract the Offaly team. Eamonn Cregan had been one of the greatest of all exponents of the game and knew all there was to know about hurling. Griffin had watched him since his schoolboy days and considered him to be strongly in the running for a place on the hurling team of the century. The midlanders were accomplished hurlers and in attacking wing-back, Brian Whelehan, the skilful and accurate Johnny Dooley, the brilliantly scheming John Troy, a tight and highly experienced full-back line and two mid-fielders who were capable of appearing out of nowhere to register scores, they had players that were well-proven on the big stage. Wexford had last beaten the midlanders in the championship in 1979. Since then the sides had clashed in 1981, 1982, 1984, 1988, 1994 and 1995. Offaly had been victorious on each occasion. All the work that Wexford had undertaken over the previous 22 months was now about to be put to the supreme test. No fouling in the backs, no solo-running, plenty of ground hurling, low deliveries, forwards tackling back, no shooting from impossible angles and accurate free taking – all had to be implemented. The players were also told to shoot with conviction. 'For today, I don't give a damn about your wides. Go for it', the players had been told. Above all, the Wexford management team felt that there were weaknesses in the Offaly back line. These weaknesses had to be exploited. The game plan had to persevered with. Not just for ten minutes. Not just for the first half. But for the entire 70 minutes or for whatever time it took for the referee to blow the final whistle. And if Offaly went ahead at a crucial stage, they had to fight, fight and fight again. Every Offaly man had to be hassled out of it.

Motivation

Motivation was easily achieved. The pages of derogatory comments about the county's hurling prowess, if placed in book form, would almost fill a branch of a Carnegie Library. Griffin grabbed every opportunity of highlighting the many occasions when sporting commentators and others danced on the bones of Wexford hurling. Newspapers headline like 'Even

Wexford Doesn't Lose Them all Greg' (a reference to Greg Norman's propensity for losing golf majors), were gleefully pasted up on in the Wexford dressing-room.

Griffin had located two photographs which he hoped would be an important motivating influence on the team. He had them enlarged and placed on the dressing room wall. The images were dramatic. One showed Stuart Pearce, the English international soccer player, in the throes of dejection, having just missed a 'sudden-death' penalty for his country in the Italia '90 World Cup. It reflected misery and utter despair. The other was the widely-seen photograph of the same spirited and wholehearted player in the moments after he had scored from a similar penalty in Euro '96. The expression of animated elation was intense. He had exorcised the personal demons that had haunted him for six years. The contrast was thought-provoking.

'What's the difference?' asked Griffin.

'He got a second chance', someone said.

'Exactly', Griffin said, 'That player got a second chance. Many of you have had lots of chances. How many more chances do you want?'

The impact of the conflicting emotions of Pearce, in victory and defeat, was a lasting one.

Confidence

Building confidence was a slower process, but was greatly aided by taking the after-match comments from the victory over Offaly in the League quarter-final. These were copied and given to the players as hand outs. Eamonn Cregan's words 'They tore us asunder'; 'We didn't perform... due to Wexford's raw determination'; 'They are playing for each other. They are hungrier and more enthusiastic' were repeated over and over to the team. Again and again Griffin emphasised the result of that match. It was crucial for the players to remember that they had hammered Offaly and they must believe that what they had done once, they could do again. This was essential for morale.

The Leinster final was also the first occasion when the team had been brought to an absolute physical peak. They were now as fit as they could be. The sharpness which had not been acutely honed for the Kilkenny and Dublin games was now clearly evident. Rory Kinsella spent many further hours working on skills and ball control. Liam and Rory occasionally quibbled over the amount of time allotted to various disciplines. It never went beyond friendly banter. Seamus Barron jokingly offered to act as peacemaker. It was never necessary as the three men were now like brothers. They were 'The Three Musketeers' of Wexford hurling and like their fabled French counterparts it was 'All for one and one for all'. During matches, Seamus paced the sideline, watching and noting carefully the mental state of each player. Whether he was ready. Whether further improvement could be coaxed from certain individuals. He said little, but what he did say was incisive and enlightening. Niamh Fitzpatrick and Liam Griffin were also satisfied that mental alertness and concentration were peaking. Guiney and Laffan were like young bulls, just let loose in a verdant meadow. If Griffin had ordered them to jump over the stand in Wexford Park, they wouldn't have hesitated.

'We Have Decided!'

As the Offaly game drew nearer, a conviction became evident among the Wexford players which was difficult to explain. This was their fourth Leinster final appearance in 5 years. Each of the others had ended in defeat. Yet every player was confident that this time Offaly would be beaten. Griffin's positive attitude had transferred to the team members. He was so certain. Or he appeared to be.

On the Wednesday night before the Offaly game, the team had sat down in a room in the Talbot Hotel in Wexford. Niamh had put a notice on the wall. It read 'Wexford 1996 Leinster Champions'. She had then asked the players to outline their arguments as to why Offaly would be beaten. Every member of the team contributed in what was a display of breathtaking assurance. 36 rational reasons why Wexford would win were voiced. 'We are a family'; 'Defeat is not an option'; 'We are prepared to bleed from first to final whistle'; 'We have faith in our preparation'; 'We trust each other 100 per cent'. Liam Dunne's contribution was the most telling of all. It succinctly summed up the mood of the team. 'We have decided that we will beat Offaly.'

'We'll Do It for Ourselves'

Many of the players had grown tired of the abuse that was directed their way after championship defeats. At the last training session before the Offaly game, they had stood around in groups after the physical end of things had been completed. Griffin told them to talk among themselves – about their attitude; about being positive and about winning. Someone had said, 'We'll do it for George and Billy'. Someone else had said, 'We'll do it for our families. Another said, 'We'll do it for the supporters'. Ger Cushe was the strong silent type. He rarely became emotional and no one had ever heard him give a rallying speech. Suddenly the Gorey giant began to speak. There was passion in his words. 'To Hell with all that, we'll do it for ourselves. For ourselves!', he shouted. It was one of the shortest speeches that any of them had ever heard. But it was also one of the most effective. Ger was right. The words had a major impact.

Growing Faith in Selectors

The methods employed by the three men that had the future of Wexford hurling as their responsibility had taken awhile to gain overall acceptance among the players. Their insistence on ground hurling, their arguments over sacrificing the individual approach in favour of a team effort and their unconditional edict on strict adherence to the game plan appeared to be bearing fruit. So far the formula had worked. Offaly however, was the real test. At a team meeting before the Leinster final, Larry Murphy had been frank in Griffin's presence. 'When you took over I thought that most of what you said was nonsense. I rarely agreed with your methods or your game plan, but damn it, it appears to work. You've got us this far so I think we should have faith enough to continue to do it your way,'

Larry's Inspiration

Larry Murphy is an enigma. Possessed of blinding speed, great control and a left-hand reminiscent of Jimmy Doyle of Tipperary, the Wexford-based bank official often threatens to take over a game. He eats and sleeps hurling. From the time he was a boy in Cloughbawn he dreamed of following in the footsteps of the celebrated forward maestro, Tim Flood. He learned his hurling at Good Counsel College in New Ross and made his Wexford senior debut in the League against Limerick in 1993. He had a memorable match and continued the performance against Cork in the trio of League finals of the same year. Since then he has invariably promised more than he has delivered. Peter Finnerty in his *Sunday Independent* hurling column had written that Larry could play like Roy of The Rovers one day and like Jack Duckworth of The Rovers the next. It had resulted in prolonged ribbing from his team mates. In the earlier victory over Kilkenny, he had some scintillating runs and often left defenders floundering in his wake as he surged towards the Kilkenny goal. The final nail, however, was never driven home.

The Walter Mitty of Wexford Hurling had yet to explode.

Despite regularly falling when in possession, the problem is not in his feet. Despite often dropping the ball, the problem is not in his hands. Despite sometimes running directly into trouble, the problem has little to do with vision. His quandary is related to concentration. He often seems to be thinking so fast that his body isn't able to keep up with his brain. It's all a question of focus. Larry is well aware of his predicament. He knows that he can beat any man he faces on the hurling field. But somehow, in the maelstrom of championship hurling, little things always seem to get in his way. He decided to try to improve his concentration. He had thought long and hard about his approach to the critical Offaly game. He knew that Wexford needed a good performance from him if the 19-year hoodoo was to be broken. His direct opponent would be the great Brian Whelehan, a man who many were saying was currently the finest hurler in the country. Unless he could lift himself well above recent performances then Whelehan would take him apart.

He decided to focus on a proven winner in the sports world. For a week prior to the game he tossed names back and forth. Then it hit him. The entire country had been floating in the realms of a sporting paradise over the achievements of Irish middle distance runner, Sonia O'Sullivan, in the build up to the Olympic Games in Atlanta. As a sports lover Larry had been utterly enthralled by the supercharged feats of the Cobh dynamo. He decided to concentrate on Sonia. Her deeds would inspire him. He took the field against Offaly with the vision of the long-striding confident O'Sullivan imbedded in his brain.

With Heart and Hand

The team set out from Wexford as usual, on Sunday morning. Picking up players, at preordained points along the way, the coach finally pulled out of Gorey and stopped, just outside the town, to pick up the last of the team, Eamonn Scallan. Then it continued on its way to Dublin. Near Scarnagh Cross there is a spot that marks the border of counties Wicklow and Wexford. Griffin ordered the coach to stop. To the players' surprise he ordered them to disembark.

Griffin was convinced that if Wexford did not win something before the year 2,000, a way of life would have passed. Already it was late in the day. Tremendous pressure would ensue for Wexford to win in 1998, the year that marked the bicentenary of the Insurrection of 1798. The pressure would be so overbearing that it would make the task almost impossible to achieve. He wanted the team to realise that it was only a game of hurling and that great Wexford hurling men had undertaken similar journeys and had survived them. But it was also about the reclamation of a fast-eroding culture and tradition. Wexford had that tradition. Hurling – the warrior game. The game of Cuchulainn. The authentic beautiful game of innocence and purity. But Wexford could be gone as a hurling force. Something had to be won – and soon.

Many years earlier, on Griffin's first day playing minor for Wexford, the team had been addressed before a championship game by a Wexford selector. The speech was all about 1798, blood sacrifice and pikemen. Griffin thought that it was ridiculous. It was standard practice for Wexford teams to be sent out to play important matches with the deeds of the '98 men ringing in their ears. Griffin vowed that he would never try to motivate a team with such historical representations. Throughout his coaching career he had always refrained from invoking such images. Now however, he was about to break the rule of a lifetime. He did not believe that he would ever have to do such a thing, particularly as it was his belief that, in this the age of communication and enlightenment, all matters of territorial, cultural and religious dispute should be capable of being solved by negotiation. He would not throw a stone at a man for Irish freedom, not because he doesn't love freedom, but because there is a better way to achieve that objective. The way of discussion, compromise and agreement. But now certain things had to be said. The issue of the quality of the blood that coursed through the veins of Wexford people kept recurring. It was distasteful, but he hadn't raised it. Commentators kept referring to it. That and the pouring of ridicule and scorn on himself and his fellow countymen hurt him deeply. Griffin loved his native county, and Wexford, because of the vitriol of certain widely read journalists, was in danger of becoming a place very much disrespected. Damn them and their calumny! It is a fact of Irish life, that the deeds of 15 sportsmen picked to represent their county, whether that county be Wexford, Kilkenny, Cork, Tipperary, Meath, Galway or Dublin, can have a major bearing on how others view that county and the character of its native sons and daughters. Griffin was intensely concerned about this image and he was worried about the future. Kavanagh's lines kept repeating in his mind:

> *You flung a ditch on my vision*
> *Of beauty, love and truth*

> Patrick Kavanagh, *Stony Grey Soil*

He firmly believed that all momentous happenings in life are marked by great dates in time. This was Wexford's date and today was Wexford's time. So although it was just a hurling game, in another sense it was much bigger than that.

He felt that he had to get all this across to his players. He admits that he wrote only one speech throughout 1996. As they stood on the side of the road, being hailed by dozens of enthusiastic supporters in the Wexford cars flashing past, he launched into that speech. He spoke calmly and in a low voice:

> *'Who are you? Who are you? I'll tell you who you are. When I'm finished speaking we are going to walk out of Wexford. Our goal is that the next time we set foot in this, our county, we will be Leinster Champions. On Friday night there was a report, on television, from Offaly and in mentioning the word tradition they sang their anthem. It made me think about tradition and its importance. And about this fantastic county of ours. A county of which we should be so proud. From the beach outside there to Courtown, Gorey, Ardamine, Blackwater, Curracloe, Wexford, Rosslare, Kilmore, Cullenstown, Fethard and The Hook. And back again to Ross, Mount Leinster, Rathnure and Enniscorthy. And of course Boolavogue.*

> *That's who we are and that's where we come from.*

> *Our people have real songs to sing. When they question the blood in*

our veins don't you ever forget that our county has a proud past and when other counties failed, ours was the only one of 32 counties wherein the people, your forefathers, rose and shook off the chains of bondage. Listen to 'Boolavogue' and 'The Boys of Wexford' and then think of Offaly. Why should we fear Offaly or Kilkenny or any other Irish county? Nothing in our past suggests that we should. Look at your names. Great Wexford names. Think of all the memories that this county of ours holds for you. For many of the bones of our nearest and dearest lie buried in the clay beneath your feet. Like yours will. Much sooner than you ever thought. This is our chance to make history. For which you will never be forgotten. You come from a fighting tradition and don't ever forget it.

Now we are going to walk up this road in silence. Out of our county. With the promise to each other that we will fight to the last – and remember it is only for 70 minutes. Not like your forefathers who had to fight for days on end. We will promise to give absolutely everything in order that the next time we set foot on Wexford soil we will carry back the Leinster Cup.

Today we are playing for a way of life.

Breathe in now, long and hard and as you walk, think of yourself since childhood; all of the matches you played; all of your friends both alive and gone; and make this promise to yourself. Today is the day we will be proud again. And remember:

> *"We are the Boys of Wexford*
>
> *Who fought with heart and hand."*

That's real tradition. Let's go!'

It was an eerie experience as the slight figure of Griffin walked purposefully up the road followed by about 30 men. Silently they paced along the tarmacadam on that summer morning. No further words were exchanged, but the players were deeply moved. Then the empty bus was driven across the Wexford border and the team took their seats. A team on a mission. A team determined and focused. A team confident that this was the day.

Ahead lay Croke Park, Offaly and destiny.

Wexford Team Selection

The Wexford team and selectors played their cards close to their chests. No one would know their hand. They made a positive decision to keep the line out to themselves. It was all designed to put their opponents on the wrong foot and sow confusion in the minds of the reigning Leinster champions. During the week, the players had been informed of the legitimate line-out. They had been sworn to secrecy and cautioned to tell nobody, not even their wives or girlfriends. They kept their word. Griffin had banned supporters and press from the last of the training sessions before the Leinster final. Some members of the press and a number of the supporters complained about this. He wanted no one to see the game plan as he was afraid that it would reach the ears of the Offaly men.

The team which was announced to the press and the one which appeared in the Croke Park match programme differed in a number of important points from the actual line-out that faced Offaly. Larry O'Gorman was selected at left corner-back but played at midfield, while Sean Flood played at left half-back, not at corner-back as indicated. John O'Connor, not named on the original selection, which had A.N.Other at centre-forward, took up his position at left corner-back. The indications were that George would play at centre-forward, but this is not how it turned out. Martin Storey, named as right half-forward played instead at centre-forward, while Rory McCarthy moved from midfield to the half-forward position vacated by Storey. To further confuse the Offaly men and make full use of their potential, Tom Dempsey, selected at right corner-forward in direct opposition to Martin Hanamy lined out in the opposite corner, still wearing number 13, where he was marked by Shane McGuckian. Tom had scored well off Shane in Thurles and favoured coming in off his left side, as he would be doing if played on the right. Griffin aided and abetted the deception by commenting on the selection. 'Larry played extremely well in the corner against Dublin, while Sean Flood is fast, aggressive and very good to hook and block', he told the *The Wexford People*. 'George got a belt on the hand against Dublin which hasn't healed up fully yet. He will probably be available, but we won't make up our minds until the very end', he added. The circumstances of George's injury had given the Wexford selectors an ideal opportunity to camouflage their real intentions.

When the teams stood to attention for the National Anthem, the deception was continued by some of the players. Liam Dunne, John O'Connor and Larry O'Gorman stood to attention around the centre half-back position. Larry, seeing Billy Dooley standing at right corner-forward, shouted in to him, 'I'll be with you in a minute, Billy'. When Tom Dempsey took up his position on Shane McGuckian, who assumed that he was playing on Eamonn Scallan, it upset his concentration. It wasn't that he thought that Dempsey was a tougher proposition. It was just that he had focused on Scallan and now Dempsey was standing beside him. It was off-putting. Tom, on the other hand, was more than contented.

The First Half

An attendance of 34,365 of which by far the majority were from Wexford, saw the challengers start nervously and register five wides in the first eleven minutes. Indications that this was a Wexford team with a difference came when Martin Storey twice beat Hubert Rigney to the pull in the early exchanges. This was a different Storey. A Joe Dooley point was answered by a pointed free from Scallan and another from Johnny Dooley before the third Dooley brother, Billy, evaded his marker John O'Connor to get his hurl to a John Troy centre. There were some doubts about the legality of the goal but they mattered little as the score now read. Wexford 0-1 Offaly 1-2. Each side sent over the bar before Larry O'Gorman hit an inspirational point which was quickly answered by Declan Pilkington. Two more points left it 0-4 to 1-5. Then Larry Murphy grabbed the sliotar and took off like a man possessed. Kevin Kinahan confronted him and a penalty was awarded. Sections of the Offaly crowd were unhappy with the referee's decision. Fitzhenry sprinted from goal and gave an encore of his Dublin performance. The purple and gold flags waved as the Croke Park score board flashed: 1-4 to 1-5. Another point was scored by each side before Brian Whelehan was moved off Larry Murphy, as the Cloughbawn man was causing havoc with his runs. Fitzhenry made a great save from Joe Erritty and Rory McCarthy had a point: 1-6 to 1-7. Then came a score which clearly illustrated that the Griffin way had definitely become part of the new Wexford hurling culture. Larry Murphy collected in the Wexford half-back line and transferred low down the left wing to Tom Dempsey. Dempsey, under pressure, centred it low into Eamonn Scallan. Scallan took a quick look and sent over the bar. It had the hallmark of the famous Eamonn Morrissey point which drew the Leinster final of 1993. But this time it was scored by a Wexford man. Each delivery had been precise and intentional and it was a seminal incident in Wexford's development into a team of maturity and control. The scores were level. Further points were exchanged before Billy Dooley broke clear and five yards out, with only Fitzhenry to beat, was hooked by Sean Flood in a repetition of his last ditch rescue act of the Kilkenny game. The result was a weak shot which was easily saved by the Wexford keeper. The Wexford backs were now playing well and John Troy and Joe Erritty changed places. Johnny Dooley then swapped with Declan Pilkington. A Wexford brace of points was answered by another Offaly point.

Wexford 1-10 Offaly 1-9.

The Second Half

The first half had seen both sides play excellent hurling. The second half witnessed the best hurling of the season. It was unforgettable. And not just from a Wexford viewpoint. The Slaneysiders played magnificently; Offaly also played superbly. They were the reigning Leinster champions and they had no intention of relinquishing that crown. Liam Griffin's phrase of the sporting season 'The Riverdance of Sport' aptly described it. Offaly introduced Daithi Regan but Wexford started well with a Storey point before Sonia O'Sullivan took an unlikely hand in the proceedings. Larry Murphy proceeded to shoot three points in five minutes. His first came from a poor Offaly clearance. Then he latched on to the puck out and drove through for another. His third was the piece-de-resistance. He gathered the ball under the Cusack Stand about 60 metres out and under pressure from Offaly he launched it skyward towards the posts. It was a beautiful left-handed shot and Larry admitted after the game that it was not in keeping with the Griffin philosophy. It was a sinful hit-and-hope attempt. Sonia intervened however and saved Larry from excommunication. The sliotar sailed through the air and as the enthralled spectators watched, it continued, on and on, over backs, over forwards and finally dropped on top of the Offaly net. It was one of the points of the 1996 championship season. 1-14 to 1-9. Four further Offaly points and one from Wexford indicated that Offaly were far from finished. Dempsey pointed to leave it 1-16 to 1-13. Laffan was causing Kinahan severe problems with his pace and he had three goal attempts early in the second half. Then a magnificent 70-metre line ball from Adrian Fenlon was flicked on by Garry Laffan. He was shattered to see it hit an upright, but Tom Dempsey, now playing out of his skin, connected in the scramble that followed and the ball was in the Offaly net. 2-16 to 1-13. Suddenly, the free flowing Wexford celebrations were cauterised by a terrific Offaly goal. Duignan ran at the Wexford defence and passed to Erritty. Erritty returned the ball and Duignan blasted to the net. 2-16 to 2-13. Then Daithi Regan who had entered the fray as a sub got the ball to Johnny Pilkington. Another Offaly point. But Larry Murphy was now on fire. Dempsey ran over to him. 'You're on a 'Man-of-the-Match' award today. For God's sake, don't stop now.' Images of Sonia O'Sullivan, Liam Griffin and Tim Flood fused into a kaleidoscopic vision of inspiration. He could do anything. 'Scorcher' hit the sliotar towards him. He gathered and even before his hurl connected he knew, for certain, where it was going. Thanks Sonia, that's your fourth point. 2-17 to 2-14.

The hurling was now awe-inspiring. This was the great game at its best. The Wexford men were hurling like champions. Offaly matched them stroke for stroke, but the signs were ominous for the midlanders. The Wexford players were not sticking to the script. In former years it was at this juncture that they would have been expected to wilt. 'You are not hanging your heads like you are supposed to,' Johnny Pilkington remarked to Murphy.

Overhead strokes, fast ground pulls, speed, courage and death-defying defence enthralled the watching thousands. Nine minutes of Elysian field splendour passed. With six minutes left there was still only three points between the teams. Tom Dempsey finally broke the deadlock with another glorious point. After that it was all Wexford. The national hurling correspondents sat transfixed as they watched their predictions cast to the winds. The Wexford forward line was unstoppable. Their hurling inscribed the indelible message across the legendary lawns of Croke Park. This is our day. And it will not be taken from us even by a Panzer division of Offaly men. Pride, determination and a Griffin-inspired recollection and reinstallation of a nearly forgotten tradition took the match in a grip of steel. The Wexford contingent watched in amazement as Storey, Dempsey and Storey again hit points. Dempsey's effort was from a difficult angle way out on the left wing. Johnny Pilkington pointed to leave it 2-21 to 2-15.

Liam Dunne had been requested by the Wexford selectors to play a different game than normal. 'We are asking you to sacrifice your normal game for the sake of the team', they said. 'Don't cover the whole field. Do a minding job on John Troy and hold the centre of the defence together.' Liam did as he was asked and during the game whenever he felt the urge to go forward he resisted. Therein lay one of the main reasons for Wexford's victory. Now Liam heard John Troy speaking to him. 'Well done, Liam, you deserve it'. The Wexford man knew that there was six points between the teams and the seconds were ticking away. He ignored the words of congratulation. He wanted to see his team leading by at least seven points. He could recall the bitter taste of 1991 and 1993. There were two minutes left when the Wexford supporters slowly began to realise that their 19-year torture was about to end. Until then they hadn't dared to believe it. Kilkenny and Offaly had snatched the laurels before, while all Wexford had waited for the glorious finale that never came. Now they were six points up with two minutes to go. Even if Offaly scored two goals, it would only bring the sides level. The doubts evaporated, to be replaced by a floating sensation of extreme elation. God!, its going to happen. Tears welled up in many Wexford eyes as they watched 'The Galloping Nurse' hit his fifth point. Liam Dunne finally acknowledged John Troy's sporting gesture. 'Thanks very much John.' A premature pitch invasion was halted before Billy Byrne set up the born-again Tom Dempsey for the final point and a personal contribution of a whopping 1-5. Billy had replaced Garry Laffan and a raucous cheer greeted the arrival of George who had come into the action to replace Rory McCarthy. Thus, the two rejuvenated old warriors experienced the exultation of a Leinster final victory for the first time in their careers. A number of the Wexford players were visibly crying with joy. The final whistle sounded. Seconds before, Storey had asked the referee to call for a short puck out, if he was about to blow the final whistle. Martin wanted the match ball to add to the two that he already had in his possession from the Kilkenny and Dublin matches. Aodain Mac Suibhne obliged him and raised his hand as an indication to the Offaly goalkeeper. However, the ball was pucked out long and high as usual. Storey set off like a hare and gathered the priceless souvenir. His team mates would later rib their captain with the claim that it was his fastest sprint of the day.

Wexford 2-23 Offaly 2-15. An eight point victory margin. Thousands invaded the pitch. It was Clare and 1995 all over again.

From that point on, the sporting people of County Wexford became inhabitants of Tir na nÓg and the New Jerusalem.

Both Teams Contributed

Offaly had made a huge contribution to the hurling game of the year. The players accepted the defeat with dignity. One time Leinster Secretary, Wexford man Martin O'Neill had bestowed the name 'The Faithful County' on Offaly in the 1930s and faithful to the rules of good sportsmanship they certainly were on this occasion. The noble bearing adopted in this, their hour of defeat, did themselves and their county proud. They later joined the joyous Wexford players in the Croke Park reception area and warmly congratulated their adversaries.

Martin Hanamy gave a faultless display and Michael Duignan was defiant to the end. Johnny Pilkington hit four good points and Billy Dooley and his brother Joe, before an accidental injury, were always dangerous. Joe Erritty and Kevin Kinahan hurled with passion throughout.

Wexford had many heroes. The forecast of the Wexford management team had come true and the Wexford half-forward line had outwitted their Offaly opponents and contributed 0-12 from play. Larry Murphy, the sleeping giant of Wexford hurling, had awoken and was named Man-of-The-Match. Apart from the Sonia-inspired Larry, Tom Dempsey and Storey were magnificent. Fenlon and particularly Larry O'Gorman were excellent throughout. Sean Flood did his job with aplomb and rendered Johnny Dooley largely ineffective. The central battle between John Troy and Liam Dunne was won by Dunne in emphatic fashion. Skill, marvellous footwork and the balance of a tightrope walker highlighted the Oulart-The-Ballagh man's performance.

The Wexford backroom team were delighted with one after match statistic supplied by the hawk-eyed John O'Leary. The Wexford backs had given away only two frees in the first half, courtesy of Liam Dunne and Sean Flood. In the entire 35 minutes of volcanic action of the second half the backs had conceded no free. It was a remarkable accomplishment against a top class forward line.

Colm Kehoe and Ger Cushe played tightly and impressively and Cushe won out over John Troy when the Offaly man moved in full-forward. John O'Connor, after an understandably slow beginning, contributed greatly, as he acclimatised to the pace of the game. With 11 minutes left he flicked the ball off Joe Erritty's hurl when the Offaly man looked certain to score a goal. Between the posts, Damien Fitzhenry showed that he was fast becoming the number one goalkeeper in hurling. Absolutely confident under the dropping ball, he stopped several well-placed Offaly goal attempts and his puck outs were long and well-placed.

The Aftermath

Following the end of the game Liam Griffin had run towards George, who was surrounded by fans. Spotting the Wexford manager he grabbed him in a bear-like hug. 'Griffin, I love you', he shouted. Griffin felt his neck click and go into spasm. He grimaced in pain. Three months later, despite constant physiotherapy, he still carried the reminder of that moment.

Brian Carthy of RTE collared Griffin near the Hogan Stand. The words of the emotional Wexford manager went out on Radio One. 'This place has so many memories for me. The first Leinster final that I can remember was in 1957 and I stood in the Cusack Stand and watched all my heroes die. I cried all the way home.' He was referring to Wexford's defeat by Kilkenny in the 1957 Leinster final – the day that the reign of the great team of the 1950s finally ended. High in the Cusack Stand, at that moment, stood a man with a transistor radio held close to his ear. He too had shed bitter tears in 1957 and now, in the moment of victory, tears of joy were streaming down his cheeks. He was a Dublin man, but from the time he was a boy, he had been a passionate follower of Wexford hurling. The years of defeat had done nothing to dim his ardour as he criss-crossed the country to be present at almost every game that Wexford played. An international banker, he had travelled from Vienna to attend the Wexford GAA Supporters Club function in late 1995. Now, on this day of days, Terry Carroll was in a hurling Valhalla.

Rory Kinsella had surged on to the field with the rest of the Wexford crowd at the final whistle. There was bedlam as he looked around for Colm Kehoe and Damien Fitzhenry. Finally, he spotted Damien just as the goalkeeper's mother, Nancy Fitzhenry, descended upon her youngest son. He watched as the Wexford goalkeeper disappeared under a generation of exultant Curaduff Fitzhenrys. Rory then made his way to the Hogan Stand and watched the presentation from the steps. Seamus Barron stayed on the pitch and was swamped by waves of hysteria as thousands of Wexford people celebrated their release from hurling bondage.

The presentation and Storey's speech passed in a fog of ecstasy. It was fitting that the Leinster trophy, the Bob O'Keeffe Cup, was handed over to the Wexford captain by another Wexford man, Jim Berry, the chairman of the Leinster Council. When Wexford had last won the trophy, 19 years earlier, a Wexford man, the late Jimmy Roche, had also been chairman and had done the honours.

It took Tom Dempsey an hour and a half to get across the pitch. He kept thinking of Niall Glynn, his brother-in-law, who had died just a few weeks earlier. He hoped that he was looking down on the scene in Croke Park. He had thought about him during the match and at times had said a silent prayer and asked for Niall's help. Tom's hand was now sore from well-wishers. His back was black and blue from slapping. He saw two men, with tears in their eyes approach. Two men from his own parish who had nurtured and encouraged him as a young hurler with Buffers Alley. Tony Doran and Mick Butler threw their arms around him. He knew they were close to breaking down. Tom could smile now and laugh at the day, a bare three months ago, when he was leaving Limerick after the loss to Galway in the Church & General National League semi-final. He was in the company of two other Wexford players, when they passed a group of supporters. One of them, an old-age pensioner, had lifted his stick and lunged at Tom. He had stepped nimbly aside but it had been unpleasant, as had the hate mail which he had received over the years. The fan mail had always greatly outnumbered it but he had been deeply upset. The catcalls from the sideline, directed at his determination to play the skilful game and not the one that had cost Wexford dearly in other days, had been hell to listen to. He hadn't even made the team for the Kilkenny match. Once or twice he thought that the selectors considered him a spent force. Now that was all in the past. He saw young Rory McCarthy with tears streaming down his face. Rory's three points had signalled that a man had stepped into the shoes of the youngster who had just left the minor grade. Everyone was emotional. Cyril Farrell in the RTE studio admitted that lesser men than George, Billy Byrne and Tom Dempsey would have thrown in the towel years ago, having suffered such narrow defeats in their attempts to win a Leinster medal.

Did You Cry?

During the days that followed strong, tough, Wexford men, not usually given to outward signs of emotion, blissfully greeted each another. The match was discussed from Bunclody to The Hook. Every puck, every clearance and every heart-warming score was analysed and replayed in engrossing detail. The same question cropped up in many conversations. 'Did you cry?'

Outward signs of emotion are not conspicuous character traits among the male of the species in Wexford, but most were happy to admit that the occasion had, indeed, brought them to tears.

Higher Peaks Beckon

The Supporters Club held a function in the Talbot Hotel following the victory. The charge was £500 for a table of ten. It was sold out in two days.

Supporters had to be accommodated in a second function room from where they watched the proceedings on closed circuit television. Liam Griffin's speech brought a rapturous ovation. It was the first time that he had mentioned his wife's illness in public. He used the word 'neglect' in reference to his behaviour in relation to his family. Some of those present thought that he was laying down a marker for events that were to unfold in the wake of the 1996 All-Ireland final. Micheál Ó Muircheartaigh was there and enthralled the full house with stories. The climax of the evening was dramatic. Spotlights had been borrowed from Wexford's famous Theatre Royal. The darkened room reverberated to the music of Riverdance and as it reached a crescendo the spotlights picked out County Secretary, Mick Kinsella, standing with the Bob O'Keeffe Leinster trophy held aloft. A standing ovation ensued. Autograph hunters filled the lobby outside. An auction followed at which Martin Storey's Leinster final jersey fetched £500. A hurl autographed by the team and an original team photo of the Leinster final winners fetched £700 and £800 respectively. Celebrities were present from all walks of Wexford life.

The most important group, however, was absent. The players had reached an important decision. The adulation and the celebrations in the Talbot Hotel were forsaken. The inflexible preparation to achieve further laurels was being continued. Higher peaks beckoned.

The great adventure was to continue.

LEINSTER SENIOR HURLING FINAL
Croke Park, 14/7/1996

Referee: Aodain Mac Suibhne (Dublin)

WEXFORD

Damien Fitzhenry(1-0f)
(Duffry Rovers)

Colm Kehoe
(H.W.H.Bunclody)

Ger Cushe
(Naomh Eanna)

John O'Connor
(St Martin's)

Rod Guiney
(Rathnure)

Liam Dunne
(Oulart-The-Ballagh)

Sean Flood
(Cloughbawn)

Adrian Fenlon
(Rapparees)

Larry O'Gorman (0-2)
(Faythe Harriers)

Rory McCarthy (0-3)
(St Martin's)

Martin Storey (Capt)(0-5)
(Oulart-The-Ballagh)

Larry Murphy(0-4)
(Cloughbawn)

Eamonn Scallan (0-4,0-3f)
(Liam Mellows)

Garry Laffan
(Glynn-Barntown)

Tom Dempsey (1-5)
(Buffers Alley)

SUBS: Billy Byrne *(Naomh Eanna)* for Garry Laffan; George O'Connor
(St Martin's) for Rory McCarthy

OFFALY

Liam Coughlan
(Seir Kieran)

Shane McGuckian *(Capt.)*
(St. Rynagh's)

Kevin Kinahan
(Seir Kieran)

Martin Hanamy
(St Rynagh's)

Brian Whelehan
(Birr)

Hubert Rigney
(St Rynagh's)

Kevin Martin
(Tullamore)

Johnny Pilkington (0-4)
(Birr)

Michael Duignan (1-1)
(St Rynagh's)

Johnny Dooley (0-4,0-2f)
(Seir Kieran)

John Troy
(Lusmagh)

Joe Dooley(0-3)
(Seir Kieran)

Billy Dooley(1-2)
(Seir Kieran)

Joe Erritty
(Birr)

Declan Pilkington(0-1)
(Birr)

SUBS: Daithi Regan *(Birr)* for Declan Pilkington; Pat O'Connor *(Coolderry)* for
Joe Dooley; Paudie Mulhaire *(St Rynagh's)* for Daithi Regan

∞ CHAPTER 8 ∞

THE PENULTIMATE HURDLE

Bliss at The Stillorgan Park

The winning team's first stop after leaving Croke Park was at the Stillorgan Park hotel, owned by Wexford businessmen, Des Pettitt and Brian Brennan. Pettitt, had sponsored the meals for the Wexford panel, in his Talbot Hotel in Wexford after the training session. The compliment was now returned and the hotel became the Dublin-based headquarters for the Wexford GAA. The scenes in the hotel after the Leinster final were unforgettable. The fans were hanging from the rafters. They feted the players like conquering heroes. The building was bedecked with balloons, flags and purple and gold banners. The large car park was filled to overflowing and the streets around the hotel were crammed with Wexford-registered cars. After the Offaly game the lounge bars ran out of alcohol. This unfortunate error was not repeated and extra supplies were ordered for the following games.

The Welcome Home

County Wexford was now on honeymoon. Many thousands turned out to celebrate the hurling heroes. The heather and gorse that bedecked the slopes of Tara Hill, the lower Blackstairs, and the bluffs of Carrigbyrne and Forth Mountain, seemed to sway in harmony with the conspicuous expanse of purple and gold flags and banners. The county had never seen anything like it. Wexford welcomed home its Leinster champions with a display of fervour that had never previously been experienced. Gorey's celebrations were stupendous and Enniscorthy and Wexford were not far behind. The players were flabbergasted at the scene. They had expected some festivities but this was unbelievable. After all, they had only won a Leinster final.

In Wexford town a civic reception was laid on. It was unprecedented. Never before had a mere Leinster final-winning team been awarded such an honour. Between the old waterfront and the winding main street stands a large open space in the shadow of the Church of St Iberius. Normally it is a public car park controlled by Wexford Corporation. Here, on the Monday night after the victory over Offaly, the men, women and children of Wexford, numbering nearly 8,000 turned out. The players couldn't believe their eyes. Dominic Kiernan, the Mayor of Wexford, officiated. A former member of the Olympic Council he had been, for many years, physio to the Wexford hurling team. His enthusiasm was infectious. South East Radio had broadcast all of Wexford's matches and their inimitable match commentator, Liam Spratt, took the microphone and kept the eager crowd entertained until the arrival of the team. Earlier that day, Wexford captain, Martin Storey, had taken the Bob O'Keeffe cup to his home area of Oulart-The-Ballagh. He was mobbed. When he arrived in the car park that evening, he was the centre of attention once again. It seemed that everyone in Wexford wanted to shake his hand.

Sponsors Smiling

Out in Rocklands, on the edge of the town, there were broad smiles all round. Seamus O'Beirne is the managing director of Wexford Creamery. His company had become the sponsors to Wexford GAA in the autumn of 1991. Although primarily an export company, vast numbers of their suppliers provided milk to Wexford Creamery through their co-op, Wexford Milk Producers. Many of these suppliers were intimately involved with GAA in Wexford. In the early years of his company's involvement with the Wexford teams, Seamus had been happy with the goodwill that the sponsorship generated. Although they had watched the teams exit the championship year after year, they kept the faith. The hurling team's memorable performance in 1996 was a just reward for their perseverance. Now, thousands of people were wearing jerseys upon which was emblazoned the Wexford Creamery name. And the numbers were growing by the day. Further exposure was coming from television and photographs. Their confidence had been vindicated and Wexford Creamery's profile received massive recognition around Ireland.

Beatification of Liam Griffin Begins

Liam Griffin was now being hailed as the hurling saviour of his county. The beatification process was underway and canonisation would follow. 'The Rosslare Messiah' was the most popular man in County Wexford. He had been deeply concerned by the results of the Wexford Hurling Survey and the stark realities that it portrayed. Now a major chink had appeared in the clouds of hurling pessimism and opportunities to spread the hurling gospel presented themselves on a daily basis. The game had a lot of ground to make up. The empty spaces in the Wexford GAA trophy cabinet had fertilised the popularity of other sports. Griffin had no problem with these sports but felt that it was unrealistic for young Wexford people to aspire to top-level involvement in these activities. Young soccer players were unlikely to emulate their Liverpool or Newcastle United heroes. The county didn't even have a soccer or rugby team playing at senior level. He also felt that Gazza and his ilk were not necessarily good role models for the youth of the county. The lure of monetary reward, rather than the urge to reach maximum potential in their chosen sport seemed, too often, to dominate their ambitions. The problems associated with full-time professionalism and the corporate baggage that they bring often tarnished the soul of these sports. Soccer was no longer the innocent cloth cap game of the English working classes. It was now a multi-million pound stock exchange dominated business. Rugby was quickly heading in the same direction.

Hurling, on the other hand, was genuine, free-flowing, beautiful and innocent. And its heroes were Corinthian-like warriors and pure amateurs who played solely for the love of the game. They were ideal role models for the youth. George O'Connor, Billy Byrne, Tom Dempsey and the others presented an image that was unlikely to be splashed across the pages of the tabloids, in lurid exposures that would cause anxiety to parents. And hurling, when played properly, was the greatest of all field games. Someone had to assume the role of hurling evangelist in County Wexford. There would never be a more fertile time.

Cometh the hour, cometh the man. Griffin took on the job of spreading the hurling gospel and his ensuing performances warmed the hearts of all those who love hurling. His involvement with the Wexford senior hurling team and his role as managing director of a busy hotel group left little free time. However, the circumstances presented could not be ignored. He entered into his new persona with gusto. On the Saturday following the Leinster final victory, he addressed a large congregation of mainly young people, during a Mass celebrated by Bishop Brendan Comiskey, at St Aidan's Cathedral, Enniscorthy. The message delivered was clear and from the heart. Get involved in sport and, in particular, hurling. Support the teams that represent your area. Have pride in your place, in your team and in your game.

Within the county, the manufacturers of hurls began to notice a remarkable upsurge in business. The sports shops sold out of purple and gold jerseys. Demand was extraordinary. Everyone wanted to wear the Wexford colours.

The Wild Swans

Paul Bell and Brendan Wade form the band known as The Wild Swans. They proceeded to rewrite their single *Dancing at The Crossroads*, a rousing celebration of Wexford's last All-Ireland win in 1968. *Dancing at The Crossroads 1996*, celebrated the Leinster champions and in a tongue-twisting segment towards the end of the song, all members of the panel are named. A cassette entitled *The Hurling Songs* which included a new Model County hurling hymn, *The Purple and Gold* was released in the weeks following the Leinster final victory. Soon it was being played regularly on South-East Radio. It became the anthem for the 1996 Wexford hurlers and from then on was always played on the way to matches in the team bus. Wherever one travelled in Wexford in the memorable summer of 1996 the voices of *The Wild Swans* were heard. Despite the apparent reluctance of RTE to play the song, it became the first GAA song ever to reach the No. 1 position in the Irish charts.

Unfamiliar with Adulation

Talk of an All-Ireland win began immediately. Griffin and the selectors were worried. The team appeared to be keen to reach further heights, but the dangers of deflation of impetus and growth of self-satisfaction were always prevalent. The goal had been achieved. The gap had been bridged. Already they had tasted success. Was the taste of that success palatable enough to inspire a further drive? A drive that could end with the ultimate achievement in hurling, to be crowned All-Ireland champions. Or would the team sink into a satisfied state of euphoria and bask in the glow of hero worship and back-slapping. Everyone wanted to shake their hands. It could easily go to their heads. This was a group of men who were not familiar with such adulation. It was the first major win of their careers. A few might decide that their lifetime ambition had been realised. Even if only one of the team settled into that state of mental contentment, it would be one too many.

– I had my day with kings

Drinking mead and wine:

Old Woman of Beare, Translation by Kuno Meyer

Have You Had Enough?

Following the Leinster final victory, Griffin had taken the players for a long run on the beach at Curracloe. Then, the following night, they got together again for a chat in Wexford Park. 'Have you had enough?' he asked. 'Only you can decide. Deep down you know that no matter what happens from now on, your season has been a success. Some of you may feel that you have achieved your target and that you have had enough glory for one year. If you have, that's okay. On the other hand, you can decide now that you want more. You can put your names in the history books for ever. Not just as Leinster champions, but as All-Ireland champions. It's your decision.'

Niamh Fitzpatrick arrived the next day and, without any prior consultation with Griffin, asked exactly the same question.

Griffin knew that the team was now merely one of eighteen Wexford teams that had won Leinster senior hurling titles. Only five of them went on to become All-Ireland champions. Did they want to be the sixth? Then, instead of being remembered as one of eighteen they would be numbered amongst one of only six. But how badly did they want it? He had been blunt with the players at the Wexford Park meeting:

'How many All-Ireland senior hurling semi-finals have you played in?'

There was no answer. He repeated the question twice. Eventually someone answered, 'none'.

'How many more All-Ireland senior hurling semi-finals will you play in, during your hurling careers?' he had asked them rhetorically.

'How many All-Ireland semi-finals have Galway played in since Wexford's last appearance in 1976? 'The answer is 19.'

'We have worked very hard to get to this stage, but it has been 20 years since Wexford last played in an All-Ireland semi-final. Do you realise how many hours have elapsed since a Wexford team last togged out in August to play in an All-Ireland semi-final? The answer is 175,200 hours. Put that against the time that you have trained to reach the semi-final this year and it sounds very little.'

The figure made a huge impression on the players. They had seen the reception that the Leinster final victory had brought. It was beyond their wildest dreams. They could hardly imagine what would happen if they won the All-Ireland. Resolve grew and determination increased.

We never know how high we are

Till we are asked to rise

And then if we are true to plan

Our statures touch the skies –

> *We never know how high we are,* Emily Dickinson

To a man they wanted more.

The Classics Are Over

The Wexford mentors knew that a further adaptation in style would have to take place if Wexford was to win the All-Ireland. There would be less free-flowing hurling. The Riverdance was likely to become a barn dance. The pure-bred Wexford hurling colts would have to mutate into stubborn and dogged hurling mules. The All-Ireland hurling semi-final and final were more noted for courage, perseverance and hunger than for artistry and dextrous play. Bobby Charlton, in hurling terms, would have to crystallise into his older brother Jack. Griffin began to enlighten the Wexford players on the type of hurling that they would face from now on. 'Kilkenny and Offaly are now gone so the classics are over. It's now a different style of hurling. From now on it will be a war of attrition. That's what faces us and that's what we will be preparing for.'

Galway's Pedigree

Neither players, selectors, or fans had looked beyond the Leinster final. The Offaly hurdle had frustrated them so often in the past, that everyone had focused on that match to the exclusion of all other distractions. Now the new Leinster champions were to play Galway in the All-Ireland semi-final at Croke Park on 4 August. Galway had beaten Roscommon in the Connaught final by 3-19 to 2-10. Their corner-forward, Francis Forde, contributed a majestic 2-8. In the quarter-final they faced New York, who had accounted for London and Derry in preliminary rounds. Six days after the Leinster final, Galway routed New York by 4-22 to 0-8 at Athenry. Forde scored 1-5, but this time the star of the Westerners' attack was under-21 player, Kevin Broderick, who scored 3-1 before being substituted after 30 minutes. Although the opposition was weaker than that faced by Wexford in their march through Leinster, it was clear that Galway had potent attackers and presented a formidable challenge. They were the reigning Church & General National League champions, having beaten Tipperary in the final in May. No one in the Wexford camp needed reminding of whom Galway vanquished in the semi-final of that competition. The Westerners had been among the best teams in hurling for the past 16 years. Their second All-Ireland win, in 1980, had been added to by further wins in 1987 and 1988. Their under-age structures had continued to yield a rich harvest. All-Irelands had come at under-21 in 1991 and 1993 and the county had been finalists in 1994. Minor All-Irelands had been won in 1992 and 1994. Under manager Mattie Murphy, the Galway men were the pundits' favourite to advance to meet the winners of Limerick and Antrim in the All-Ireland final.

Wexford – Unbeaten in All-Ireland Semi-Finals

Since the All-Ireland series began, Wexford has never lost an All-Ireland semi-final. Remarkably, every time the team had won the Leinster title it had gone on to play in the All-Ireland. Sometimes it had got a bye and on other occasions the champions of Ulster, Connacht or Munster had been encountered. Always Wexford had been victorious. Since the first hurling resurgence of the county in 1951, Galway had been Wexford's opponents four times in All-Ireland semi-finals – in 1951, '56, '70 and '76 (after a drawn game). Wexford had won them all. It was a record that could be matched by few, if any, other counties.

Accurate Predictions

Griffin, in the eyes of the players, seemed to develop a rare ability to predict events, in hurling terms, at least. All the trends that he had forecast in the earlier games had come true. John O'Connor said that he began to feel that the manager's unusual faculty was spooky. 'It was uncanny. It was as if he was listening in on the opposition's team talks. It became almost ridiculous. Everything that he had forecast began to happen with eerie regularity.' Griffin told Rory McCarthy that he could possibly, at some stage, be moved to the half-back line and pointing at Sean Flood casually remarked, 'he might break his leg'. The words spoken almost in jest, turned out to be prophetic. Sean was injured in the Galway game and although his leg was not broken badly, it later turned out that he did indeed fracture a bone in his shin and Rory did have to move into the backs in the latter stages of the second half.

The players knew that mistakes had been made during the early reign of the Wexford management team. It was all part of the learning process. It was becoming clear, however, that these three men had developed into a cohesive and extremely effective force. They never made the same mistake twice. Any remaining sceptics were won over by the manner of the victory over Offaly. Everything turned out as they had insisted that it would. Consequently the players now had the utmost trust in the abilities of the manager and his selectors. 'Liam Griffin is the thinking man's manager,' said John O'Connor. Whatever game plan he came up with would be carried out, to the letter, by the team.

Sean Flood's Struggle

Sean Flood, at 10 st. in weight and 5 ft. 6 ins. in height is the smallest man on the Wexford team. He is the son of the legendary Tim Flood, one of the greatest of all Wexford forwards. Sean made his Wexford debut in 1987 and since then has usually been a member of the Wexford back division. Possessed of a great turn of speed and a big heart, he matured into a much tighter player in 1996 and gave dazzling displays in all the games in which he figured. He is extremely skilful in the art of 'hooking' and on more than one occasion in 1996 he saved certain goals. Like his father he is a talented musician and plays guitar and banjo. His rock band, Running On Empty is well known in the south-east.

During the nights spent in the army tent at Ballytrent with the other Wexford hurlers, Sean was in great demand for his musical abilities. He always brought along his guitar and led the communal singing. When the training, eating and singing were over, the members of the team retired to sleep. They slept in survival bags and the oil-fired generator, which supplied the power for the lights, had to be switched off by someone each night. The generator was situated outside at the back of the tent and some person, reluctantly, had to volunteer to go into the dark, cold, night and switch it off. One night it was Sean Flood's turn and, returning to the tent in the darkness, he had some difficulty finding the zip on his survival bag. The diminutive Wexford defender struggled manfully for a few minutes whereupon the voice of Tom Dempsey was heard to remark, 'Lads, I think Sean is trying to get into his pillow case'.

The panel was required to be out on the beach by 6 a.m. to undergo further torture under the watchful eye of their tireless management team. Griffin encouraged the players as they struggled from their slumbers. 'The Galway men are still tucked up in bed. This will give us the advantage.'

The Unbreakable Bond

Before the Kilkenny game, the selectors had chatted to the players about their attitude to the consumption of alcohol while in training. The management was happy that the team had freely decided to refrain completely in the weeks leading up to matches. A few drinks to celebrate was in order, after victories, but then abstention was observed. Griffin now spoke of the 'unbreakable bond' that had formed among members of the panel. He said that all of them, panel members, backup staff and selectors would remain friends for ever, irrespective of the outcome of the remaining matches. They had been through a great experience together. They were the 'brotherhood of Wexford hurling'.

Predictions of National Hurling Correspondents

A few of the national hurling correspondents were tipping Wexford to beat Galway. Among these were Liam Horan of the *Irish Independent*, Aoife Kavanagh of *The Examiner* and Paddy Hickey of the *Evening Herald*. Paddy was the man who had given the team an incentive in the lead up to the Kilkenny match, with the headline 'So Sorry, Wexford'. Now he appeared to have been won over by the style and panache that the team showed in the Leinster final. The majority of commentators, however, were tipping Galway. It was hard to blame Peader O'Brien of *The Sun*, Sean McGoldrick of *The Sunday World*, Martin Breheny of *The Title* and Brian Carthy of RTE, as the Galway hurlers were a proven force and well used to the big stage of All-Ireland semi-finals and finals. The few journalists who thought that Wexford would win were basing their assumptions on the gathering momentum that seemed to be propelling the county's hurlers. The comparison with Clare in 1995 was unavoidable.

It also became apparent that the great majority of hurling counties wanted to see a Wexford victory. The memories of the great team of the 1950s had created a fan club for Wexford hurling. In Carlow, Wicklow and Dublin, the support for Wexford had been kindled by the magnificent group of sporting hurlers who had made the breakthrough in 1955. Now the generation who watched the deeds of the Rackards, Tim Flood, Ned Wheeler and Jim English were warming to their successors in the purple and gold, forty odd years later. The children and grandchildren of that generation who had listened to their elders recall in cherished tones the feats of the Wexford teams of the 1950s, now found themselves drawn towards the young Wexford men of 1996 and their attempt to come out of the hurling shadows.

Wexford, at this time, was being quoted at 3/1 to win the All-Ireland title, but 4/1 was readily available to any keen betting man. The general view was that if the Wexford men reproduced their Leinster final form, no team would beat them. Anything less than that, however, and Galway would advance.

Wexford Selection and Game Plan

The team was usually picked in the dressing-room or sometimes at the Ferrycarrig Hotel. It was always a long drawn out process as permutations were tossed back and forth. It usually took many hours and often days, before a final selection was decided upon.

The game plan to beat Galway was speed and adaptability. Griffin repeatedly stressed that individual members of the team should be prepared to play in any position. On one occasion, in order to emphasise this point, he rounded on George, and told him that he could find himself playing in goal. George was not amused.

The Westerners had not been tested in the championship and the Wexford selectors believed that the Wexford men would have an advantage in fitness and speed. They knew that Galway had a strong team and felt that their men were going to have to do something remarkable if they were to get the better of the Westerners in the physical exchanges. They decided that the pattern of the game must be set by Wexford. Galway must not be allowed to dictate it. This approach became an indelible part of the mental preparation and dominated the players' attitude to the game. Speed and ground hurling were deemed to be Wexford's best counter weapons. It was felt that a number of key encounters would have to go Wexford's way if the team was to reach its first All-Ireland final for 28 years. Adrian Fenlon must come out on top in his duel with Michael Coleman. Ger Cushe had to have a game plan that would nullify Joe Cooney, the schemer-in-chief of the Galway attack. Cushe was told to play Cooney from in front. Above all else, Griffin and his colleagues knew that they had to neutralise Joe Rabbitte and stop him from recreating the havoc of the League semi-final.

The Wexford mentors once again published a team which was not exactly the formation in which the players lined out. Sean Flood, selected at left half-back and John O'Connor named at left full-back changed places when the teams lined out. This move was readily foreseen by astute hurling people. It was clearly obvious that the 5 ft. 6 ins., 10 stone, Sean Flood was not about to be asked to mark the towering Rabbitte. The Cloughbawn man's responsibility at corner-back, however, was no less onerous. The new Galway scoring sensation, Kevin Broderick, was now his direct opponent and this confrontation was another that the Wexford men felt had to go their way. Rabbitte versus O'Connor was seen as one of the key contests of the match. John was now 33-years-old and an experienced hurler who could fill any defensive position. He had won three Fitzgibbon Cup medals with the great UCC three-in-a-row team of 1983-85, which was masterminded by Canon Michael O'Brien.

Tom Dempsey was selected this time at left corner-forward, the position that he had occupied in his five-star Leinster final performance. To the surprise of many, he played in the opposite corner where he was marked by Gerry McInerney. Particular note had been taken by the Wexford management team of McInerney's performance in the League semi-final. Tom Dempsey was now a different hurler to the hesitant forward of the previous year. His ability, stick work, class and shooting expertise had been brought to a pinnacle by an ingredient that he had not always previously possessed – confidence. McInerney was an experienced hurler and usually reserved his really spectacular performances for the big occasion. When playing in the Galway half-back line, he had been the star of a number of All-Ireland finals. Corner-back was not his best position and the Wexford selectors felt that Dempsey could take him.

Garry Laffan was to be fed with low deliveries. In the event that Garry was proving ineffective against Galway's full-back, Brian Feeney, then Wexford would introduce a powerful weapon from the substitutes' bench. That weapon was Billy Byrne, who had that rare ability to continually find space when in possession. The dark moustached Gorey veteran was happy to play whatever part that was required of him.

Motivation

The Galway management had said that they could not see a hurling team in the country that was capable of beating their charges. It was a statement presumably designed to give their players confidence in themselves. Whether it achieved that objective is a moot point, but it certainly worked the oracle in helping to motivate the Wexford team. The Wexford management was surprised at the utterance and naturally used it to spur on their men. They drilled it into the players that only two teams had beaten Wexford in recent times. Two of these were among the three teams that stood between Wexford and All-Ireland victory. The first one was Galway and if they slew that particular dragon, only one would stand between them and glory. Antrim could beat Limerick but Wexford would prefer to face the Munster champions. 'We can lay all of the bogies. First we must concentrate on Galway. If we beat them, there is only one hurdle left.'

Tickets

Almost 62,000 crowded into Croke Park. Wexford had been allocated 15,000 tickets and a further 5,000 were estimated to have been secured by begging, coaxing and the bartering of football tickets from other, non-hurling, counties. The demand for tickets in Wexford had been phenomenal. County Secretary, Mick Kinsella, had been bombarded from all quarters. The phone rang incessantly and the Gorey man was driven to distraction. Threats, appeals and invocations came from all quarters. Bribery was even tried by some, but to no avail. The GAA in Wexford had got their allocation from Croke Park and nothing more could be done. Miracles could not be worked, except perhaps on the hurling field, by the young men who wore the purple and gold jerseys. The hard-pressed Mick could have named any price for the precious piece of paper that would guarantee entry to Croke Park and it would willingly have been met. He thought about going into hiding. From the time that Wexford won the Leinster final until the end of the All-Ireland final, Mick Kinsella was the most powerful man in County Wexford.

It was an experience that he did not relish.

The First Half

Limerick beat Antrim by 1-17 to 0-13, without playing impressively. The Wexford crowd sat back nervously as the broad-shouldered, maroon-clad, men of Galway took on the rejuvenated hurling men of Wexford.

Martin Storey had an early point, and a foul on Tom Dempsey after 5 minutes resulted in a pointed free by Eamonn Scallan. Then Francis Forde brought alarm to the Wexford bench when he easily rounded Colm Kehoe and put the ball over the bar, followed by a similarlike score from Galway centre-forward Cathal Moore. 0-2 to 0-2. The Wexford selectors saw that Forde was causing Colm Kehoe problems. They refused to panic because they suspected that the Bunclody man would settle, learn from the early errors and get the measure of his man. They were proved right and Colm went on to play a stormer. Sean Flood was playing well and his clearance was sent over the bar by Larry Murphy. Two minutes later Tom Dempsey sent over a marvellous long range point. Then a Storey point was answered by Brendan Keogh. 0-5 to 0-3. In the 18th minute the Wexford selectors took off Eamonn Scallan and sent on Paul Finn. Tom Helebert was playing brilliantly for Galway and it was felt that something had to be done to curtail his effectiveness. John O'Connor converted a '65. Two minutes later Liam Dunne slipped when tackling Cathal Moore, who had his shot blocked down by John O'Connor. The loose ball was doubled on by Joe Cooney and sent to the back of the Wexford net. Shortly afterwards, Forde pointed a free. Galway were in the lead by 0-6 to 1-4. It was the only time that the Tribesmen were in front. Dempsey pointed a free and then came a crucial moment.

The Rabbitte Incident

In the 24th minute, John O'Connor and Joe Rabbitte clashed for a high ball under the Hogan Stand. Rabbitte's elbow was seen to make forceful contact with O'Connor's head. O'Connor fell motionless to the ground. Dr Stephen Bowe, Liam Griffin and tended to the stricken St Martin's man. Words were exchanged between Rabbitte and Griffin. The Wexford manager had to be sure that John was incapable of resuming before bringing in a sub. Across on the other side of the pitch, under the new Cusack Stand, Seamus Barron waited with the Wexford substitute George O'Connor. George was limbering up under the watchful eye of Wexford physio, Sean Collier. He was later described by the Wexford bench as 'prowling the sideline like a caged lion'. George watched the futile attempts to revive his stricken brother. Barron was his usual cool self. Griffin put up his hands as a signal to Seamus that they had not yet reached a decision regarding John O'Connor's predicament. John made a valiant effort to stand upright, but he appeared punch drunk and in no fit state to continue. George entered the fray and frantically tried to attract the referee's attention. Following a two minute delay, Wexford played on with 14 men. In the 27th minute a free by Liam Dunne was broken down by Paul Finn into the path of Rory McCarthy. The young St Martin's man showed great skill in controlling and striking in one movement, to send a blistering shot high into the Galway net. It was the best goal that Wexford had scored in the 1996 championship. Throughout that first half the Wexford half-forwards had run, at speed, at the Galway half-backs. On many occasions they had succeeded in losing their men. The tactic paid rich dividends with McCarthy's incisive strike. Only then was George officially allowed into the match. McCarthy was now popping up all over the place and in the 30th minute he executed a quite superb turn to send his opponent Michael Donoghue in the wrong direction, before striking left-handed over the bar. 1-8 to 1-4. Cathal Moore had a point from a tight angle before Joe Cooney flicked the ball out to Moore who hand-passed to Forde. Forde's shot was saved but Moore got to the rebound and goaled. Just on half time Dempsey was fouled and pointed the free.

Wexford 1-9 Galway 2-5.

Wexford had appeared to be the better team in the first half. Still, they had a slight wind advantage and were only leading by a point. In the first half, the only Galway forward who looked impressive was Cathal Moore.

Tom Helebert and Brian Feeney in the Galway full-back line were blotting out their immediate opponents, Paul Finn and Garry Laffan. Ominously for Galway, Joe Rabbitte had not figured prominently in the game and had appeared to be limping towards the end of the first half. He was seen to remove his boot and feel his right foot. It was heavily bandaged, which suggested that he had carried an injury into the game. He was eventually to leave the action in the 55th minute, to be replaced by Ollie Fahy.

Rabbitte's foot, thus, became Galway's unlucky omen.

Half-Time in the Wexford Dressing Room

The scene that greeted the Wexford team when they entered their Croke Park dressing-room at half-time was a dismal one. A semi-conscious John O'Connor lay stretched on the table. An ambulance was visible in a darkened corridor to the rear, its revolving light throwing eerie reflections into the shadows. A number of people hovered around the stricken player as the stretcher-bearers prepared to convey him to the Mater Hospital. The place had the appearance of a battle zone. The portents were ominous and the setting was not designed to help the focus of the team at this crucial halfway mark in their semi-final clash. Something had to be done, quickly. Martin Storey showed that he was the team captain in more than just name. 'If we ever needed a reason why we should go out and win this match, then that man there is that reason,' said Martin pointing at his colleague, John O'Connor. The gloom lifted. A handicap became an advantage.

The Second Half

Wexford resumed with George at midfield in a swap with Larry O'Gorman. Paul Finn was now at full-forward. The opening ten minutes of the second half were poor and reflected the mounting tension. Tom Dempsey, who was now hurling the socks off Gerry McInerney, had a terrific point. The game was tight and physical. Galway shot four successive wides. The Wexford defence was in death-defying mood and their attitude was typified by Rod Guiney who, having lost his hurl, flung himself full length to win the ball. Kevin Broderick was roaming well outfield resulting in more space for the Galway full-forward line. Eight minutes passed without a score until Moore had a Galway point. Dempsey then pointed another free which was awarded for a late tackle by Tom Helebert on Storey. Liam Burke gave Joe Cooney a 'hospital pass' and the Wexford goal appeared to be under severe threat. Fitzhenry advanced and flung himself at the Galway full-forward. It was a hard challenge and resulted in the ball going away from the danger area. Griffin had instilled in Damien the tactic of commanding the area in front of goal. 'You are more than a goalkeeper on this team. You are a "sweeper". That sector in front of you is your domain and you must command it', the Wexford manager had repeatedly told the young Duffry Rovers man. The Galway supporters screamed for a penalty but the referee waved play on. Fitzhenry had played the ball as he was entitled to, albeit a mite ferociously. Three minutes later, however, a penalty was awarded when Rod Guiney was adjudged to have pulled down Joe Rabbitte. Little Colm Kehoe was seen to square up to Joe Rabbitte. It was almost comical, but the Bunclody terrier did not back off. Joe Cooney took the penalty and shot hard for goal but Liam Dunne saved and cleared brilliantly. Another scoreless seven minutes passed before Rory McCarthy set off on a sparkling solo run. Rory, who had switched places with Larry Murphy, brilliantly rode a Nigel Shaughnessy tackle and passed to Storey who pointed. Liam Burke replied for Galway. Tom Helebert beat two Wexford men and then attempted to round George. He did not succeed and George had his name taken for the resultant foul. 1-12 to 2-7. Seven more torrid minutes passed.

The Second Coming of Billy Byrne

With nine minutes to go, the Wexford contingent witnessed the second coming of Billy Byrne. The Gorey man came on for Garry Laffan. Rod Guiney's determination won an almost irretrievable situation and Ger Cushe sent a short clever clearance to Adrian Fenlon. Fenlon pucked it high into the full-forward line, exactly as he had done in the Kilkenny match, where it dropped between Billy Byrne and Galway full-back Brian Feeney. The Galway goalkeeper Morgan Darcy advanced off his line but the wily Billy got the merest of touches and the ball trickled into an empty Galway net. Billy had repeated his feat of the Kilkenny game and the score this time was even more crucial.

2-12 to 2-7.

In the 66th minute Sean Flood got a bad stroke on the leg. It was completely accidental and resulted from Sean sticking his leg in to frustrate a Galway man's stroke. It was obvious that he could not continue but Wexford had used up its allocation of subs and the selectors were forced to send Flood into left corner-forward. Flood attempted to hobble down to his new position. The large crowd saw Tom Helebert approach him, put his arm around Sean and help him to limp into the corner-forward position. It was a heart-warming incident that typified the sporting attitude of the contestants. Rory McCarthy moved to wing-back exactly as the Wexford soothsayer manager had forecast. A few minutes of torrid exchanges followed, before Byrne fed Dempsey who pointed with his weaker right hand, from a narrow angle. 2-13 to 2-7. In the 70th minute Kevin Broderick found himself unmarked and scored a third Galway goal. Liam Dunne was penalised, a little harshly, for over-carrying. Cathal Moore's free was saved and sent out for a '65. Nigel Shaughnessy took it, but it was mishit and cleared by Paul Finn. The referee blew the full time whistle. Some of the players had not heard it and the ball fell between Dempsey and McInerney. Dempsey, as he had done all afternoon, once again beat the Kinvara man.

Wexford 2-13 Galway 3-7.

Summaries

Wexford did not reproduce the form shown in the Leinster final. The backroom team always knew that this expectation was unrealistic. A different type of hurling was played and the Wexford men adapted well. They were the better team and deserved to win. Wexford hit 11 wides to Galway's 16. Some commentators said that the Slaneysiders were lucky and pointed to Galway's large number of wides. An examination of these showed that Galway had six misses in the second half from realistic scoring opportunities. Two of these, a free by Francis Forde and another by Joe Cooney, were indeed inexcusable. The other four misses were either from shots taken under pressure from hassling Wexford defenders, or attempts at pointing frees from angles that could not be classed as simple. Wexford also had a close-in free missed by Eamonn Scallan in the first half and could have had a further goal from a good opportunity in the second half. It was also significant that Broderick's only score of the game, the late goal, came only after the tenacious Flood had been injured and moved to the forwards.

In the second half, Galway seemed intent on going through for goals instead of taking points, when it was clearly obvious that the Wexford backs were prepared to die rather than yield. Time and time again, they used arms, legs and bodies to block the sliotar. When the maroon of Galway did break through, they were faced by a goalkeeper who could stop a speeding swallow. Damien Fitzhenry was splendid and anchored a defence in which Liam Dunne, Sean Flood and Ger Cushe all played superbly. Dunne made one magnificent sally out of defence, turning, weaving and dodging as he carried the ball 50 metres or more. Larry O'Gorman was everywhere and his linking, running and distribution played a large part in Wexford's win. Fenlon gave his usual consistent display of ground hurling and quick ball movement.

Little Rory McCarthy was a revelation and had his best game of the championship. He was a purple and gold wasp as he buzzed around the field and when the Galway backs succeeded in making physical contact with him he expertly rode their tackles and showed the effectiveness of the Wexford upper body strength programme. The role that the Wexford management had designed for Rory came to fruition and he scored the goal of the season. That score was the turning point of the game and brought Galway to the realisation that this was not the team that they had beaten in the League semi-final.

Tom Dempsey gave another dynamic display. McInerney won four of the challenges between the pair and one was indecisive. Tom won the remaining 13. His control, skill and confidence shone like the Hook lighthouse and he finished the game with a personal contribution of 0-6, 0-3 coming from play. Martin Storey exhibited valour of a high order. The victim of a bug, he was forced to fast for a week before the game and in the early exchanges he dislocated a finger. He was seen to wince in agony as Dr Stephen Bowe pulled it back into place. Despite the discomfort he played on through the pain barrier and scored three crucial points.

Tom Helebert had a magnificent game and was Galway's best player. Three different Wexford men tried to mark him and he outplayed them all. Brian Feeney at full-back commanded his area and was unbeatable until the arrival of Billy Byrne. Cathal Moore scored 1-3 and was a huge threat to Wexford for the entire game. Apart from one or two others the remainder of the Galway team lacked the intent of purpose of their Wexford counterparts. In simple terms, Wexford were hungrier and wanted to win more badly than Galway. Pride and character illuminated their display. In fairness to Galway, Wexford's three hard championship matches had prepared them well. Galway's lack of real competitive hurling since the League final was a telling factor.

All in all, the final result was a fair reflection of the play.

In the RTE studios, Michael Duignan of Offaly said that Wexford deserved to win and their back line had been well on top throughout the game. He added that it was a great result for hurling and tipped Wexford to win the All-Ireland.

The Two Backroom Teams

The three wise men of Wexford hurling had a superb match and easily outfoxed their Galway counterparts. They acted quickly and decisively when Eamonn Scallan was being cleaned out by Helebert. They successfully counteracted the threat of Joe Rabbitte and their charges followed the game plan and remained focused throughout.

Galway's tactics seemed less than decisive. Former Galway hurler, Peter Finnerty in his *Sunday Independent* column summed it up as follows:

'Galway's inability to take their scores from the dead ball cost them dearly. Peter Kelly, who doesn't take frees for his club, was asked to convert with his first touch of the ball after being introduced as a substitute to the game. This is not good enough. Some other player should have taken the responsibility and tapped the ball over the bar... Hurling is reputed to be the fastest field game in the world. Why then was Joe Rabbitte allowed to continue when he couldn't even walk?'

Immediately following the final whistle, the Galway manager, Mattie Murphy, sportingly shook hands with Liam Griffin, who dressed for the weather and wore black shorts. The ribbing that the Wexford manager took from his players, concerning his less than muscular legs, was so unflattering that he did not repeat this sartorial experiment.

The 'Nearly-Men' Reach the Final

It was another wonderful day for Wexford and its marvellous fans. The celebrations that ensued after the Leinster final were repeated. On this memorable night, the atmosphere in the town of Gorey was beyond belief. The crowd had started to gather at about 6.30 p.m. By 12.30 a.m., when the team arrived, Gardai estimated that up to 20,000 were waiting. The team gaped in astonishment at the masses of revelling thousands. It took them almost an hour to traverse the Main Srcct. The players then climbed onto the roof of a local pub, Brennan's 64 and sprayed champagne over the crowd. The fires of celebration blazed, as the county came to a standstill. The Monday morning newspapers sold out. Wexford people pored over the accounts of how their hurling heroes had beaten 'The Men of the West'.

Wexford, the perennial losers of hurling, the limpid lemmings of the game, the men whose blood had been put under the journalistic microscope and pronounced anaemic, were one step away from the ultimate prize.

The 'nearly-men' of hurling were in the All-Ireland final.

ALL-IRELAND SENIOR HURLING SEMI-FINAL
Croke Park, 4/8/1996

Referee:Joe O'Leary (Cork)

WEXFORD

Damien Fitzhenry
(Duffry Rovers)

Colm Kehoe
(H.W.H. Bunclody)

Ger Cushe
(Naomh Eanna)

Sean Flood
(Cloughbawn)

Rod Guiney
(Rathnure)

Liam Dunne
(Oulart-The-Ballagh)

John O'Connor (0-1f)
(St Martin's)

Adrian Fenlon
(Rapparees)

Larry O'Gorman
(Faythe Harriers)

Rory McCarthy (1-1)
(St Martin's)

Martin Storey (Capt.)(0-3)
(Oulart-The-Ballagh)

Larry Murphy (0-1)
(Cloughbawn)

Tom Dempsey (0-6,0-3f)
(Buffer's Alley)

Garry Laffan
(Glynn-Barntown)

Eamonn Scallan (0-1f)
(Liam Mellows)

SUBS: Paul Finn *(Oulart-The-Ballagh)* for Eamonn Scallan; George O'Connor *(St Martin's)* for John O'Connor; Billy Byrne (1-0) *(Naomh Eanna)* for Garry Laffan.

GALWAY

Morgan Darcy
(Moycullen)

Tom Helebert
(Gort)

Brian Feeney
(Athenry)

Gerry McInerney
(Kinvara)

Conor O'Donovan
(Liam Mellows)

Nigel Shaughnessy
(Loughrea)

Michael Donoghue
(Clarinbridge)

Michael Coleman (Capt)
(Abbeyknockmoy)

Brendan Keogh (0-1)
(Athenry)

Joe Rabbitte
(Athenry)

Cathal Moore (1-3)
(Turloughmore)

Liam Burke (0-1)
(Kilconieron)

Kevin Broderick (1-0)
(Abby-Duniry)

Joe Cooney (1-0)
(Sarsfield's)

Francis Forde (0-2,1f)
(Turloughmore)

SUBS: Ollie Fahy *(Gort)* for Joe Rabbitte; Peter Kelly *(Sarsfield's)* for Francis Forde; Ollie Canning *(Portumna)* for Joe Cooney

∞ CHAPTER 9 ∞

THE GAP IS BRIDGED

The Wexford Fans

There is no disputing that the men, women and children who support the Wexford hurling team are the best fans in the game. A glance at the table below illustrates this point. Wexford dominates the figures and the county has appeared in five of the top eight attendances at All-Ireland hurling finals. It must be borne in mind that the capacity of Croke Park has been altered a number of times, with the result that today's figures are not strictly comparable. The county was also involved when the attendance records for Leinster finals and Oireachtas finals were set.

Attendance records at All-Ireland hurling finals

1954 Wexford v Cork	84,856
1956 Wexford v Cork	83,096
1959 Waterford v Kilkenny (replay)	77,285
1960 Wexford v Tipperary	77,154
1962 Wexford v Tipperary	75,039
1959 Waterford v Kilkenny (draw)	73,707
1963 Waterford v Kilkenny	73,123
1955 Wexford v Galway	72,854

Attendance records at Hurling League finals

1956 Wexford v Tipperary	45,902

Guinness and the Renaissance of Hurling

The game of hurling was undergoing something of a renaissance in the 1990s. The decision to allow live television coverage of an increased number of championship matches was one factor. The renewal of Tipperary hurling under Babs Keating and the sustained challenges from Offaly, Galway and Limerick, were others. Then came the breathtaking magic of Ger Loughnane's Clare. The All-Ireland win by the men from the

Banner County in 1995 brought a lump to the throat of all hurling people. No one involved in sport could remain unmoved by the sheer emotion and fairy-tale ending that saw the Clare men record their first All-Ireland senior win since 1914. The involvement of 'Uncle Arthur' in becoming sponsors to the All-Ireland hurling championship signalled the dawn of a new hurling era. Apart from the large sums of money which the company poured into the game, the power of the imagery in their striking advertisements for The Guinness Hurling Championship changed the perception of the game. Charisma-evoking representations of hurling as 'The Most Exciting Game on Earth' and the memorable 'No One Said It Was Going To Be Easy' advertisement, allied to a nation-wide billboard campaign of flair and ingenuity, served to eat away at the old blinkered attitudes. After all, if a forward looking company like Guinness felt it was worthwhile to become involved in hurling sponsorship, then there must be something there worth looking at. Television brought the exciting confrontations of the Munster and Leinster championships into the living rooms of the nation. People who had never seen top-class hurling began to watch. They liked what they saw. Suddenly hurling was glamorous. Suddenly it was okay to be a hurling fan.

The re-emergence of 'The Boys of Wexford' added further fuel to the blazing heather of hurling's rebirth.

'Leave the Players Alone'

The members of the Wexford hurling team were now the centre of attention within the county. Overnight, they were celebrities and in demand for all kinds of functions, openings and events. Hundreds of fans queued up each evening after training for their autographs. Often, it took each player up to an hour to sign these. It became unmanageable. Griffin appealed to the public. 'Please leave the players alone. Everyone has got to be sensible in the weeks ahead. People are coming forward with all kinds of worthy causes, but there is no cause more worthy than our own.'

Propelled in the slipstream of their senior counterparts, the Wexford under-21 hurlers had also reached the All-Ireland final. This added to the renewal of hurling fervour. Griffin castigated a small minority of Wexford fans who had boohed a Galway player when taking a free in the All-Ireland semi-final and told them that it was not part of Wexford's tradition. He told everyone to fly purple and gold flags and to enjoy the next three weeks. The population of the county took him at his word and flags and pennants in the county colours unfolded like blossoms of heather and gorse on the Wexford landscape, as an epidemic of hurling fever swept across the south-east.

Nothing Was Left to Chance

Rory Kinsella computed all training attendance figures. There had been 187 sessions in total and some of the players had 100 per cent attendance records. Many, like Garry Laffan, Dave Guiney, Mitch Jordan and Seamus Kavanagh had to travel very long distances. On the odd occasion when a player could not attend, he always furnished a genuine reason. With thirty players on the Wexford panel, it was feasible to engage in full scale matches in training. Those on the secondary panel, whose style of hurling resembled individual members of opposing teams, were encouraged to impersonate them in training. Opposing team colours were worn by the shadow 15. Before the Kilkenny match, the black and amber jerseys of local club Shelmaliers were used. Duffry Rovers' colours roughly correspond to Offaly's and these were put to use before the Leinster final. The maroon colours of FCJ Bunclody were worn to simulate Galway and before the All-Ireland final, 15 men togged out in the green outfits of the Bunclody club to represent the men of Limerick.

The team got down to minute planning for the All-Ireland final. Particular attention had been paid to the performance of Limerick corner-forward, Owen O'Neill. The Wexford selectors reasoned that O'Neill was a good straight line hurler and dangerous if allowed to get in behind the full-back and run straight at goal. But if kept on the outside, he was not a Johnny or Billy Dooley, or a D.J. Carey, and was much less effective. Keeping him to this pattern would, it was hoped, be achieved by flicking the ball away and competing in the open spaces on the outside. Before the All-Ireland final, Griffin had players bearing down from all directions on goalkeeper Damien Fitzhenry, and attempting to beat him with kicked shots in the style of the Limerick man. John O'Connor, the man who would be marking Owen O'Neill, watched the proceedings with a mild sense of amusement. Fitzhenry's expertise in dealing with this type of shot would be called upon only if O'Neill first rounded John. As far as the St. Martin's man was concerned, this was not going to happen. Wexford worked hard on their defensive tactics. The target set for them for the final was one of zero mistakes. The plan was to limit Gary Kirby to a maximum of five points from frees and to prevent the Shannonsiders from scoring a goal. This was to be achieved by speed and hassling, allied to drive and 'guts'. Each player had to be prepared to run until he dropped.

Limerick represented the last bogey for Wexford. The Shannonsiders were now the only team in Ireland who held an un-avenged victory over the Slaneysiders. In the week of the final, Griffin reminded the players of the strength and physique of the Munster champions, as portrayed when they played Limerick in the league in Kilmallock. The Wexford management team had not forgotten this game and they particularly remembered the treatment dished out to Tommy Kehoe. They observed

Limerick's progress through Munster, taking detailed notes of their methods and strategies along the way. They prepared themselves for the possibility of a repeat of the tactics adopted by Limerick in Kilmallock. The dictates of sportsmanship, as strictly laid down by Wexford's selectors, would be followed. But intimidation would not be tolerated. If Limerick attempted to play that type of game, then the Wexford players would meet fire with fire. Kilmallock would not reoccur.

'No intimidation' became the password.

The 'What If?' Scenario

The 'what if?' scenario was played out ad infinitum. This involved the laying of plans for all eventualities that could come to pass, before and during the game. What if a Wexford or Limerick player was sent off? Plans were hatched and the players were made aware that these possibilities were catered for by the Wexford backroom team. Designs were drawn up to cater for all possibilities. Blueprints to counter Limerick team switches were detailed. Injuries and the team disruption that would ensue were discussed and positional switches were considered in detail. Such was the players' appetite for discussion, planning and revision that, by the time the week of the final arrived, Griffin was forcibly having to call a halt to team talks. The players wanted to talk on and on. This was a thinking hurling team.

Any remaining doubts that this was the most united family of hurlers that ever represented Wexford, were removed by Billy Byrne when he spoke briefly on the Wednesday night before the All-Ireland final. 'I feel more a member of this team than any previous Wexford team that I have been involved in – and I'm only a sub', said the quiet, 36-year-old Gorey man.

The Wexford Team Selection

Wexford now had two injury problems. John O'Connor was making slow progress from the concussion that resulted from the blow by Rabbitte's elbow in the All-Ireland semi-final. O'Connor is the toughest man on the Wexford team and jostling with him is like coming face to face with a wall of granite. Prior to Griffin's appointment, the St Martin's man had sometimes been prone to bouts of aggression which were beyond the limits of fair play. The Wexford manager knew that O'Connor was a fine hurler and strove to eliminate this aspect of his game. Griffin spoke to John O'Connor when he was in hospital and bluntly told him that his injury would draw no sympathy from hurling people around the country. John suspected that the manager was correct, but it was disconcerting to hear such disagreeable sentiments. Nevertheless, it served to increase his determination to recover in time.

Sean Flood was still limping but, initially, it was thought that he would be fit to take his place for the final. As the climatic day drew nearer and Sean's injury failed to respond to intensive treatment, the Wexford men were left with a major selection problem. John O'Connor would make it and was selected at left corner-back, where he would oppose the tall speedy Owen O'Neill – the man whose kicked goals in the Munster final had vanquished Tipperary. The selection released to the newspapers had Larry O'Gorman at midfield and A.N.Other at left half-back. Different permutations were tossed back and forth to fill the vacancy created by Flood's enforced absence. The selectors felt that experience was a priceless asset on the big occasion. Nothing in hurling came bigger than the first Sunday in September. They would prefer to start with Larry O'Gorman at left half-back in the position vacated by Flood. That left a vacancy at midfield. They considered a number of players, but the more they pondered the more they kept coming back to the obvious solution. 37-year-old George would play at midfield in the All-Ireland hurling final. They knew that he was still the fittest man on the panel. They also knew that his right hand was a jigsaw of fragile and reset bones. The once formidable weapon that had snatched countless sliotars from the Croke Park skies was now just a battered remnant. George was still playing, but his left hand had been forced into retirement some years earlier. Still his character, his fitness level and his experience would ensure that Wexford would, at least, hold their own at midfield. Throughout his hurling career, George had often been a free-spirited hurler with an inclination to wander from his position in search of the action. He had adapted well to the new Wexford pattern and the management team felt that he could be trusted to stick to the game plan.

Griffin had another worry. Since he had become the Wexford manager he had been relieved that one piece of information had not become public knowledge. A few people close to the team knew, but the newspapers had never tumbled to the fact that George O'Connor and Liam Griffin were cousins. Griffin had known George since he was a boy and they had played on the same Wexford District team that had won a county senior football title in 1977, when George was just a 17-year-old. They knew and liked each other, but had never been bosom buddies. Griffin had dropped George for the Leinster final and when he was discussing the matter with the player, George had candidly said, 'If I were you Griffin, I wouldn't pick me either.' Still, the manager did not want the 'hurlers on the ditch' to be given the opportunity to say that he was showing favouritism in his team selections. Although Griffin would never allow personalities or relationships to enter into his selections, it would not stop the rumour factory. That could result in pressure on George and on his brother, John O'Connor. The Wexford management team was well aware that previous Wexford hurling teams had often been selected with an emphasis on maximising the representation of the selectors' own clubs. The appointment of selectors from less dominant clubs can be a good thing for a county team, as it results in less pressure on the club's representative to show favouritism to their own club. Seanie Kinsella of Naomh Eanna was an example of a hurler who got less than a fair chance to show his undoubted worth on the intercounty scene for the prolonged spell that his talents deserved. Kilkenny hurling men always felt that the speedy and skilful Seanie would have been utilised much better if he had been born in Kilkenny. The Wexford hurling team of 1996 had the largest club representation of any senior team from the county that had played in an All-Ireland final. The case of the Guiney brothers showed Griffin's single-mindedness when it came to selecting the best 15 hurlers to represent Wexford. Rod and Dave Guiney had been the mainstays of the St Mary's, Rosslare hurling team. Griffin was heavily involved with the club. He had been central to the hurling progress of the Guineys since they were children. The two brothers, with a view to improving their hurling by playing at a higher level, had transferred to senior club, Rathnure. Griffin was very unhappy to see his home club lose two such fine hurlers. He brooded on the damaging repercussion to his club. He felt betrayed and it severely damaged St. Mary's chances of advancing from the junior grade, a target that Griffin felt was well within the club's capacity. He believed that St. Mary's could become a senior club. Still, he was determined not to overreact and he never allowed it to influence the selection of the Wexford senior hurling team. Rod Guiney was picked for every match and his brother Dave was a substitute. It was the same with the O'Connor brothers, but George's age was a factor which would lend weight to the arguments of the critics. If Wexford lost the All-Ireland final, there were sure to be those who would voice opinions as to the stupidity of playing a 37-year-old at midfield. If they knew that he was the manager's cousin, well, the amateur analysts would have a field day.

On the Friday before the All-Ireland final, Griffin phoned George. 'How would you like to play in the All-Ireland final?' the Wexford manager asked. 'What sort of a stupid question is that?' retorted the delighted St Martin's veteran. 'What did he expect me to say? Sorry Liam, I have a bit of work to do on the farm!' he later joked to a hurling journalist.

The die had been cast.

Limerick's Passage to the Final

Wexford and Limerick had met twice before in All-Ireland finals. Wexford had triumphed in 1910 and the Limerick men had been victorious in 1918. The most recent championship clash was in the All-Ireland semi-final of 1955 when 'Mackey's Greyhounds' had been overwhelmed by the Wexford-led Nick O'Donnell. Two of the famous Quaid hurling clan, twin brothers, Jack and Jim had represented Limerick on that day. Their first cousin, Limerick-born Seamus Quaid won an All-Ireland senior medal with Wexford in 1960, before being tragically shot dead in the course of his duty as a member of the Garda Siochana. Jim Quaid's son, Joe, would be Limerick's goalkeeper in the 1996 final.

Limerick had opened their 1996 campaign with the impressive demolition of Cork at Pairc Ui Chaoimh by 3-18 to 1-8. Cork had no answer as Limerick hurled the Leesiders off the pitch. Next, the All-Ireland champions, Clare, went under by 1-13 to 0-15. Inspirational Limerick captain, Ciaran Carey, scored a magnificent winning point in the last seconds. It ranked as one of the scores of the decade. The Munster final between Tipperary and Limerick saw the Shannonsiders comprehensively hammered in the first half and trailing at the interval by 0-4 to 1-11. Their second half fight back was memorable and the teams finished level at 0-19 to 1-16. In the replay, Limerick appeared to be the benefactors of some very bad defending by Tipperary and a rampant Owen O'Neill kicked two goals, which saw Limerick crowned Munster champions by 4-7 to 0-16. Limerick then beat Antrim in the All-Ireland semi-final by 1-17 to 0-13. The majority of the Limerick team had already played in an All-Ireland senior decider. They had looked to be heading for victory in 1994, only for Offaly to set Croke Park buzzing in the last five minutes with an extraordinary scoring burst, to win by six points. It was a huge blow, but Limerick had recovered well and now had the longed-for opportunity to make up for their 1994 disappointment. The team was determined and fit, having been through 187 training sessions – coincidentally, the same number as their final opponents, Wexford.

It appeared to the Wexford management that some statements emanating from the Limerick camp had the effect of putting increased pressure on the Limerick team. The message was that the final had to be won or they couldn't go back to Limerick.

The Press Previews of the 1996 All-Ireland Final

Two confrontations dominated the previews of the 1996 All-Ireland final. The clash of the opposing captains, Martin Storey at centre-forward for Wexford, and Ciaran Carey, at centre-back for Limerick, was a key encounter. The two men were well acquainted, having forged a friendship at All-Star functions and both had been inspirational in their team's progress to the final. Carey was the spiritual leader of the Limerick men and his sallies upfield were liable to wreck opposing team's defensive plans. Storey was the linchpin of the Wexford attack and 'The Galloping Nurse' had contributed 0-15 from play to his team's scoring tally.

Gary Kirby, the Limerick centre-forward, was to be marked by Wexford's dynamic and skilful centre-back, Liam Dunne. Kirby had scored

1-33 of Limerick's total in reaching the final and 1-9 of this total had come from play. A player of immense character, he was generally recognised as the best free-taker in the game. At 6 ft. 1 ins. and 13 st. 7 lbs. he promised to be a handful for the diminutive Dunne. Additionally, the Limerick full-forward, Damien Quigley, had scored 2-3 in the 1994 All-Ireland final and his speed was expected to cause problems for Wexford full-back, Ger Cushe.

The Finest Defender in Hurling

Mick Jacob was the star hurler of the Oulart-The-Ballagh area when Liam Dunne was growing up. As a child, Liam used to stand behind the goal and retrieve the ball for the great centre half-back, when he practised long distance frees. Now the roles were reversed and in the natural order of things in the close-knit rural area of Oulart, Jacob returned the compliment for Dunne. Like the changing seasons, it seemed that the shadow of the great Jacob had merged into that of the equally skilful Dunne. Although Liam Dunne had not been considered good enough for the county minor team in 1985, a year later he was not just on the Wexford minor team, but also part of the under-21 selection that won Leinster honours, a feat that was repeated in 1987. He puts his omission from the 1985 minor team down to prejudice against his club, Oulart-The-Ballagh, who had not yet assumed their leading place in Wexford hurling. He made his Wexford senior debut as a 20-year-old, against Laois in 1988, winning All-Star awards in 1990 and '93. If hurling had a transfer system, Liam Dunne's price would be equalled only by that of D.J. Carey. He is a priceless asset to Wexford. A hurler of rare skill, his brilliant footwork, dazzling side-step, incisive reading of the game and exceptional ball control mark him out as the finest defender in the game. His 5 ft. 8 ins, 11.5 st. frame appears to be too small for centre-back, but his displays belie the fact. Throughout 1996, his natural instincts were reigned in at Liam Griffin's request. This was a different Liam Dunne, but a more effective one. He became a disciplined and more focused hurler. His performances appeared less spectacular than those of previous years, but by fashioning his play to the needs of the team, he contributed, arguably, more than any other player to Wexford's success.

Some weeks before the All-Ireland final, Liam Dunne phoned Griffin to discuss what the manager wanted from him on All-Ireland day. 'Liam Dunne, the great Liam Dunne', mused the Wexford manager, 'You will be the Man-of-the-Match on the first Sunday of September'. Griffin appreciated the greatness of Dunne and was convinced that he would show it on All-Ireland day. Dunne was chuffed. He still had to figure out how he was going to combat Gary Kirby, but it was nice that Griffin had such confidence in him.

He studied videos of Limerick in action and paid special attention to the performance of Gary Kirby. In the tent in Ballytrent, Liam had deliberated at length on the style and pattern of the Limerick centre-forward's game. He gained confidence by observing particular aspects of his opponent's methods. As the day of the final drew nearer, Liam Dunne intimated to the Wexford selectors that he was convinced of his ability to hold Gary Kirby. The Wexford management team was greatly reassured by the centre-back's attitude.

A few days before the All-Ireland final, Niamh Fitzpatrick asked Liam Dunne a question. 'Which was your best game in the championship?'

'I haven't had my best game in the championship, yet', retorted Dunne quietly.

Glory Storey

Martin Storey made his Wexford senior debut in 1985, having progressed from the Wexford junior team that won the Leinster final that year. He made the right half-forward position his own and soon became one of the finest forwards in the game. Fast, strong and brave, his electrifying runs are a feature of his game that send Wexford fans into rapture. His ability to get the ball into his hand in the twinkling of an eye is one of his greatest assets. For many years he has been Wexford's most productive forward. He deserved many more than the one All-Star award that came his way in 1993, but the failure of Wexford to escape from the confines of Leinster resulted in his under-exposure on the big days which dominate the selection of these awards. His club, Oulart-The-Ballagh were county Wexford senior hurling champions in 1994 and 1995 and Martin became Wexford captain for the 1996 season. Now 32 years of age, this year has seen him become a more rounded player than heretofore. He proved to be an inspirational captain and 1996 marked his maturity into a fine team player. While still an effective scoring machine, he added ground hurling and guile to his game and as a result the Wexford team benefited enormously. Storey is a fine athlete and as well as playing hockey competitively, he is a keen follower of all sports. Very popular among hurlers of other counties, he had up to 20 phone calls and cards from Kilkenny officials and players before the 1996 All-Ireland final, wishing him the best of luck.

Liam Dunne adjusts and grafts hurls for many of the Wexford panel. The popular hit song from English group Oasis, *What's the Story – Morning Glory?* and his scoring exploits in 1996, resulted in a now familiar label being applied to the Wexford captain. Liam Dunne copperfastened it by inscribing all of Storey's spare hurls with the legend 'Glory Storey'. Martin was selected as National Irish Bank GAA Personality of the Month for July 1996, as a result of his display in the Leinster final.

Ger Cushe

Ger Cushe had been picked to play minor hurling for Wexford in 1985. The team came out of Leinster that year and Ger was part of the under-21 team that won successive Leinster titles in 1986 and '87. He attracted the attention of the senior selectors and was picked at full-back to face Limerick in the league in Gorey in 1990. Ger is the biggest man on the team, weighting 14 st. 5 lbs. and standing 6 ft. 2 ins. The Wexford masseurs, Pat Whitney, Sean Collier and Chris Culleton, joked that when working on Ger they should charge by the acre. Ger, because of his bulk, always had problems with fitness levels. Several of the Wexford training routines to increase speed, were designed specifically with Ger in mind. His hurling ability was never in question and he entered into the fitness regime of 1996 with enthusiasm and an increased sense of purpose. The results were clear, as he outplayed a succession of opponents.

Liam Dunne and Ger are close friends and in the days approaching the All-Ireland final they had chatted about their hurling careers: 'They keep saying that I'm too small and too dainty for centre half-back', said Liam, 'and you have been crucified for the past three years for one score that you conceded.' Liam was referring to the famous equalising point scored by Kilkenny's Eamonn Morrissey in the Leinster final of 1993. 'Ger, you and I are going to shut up all the critics, on the first Sunday in September', said Dunne defiantly.

Ger Cushe nodded in silent and determined agreement.

The View of the National Hurling Correspondents

Limerick was favoured by the following: Martin Breheny of *The Title*; Peader O'Brien of *The Sun*; Sean McGoldrick of *The Sunday World*; Roy Curtis of *The Star* and Micheál Ó Muircheartaigh of RTE.

Martin Breheny of *The Title* wrote:

'Gary Kirby v. Liam Dunne and Damien Quigley v. Ger Cushe could emerge as two of the more vital personal duels ... However, Limerick have one distinct plus. They have been through the All-Ireland mill before, a factor which could sway what is certain to be a fascinating contest.'

Liam Hayes of *The Title* also went for Limerick:

'Wexford are the most popular team in the country but, of course, if they were not so inoffensive they might have won something big these last twenty years ... 'It's unlikely that Wexford will show any teeth this afternoon. In a fight ... well, they may be surprised to find themselves in a fight! Limerick, however, have to go looking for a fight this afternoon. They've got to bully. Dictate. And if they start off like that this time around then it's a pretty sure thing that they will

continue to lay down the law until the game has drawn its last breath.'

Conor Hayes writing in *The Sunday Tribune* saw it as follows:

'Limerick will close them down and give them little space to play. I felt before the semi-finals that if Limerick got through against Wexford they would win it.'

Donal Keenan of *The Title* favoured Wexford:

'The winner takes it all and to hell with the loser. With that attitude, Wexford can be winners.'

Enda McEvoy of *The Sunday Tribune* (and *The Enniscorthy Echo*):

'Liam Griffin's team will deliver.'

Liam Horan of the *Irish Independent*:

'Though the thought of Limerick suffering another final defeat must go hard with all decent sports fans, I back Wexford.'

Among the players and managers who had first-hand experience of one or both of the teams, Wexford appeared to be the favourites. Jimmy Barry Murphy, Johnny Pilkington, Anthony Daly, Conal Bonnar and Waterford manager, Tony Mansfield, went for Limerick. Dublin manager, Jimmy Grey, Dominic McKinley of Antrim, D.J. Carey, Joe Rabbitte, Shane McGuckian, John O'Sullivan of Laois and Michael Walsh felt that Wexford would win. Geographical and provincial allegiances were clearly obvious in the forecasts.

Before the game, in the RTE studios, Tomas Mulcahy and Ger Loughnane plumped for Limerick while Offaly's Michael Duignan tipped Wexford. 'Overall Wexford are a better balanced side and I think that they'll do it', said Duignan.

The Day of the All-Ireland Hurling Final

The roads through Enniscorthy, Gorey, Arklow and Bunclody were pregnant with the snake-like procession of Wexford registered cars and vans. The occupants were on their way to watch their heroes play in the All-Ireland hurling final. The pensioners, with cherished memories of the golden era of the 1950s and 1960s, the middle-aged who still dreamed of their one great day in 1968, and those under 19, who never saw a Wexford team playing in an All-Ireland hurling final, made the pilgrimage. Since 1968, dozens of defeats, many of them unlucky, and the consequent sad homeward journey along by the dark, age-old hills and upland meadows of the brooding Blackstairs, had failed to diminish the incurable optimism of the Wexford hurling followers. No other team in Ireland has such forgiving, such faithful, and such steadfast supporters as the hurlers of the Model County. Disappointment, frustration and last minute defeat was

Martin Storey, the Wexford captain, hoists aloft the Liam McCarthy Cup after the 1996 All-Ireland final victory over Limerick, the first since 1968. (Photo: Adrian Melia).

Inset, Liam Griffin, team manager, hugs the Bob O'Keeffe Cup after the 1996 Leinster final win over Offaly, a first provincial success since 1977. (Photo: courtesy of The Star).

*Some exultant Wexford players in the Hogan Stand after the All-Ireland final 1996.
L to R: Tommy Kehoe, Rod Guiney, M.J. Reck, Larry Murphy, Dave Guiney and
trainer, Sean Collier.*

(Photo: Ray Flynn, People Newspapers)

*Rod Guiney is chaired from the field
by supporters after the Leinster final
win, cradling his nephew Jack (son of
Rod's twin and panel member, Dave)
in his arms.*

*An emotional county chairman,
Paddy Wickham, is embraced by
team captain Martin Storey, after the
semi-final victory over Galway.*

(Photos: Paddy Murphy, People Newspapers).

Ger Cushe is first out to this ball, as he was so often during 1996, leaving Limerick's Padraig Tobin in his wake. Quiet man Cushe made an inspirational, motivating speech to his team mates at one stage during the preparations. (Photo: Paddy Murphy, People Newspapers).

Larry O'Gorman has the ball clutched in his hand and his eyes fixed firmly on the posts though under severe pressure from Offaly's captain, Gorey based Shane McGuckin, during the 1996 Leinster final. (Photo: Adrian Melia).

Before the 1996 All-Ireland final, the Wexford team continues on alone in front of the massed ranks of purple and gold on Hill 16 in the pre-match parade after Limerick had broken away prematurely, with manager Liam Griffin on the sideline urging them to keep on going.

(Photo: The Examiner)

Sean Flood is still cheerful before the All-Ireland final despite being unable to take his place due to injury.

George O'Connor gets his reward at last as he raises the McCarthy Cup.

(Photo: Adrian Melia).

A special moment for Martin Storey as his daughter Ciara gets a greeting from a smiling President Mary Robinson.

(Photo: Ray Flynn, People Newspapers)

The Gardaí are under pressure to clear a way into Gorey for the open top bus bearing the All-Ireland champions on the Monday evening after the 1996 final.

The crowds on Gorey's wide Main Street stretch as far as the eye can see for the first of the tumultuous Monday night welcomes for the new champions. Gardaí estimated the crowd at 25-30,000 people. *(Photo: Pat O'Connor, People Newspapers).*

The Loving Husband
- with his wife, Mary, who has been such a support to him during his time in the Wexford job.

The Team Manager
- in action at Croke Park.

The Evangelist
- on his crusade for hurling.

The Family Man
- with his mother Jenny and youngest son, Rory, and the MacCarthy Cup on the return home.

LEINSTER AND ALL-IRELAND HURLING CHAMPIONS — 1996

1996 Wexford senior hurling panel and backroom team.

Back row, L to R: Rod Guiney, Seamus Kavanagh, Sean Collier, Joe Kearns, George O'Connor, Jim Byrne, John O'Connor, Tomás Codd, Ger Cushe, Declan Ruth, Larry Murphy.

Middle row, L to R: John O'Leary, Dave Guiney, Mitch Jordan, Liam Turley, Larry O'Gorman, Paul Finn, Adrian Fenlon, Billy Byrne, Garry Laffan, Shane Carley, Tom Dempsey, Paul Codd, Liam Dunne.

Front row, L to R: Rory Kinsella, Seamus Barron, Eamonn Scallan, M.J. Reck, Rory McCarthy, Damien Fitzhenry, Martin Storey, Sean Flood, Tommy Kehoe, Colm Kehoe, Liam Griffin.

Trophies, L to R: Bob O'Keeffe Cup (Leinster Champions), Liam McCarthy Cup (All-Ireland Champions), Walsh Cup (Leinster Tournament).

(Photo: Image Studio)

their lot for 27 barren years. But the renewal of confidence took place annually. Like the crocuses of springtime they came out in April or May, bedecked in banners of purple and gold, only to fade like the last rose of summer before the end of July.

But 1996 was different. 1996 saw the emergence of a team of hurlers with new enthusiasm, with new attitudes and with those important elements that heretofore had been noticeably absent; discipline, passion, tactical awareness and togetherness.

A team that had been written off was in the All-Ireland final. A county where, according to the hurling experts, the standard of the game was on an accelerating downward spiral, had two adult teams in All-Ireland finals. Players, whom the experts said were too set in their ways and too old to change their style, had confounded their critics and dramatically altered their game. The team had played four hard championship games and reeled off four impressive and, with the exception of Dublin, unexpected victories.

The caterpillars of winter had crystallised into the hurling butterflies of summer fields.

The Hours before the Final

Sean Flood was heartbroken when he learned that he would miss the All-Ireland final. What was assumed to be a bad sprain, turned out later, to be much worse and the Cloughbawn defender was out of hurling until the end of the year. A week before the big match, it finally became obvious that Sean was not going to recover in time to take his rightful place in Croke Park. On the day of the final, his torment was acute, but he managed to put on a brave face. Before the team left the Stillorgan Park hotel for Croke Park, Sean indicated that he would like to say a few words to his team mates. He spoke from the heart. 'I spent all my life waiting for this day to happen. You must realise the great opportunity that you have. I didn't realise what I had, until it was taken away from me ...'. Then he broke down. The room became charged with emotion and many were on the verge of tears. It was another indication of the unbreakable bond of friendship, trust and utter reliance on one another. Many of the Wexford team later referred to the incident as a critical one. It cemented the close knit body of hurlers into an intimate bond of steel. It supplied another motivation in focusing on their last great objective. Each player then placed his hand on the shoulder of the man opposite him and deliberately and earnestly vowed to bring the laurels back home to Wexford. Those who watched the moment were convinced that they were looking at a team that had but one inflexible objective. Defeat was not on the agenda. Sean Collier of the backroom team had watched the proceedings. He had never wielded a hurl in his life, but now felt thoroughly stimulated. 'I wanted to get out there and hurl myself', he said.

The flood of emotion, however, served another purpose. The tension of the long build-up, the pressure and the stress was abated in those few minutes of empathy. Since well before the Kilkenny game, the Wexford players had been warmly receptive to ideas that improved their mental preparation. Life skills were being absorbed by the team. Skills that would be used throughout their lives, for the betterment of their families and while engaged in their occupational pursuits. Niamh Fitzpatrick's involvement with the Wexford hurling team was no 'quick fix'. She travelled from Dublin, two and sometimes three nights per week for prolonged sessions with the team and individual players. Liam Griffin and Niamh showed remarkable harmony in their techniques. They had talked to the players at length about 'the ideal performance state'. This had first been discussed the previous year, for the Leinster semi-final against Offaly. It is an involved process and contains 12 different elements. It had not worked in 1995, because many other factors necessary for its success were not in place. In 1996 the team had absorbed the concept and it played a major part in the success. The 'ideal performance state' is the honed-in, focused, penetrating, mental state of an athlete who is ideally prepared for the coming contest. Many hours had been spent in preparing the team to facilitate their entry into this indissoluble state of being. They must be able to switch into it at will. It was code-named 'green'. All distractions must be cast aside. A surfeit of emotion could have served as one of these distractions. It was now behind them. The players were now encouraged to enjoy the lead up, to savour and enter into the occasion of the ceremonies of the All-Ireland hurling final, as something they could look back on with pleasure for the rest of their lives. They were advised to enjoy the formalities of the big day and to play their parts with dignity. This mental state was code-named 'amber'. They were to leave the dressing-room on 'amber'. At the end of the formalities they were to switch from the relaxed pre-match state of enjoyment. Then, and only then, were they to enter into 'the ideal performance state'.

The referee's whistle would be the signal to switch to 'green'.

Those who witnessed the occasion of the 109th All-Ireland hurling final and its pre-match ritual know that these objectives were splendidly achieved by the hurlers of Wexford.

The Pre-Match Ceremonies

The availability of tickets for the final was, once again, the focus of everyone's attention. The touts were charging £80 for a terrace ticket and between £100 and £140 for the Hogan or Cusack Stand. A crowd of 65,849 crammed into Croke Park. Apart from 1981, it was the biggest attendance at a hurling final for 24 years. Wexford fans appeared to number about 20,000 with their Limerick counterparts little, if any, behind. The Canal End was a sea of green and white and Hill 16 was festooned in Wexford colours. Liam Griffin had spoken a few calm words to the players in the Stillorgan Park Hotel. 'This is the last occasion when this body of men will assemble together as players in the Wexford jersey. You will be remembered for what you achieve today. For this particular group of men it will be your last hurrah. This is our last battle.' Even in the heat of the moment, Griffin picked his words carefully. Many of those present suspected that, win or lose, there would be at least one retirement among the players, following the final. Griffin knew who it would be and so did the players. Seamus Barron and Liam Griffin's impending retirements were other unspoken implications. Now, in the Croke Park dressing room, before the most important match of their lives, the joker in the pack, Larry O'Gorman was encouraged to crack jokes. Soon the livewire Faythe Harrier had his team mates at ease and smiling broadly. They then moved into the warm-up area and, as was now the custom, a communal prayer was offered. Griffin honed in on the key words. 'Drive and hassle, multiplied by a million. Every ball is important. One lost ball can lead to losing an All-Ireland final ... The next ball! The next ball!'

Martin Storey made a short speech There was no shouting, no final frenetic exhortation. Motivation and planning had long since been concluded. Instead of pumping them up on adrenaline and whipping them out of the dressing room wired to the moon, everything was now controlled and composed.

All over the world, in cinemas, bars and auditoriums, wherever Irish people gathered, thousands of emigrants watched the television link-up, as the colourful spectacle unfolded. The highlight of the hurling year renewed that feeling of Irishness, whether the viewer was in Canberra or Los Angeles and made them feel, once again, a part of their country. It brought back nostalgic memories of youthful and innocent days spent hurling a leather ball on the local pitch, as they watched the warriors of Limerick and Wexford prepare to engage in the game of Rackard and Mackey in the fabled old coliseum off Jones' Road.

Both teams received rapturous receptions. The Wexford team that emerged on the first Sunday of September 1996 was probably the calmest and most relaxed group of men who had ever left the Croke Park dressing rooms on All-Ireland final day. The television commentators who had watched the teams get ready, remarked on the nervousness and tension evident among the Limerick men. Conversely, Wexford's representatives were cool, relaxed and enjoying themselves. The photographers lined up as the players took their positions. Larry O'Gorman's absence from the Wexford photo was accidental and not contrived. He broke away with the subs and the photographers focused on a 15 man line-up which was completed by the presence of Sean Flood. The fact that the injured Cloughbawn defender remained on the bench, misled the press photographers, who did not appear to miss Larry.

The behaviour of the Limerick team, while the introductions to President Mary Robinson were in progress, was in marked contrast to Wexford. The Wexford men stood like soldiers, with a manly and dignified bearing, as Martin Storey introduced the players one by one. All removed their helmets. They had already rehearsed the ceremony in training. Their fellowship was admirably captured by Storey's unpremeditated gesture of laying his hand on the shoulder of each of his team mates in turn. Protocol expert, Larry O'Gorman, was so relaxed that he did more than just shake the President's hand. He complimented her on her attire. The President of Ireland smiled and thanked him.

The Limerick men, by comparison, seemed ill-prepared. Nervousness was apparent and they looked apprehensive and ill-at-ease.

What followed was even worse and showed that something in the Limerick team's preparation for the big day was amiss.

The Parade

Both teams then embarked on the traditional pre All-Ireland final parade. Beginning under the middle of the Hogan Stand, Wexford captain Martin Storey appeared eager to gain the outside line in the parade. This tactic was designed so that the team would be closer to their supporters, when they reached Hill 16. He achieved his objective and the two columns of players proceeded to follow in the wake of the Artane Boys Band and march down to the Canal End, where the good-humoured, green-clad, thousands greeted their Limerick heroes. The parade then turned and continued down by the new Cusack Stand, as the packed house watched in growing anticipation.

Abruptly, when the teams had reached the halfway point of the Cusack Stand the Limerick players betrayed their anxiety and broke off like startled colts. Wexford marched on. Amazingly, their manager had predicted that this would happen. They continued towards Hill 16 where they were ecstatically greeted by the Wexford fans. 'You can break now', shouted a steward. They ignored him and continued. As they turned to march back towards the Hogan Stand side of the pitch, they crossed in front of the Railway goal where some of the Limerick players were now engaged in a puck about. One of the Limerick men attempted to 'psyche' his direct opponent, by staring him down. Just after the men in purple and gold turned to walk back down by the Hogan Stand, they finally broke off. Altogether, Wexford had marched for two minutes and ten seconds longer than their Limerick counterparts. Ger Canning, the RTE match commentator, alluding to the disengagement of the Limerick team, mentioned the remarkable coolness of Martin Storey and the Wexford players in continuing to march proudly on their own.

They had lived up to the Wexford emblem, 'Exemplar Hiberniae', the words which appear on their purple and gold jerseys.

Wexford had won the first battle.

Someone Should Have Warned Him

> *'With never a sound of trumpet,*
>
> *With never a flag displayed,*
>
> *The last of the old campaigners*
>
> *Lined up for the last parade.'*
>
> *The Last Parade*, A.B. 'Banjo' Patterson

Someone should have informed Sean O'Neill. Many of the famous old warriors whom George had opposed in his long hurling career were now retired. He had matched his skills with Sean Silke, Iggy Clarke and Joe Connolly of Galway; with Tim Crowley and Jimmy Barry Murphy of Cork; with Liam Currams, the late Pat Carroll and Johnny Flaherty of Offaly; with Ger Henderson, Frank Cummins and 'Chunky' O'Brien of Kilkenny, with Joe McKenna of Limerick and Sean Stack and Johnny Callinan of Clare. All were now retired from inter-county hurling. George would soon follow them, but first there was the matter of one last game. One last hurrah on the hallowed turf that he had so often adorned. One last shining hour. The length of his career was emphasised by the fact that he played against two of the managers of the teams that Wexford had beaten on the way to the final. Eamonn Cregan and Nicky Brennan were familiar with George and knew and respected his steely resolve. Tom Ryan, the Limerick manager, on the other hand, had never played against the lithe, helmeted figure who stood in the Wexford midfield with the number 17 on his back. He never had personal first-hand experience of the steel hard sinewy Wexford man. George, even in his teenage years, was never intimidated and this, the day of his final quest, the day when he had his first, last and only chance to win the coveted Celtic Cross, was not the day to attempt it.

Someone should have told Sean O'Neill that he was standing beside Mount Vesuvius. For George, this was the culmination of 18 loyal years of championship hurling. This was his 16th major final and he had figured on the winning side just once – for a few paltry seconds at the end of the 1996 Leinster final. He knew that it was his last opportunity. His ultimate farewell to the major stage that he loved and graced, as man and boy, since he first donned the purple and gold in 1979. In 28 days time he would be 37-years-old. It was time to call it a day. It would be done his own way, quietly – 'with never a sound of trumpet' and 'with never a flag displayed'. He had not discussed the matter with anyone, but he knew deep down that this was it. His final day. His last hour. And nothing was going to spoil it. Nothing was going to take it away from him. All the pent-up desire, all the frustrations of the past 18 seasons, all the days of thwarted dreams were about to be put to rest. 15 Mick Mackeys would not have deflected him from his purpose. Broken fingers, damaged hands, missing teeth and battered and bruised limbs were now forgotten as the man, known throughout hurling simply as 'George', lined up for his final battle. George was fiercely determined that he was going to do justice to himself, his family, his parish and his county and he was prepared to die, if necessary, in the attempt. He knew that if he did not play his part well, the Wexford selectors would be slated for playing a 37-year-old at midfield in an All-Ireland final. He was not about to let them down. He had never felt better. He had never felt more focused. He would do his job. Anyone who tried to spoil this day for George might as well be trying to stop the Slaney flowing.

The capacity crowd settled down, as the players took up their positions. The moment of truth was at hand. The next hour would answer all the questions. Seconds before referee Pat Horan signalled the start of the 1996 All-Ireland hurling final, the tough athletic, Limerick mid-fielder, Sean O'Neill, attempted to assert his manhood. He picked on the wrong man. Someone should have advised him.

George reacted instantly and emphatically. The volcano erupted and spat flying ash in the direction of his green-shirted tormentor. The confrontation was over in seconds and George was not the man on the ground, gasping for breath, in an attempt to come to terms with his folly. Someone should have warned Sean O'Neill.

The First Half

Limerick won the toss and elected to play against the slight wind. Within a minute, Larry Murphy had the first point of the game when he outpaced Mike Houlihan, and struck the ball over the Limerick bar. In the second minute there was an incident which resulted in damage to Gary Kirby's fingers. A high ball dropped between Dunne and Kirby. Both pulled, and shortly afterwards, Kirby received treatment from the Limerick bench. It was an accidental injury and the referee did not award a free or speak to any player. The injury however, was a bad blow to Limerick's chances and an inhibited Kirby was never effective thereafter. The exchanges were fiercely physical in the opening ten minutes, which witnessed end-to-end hurling, but from the seventh to the fourteenth minute Limerick outplayed Wexford. First Gary Kirby pointed a free, followed by another from play by Frankie Carroll. Then two points from Barry Foley were added to by another from Damien Quigley. 0-1 to 0-5.

Larry O'Gorman steadied Wexford with a point and then, in the 16th minute, he was dangerously tackled by Mike Houlihan who was booked. The Limerick man broke his hurl across the Faythe Harriers man. This was followed by an altercation between Owen O'Neill and John O'Connor. Both players were spoken to and booked, by referee Pat Horan. John O'Connor pointed the free from 71 metres. In the 19th minute a Rod Guiney side-line cut was gathered by Garry Laffan and sent towards the Limerick posts. Larry Murphy broke it down and Tom Dempsey pounced and sent a left-handed ground shot to the Limerick net. 1-3 to 0-5. Ciaran Carey responded brilliantly and surged forward for a point. A rare battle had developed between the opposing captains and Storey answered with a Wexford point. Barry Foley equalised for Limerick in the 23rd minute. 1-4 to 0-7. The Wexford selectors acted quickly to counteract 19-year-old, Barry Foley, who was causing havoc on the Wexford right wing of defence. O'Gorman and Guiney swapped positions in the 24th minute. Laffan pointed and Gary Kirby once again equalised from a free, when Frankie Carroll was fouled by Rod Guiney. The Wexford defenders were proving very adept in the art of hooking. Martin Storey was fouled when heading for goal and Eamonn Scallan pointed the free. Barry Foley then scored his fourth point, a terrific effort from far out the field, which was answered 35 seconds later by Martin Storey. Owen O'Neill had a Limerick point, just as the Limerick selectors were preparing to replace him. They changed their minds and O'Neill was given another chance to halt John O'Connor's dominance. Then in the 32nd minute came the first of two remarkable saves by Joe Quaid. Garry Laffan gathered, rounded his man, and shot for the Limerick net. Quaid reacted and pulled off a magnificent stop. Ger Canning, in the RTE commentary box, almost swallowed his microphone.

The Dismissal of Eamonn Scallan

Immediately, a mêlée occurred near the Hill 16 goal which resulted in a minor free-for-all. Mike Nash, the Limerick full-back, was seen to attempt to act as peacemaker. When the smoke cleared, Ciaran Carey and Adrian Fenlon were booked, although other players appeared lucky to escape without censure. Referee Pat Horan restored order and threw the ball in between Stephen McDonagh and Eamonn Scallan. Both players pulled hard and recklessly. Scallan, however, pulled a second time in the same fashion. Pat Horan reached for his notebook and standing in front of the Wexford corner-forward, pointed emphatically to the line. Other incidents worse than Scallan's misdemeanour had occurred, but it was hard to blame Horan, as he felt that action needed to be taken before things got out of hand. Scallan was unfortunate and paid the penalty for the disturbance that had taken place seconds earlier. Devastation descended on the Wexford supporters as Eamonn made the long, lonely walk with dignity. Limerick now had an extra man, but Wexford's pre-arranged plans went into action and they played with a five-man attack formation. This was nothing new, as regularly in their championship run they had played with one of the half-forwards helping out at midfield. Initially, Stephen McDonagh became the extra man for the Shannonsiders. It was to prove a double-edged sword for Limerick.

Just before half time Damien Quigley moved to corner-forward and Ger Cushe doggedly followed him. John O'Connor moved in full-back and continued to mark Owen O'Neill. Shortly afterwards, Dave Clarke was shouldered off the ball by Tom Dempsey, who pointed. The first half ended, having seen Wexford get 18 scoring chances and Limerick 14. The scores had been level on six occasions. It was a compelling match.

Wexford 1-8, Limerick 0-10

The Second Half

Tenor Anthony Kearns's half-time rendition of *Boolavogue* was interrupted by the Limerick team's re-emergence onto the field. There was a buzz around Croke Park as the game was restarted. Dave Clarke and later Ciaran Carey assumed the extra man role for Limerick. It did not appear to benefit the Shannonsiders and Wexford's two man full-forward line was showing to greater advantage in the wide open spaces near the Limerick goal area. Garry Laffan had the measure of the Limerick full-back, Mike Nash, and had two early wides before sending over the bar. In the 40th minute, play was halted while an injury to Colm Kehoe was attended to. John O'Connor was seen to turn towards Hill 16 and the massed assemblage of Wexford colours. He raised his arms in supplication. The Wexford fans responded and lifted the decibel level even higher. T.J. Ryan had a Limerick point and then came one of the greatest saves ever seen in Croke Park.

Larry Murphy let fly from just outside the square. The Limerick goalkeeper appeared to be unsighted and Murphy's perfectly struck left-handed shot headed like a bullet for the top left-hand corner of the Limerick net. Joe Quaid reacted instinctively and pulled off a miracle save, with his hand. It was the second time that the goalkeeper had rescued his team. The save drew a barely audible, awe-struck expletive from co-commentator, Tomas Mulcahy. Laffan gathered the rebound and pointed. 1-10 to 0-11.

Owen O'Neill was replaced by Padraig Tobin in the Limerick attack. Damien Fitzhenry made two fine saves for Wexford. The Slaneysiders were now on top and were taking the game to Limerick. In the 48th minute Tom Dempsey pointed a free for a foul on Rory McCarthy. Then Larry O'Gorman had his second point. Ciaran Carey again broke upfield and rallied his team with a great point. Storey was fouled and Dempsey pointed the resultant free. 1-13 to 0-12. Twelve minutes elapsed without a score as Limerick hit four wides and Wexford two. A further Limerick substitution saw Brian Tobin introduced for T.J. Ryan and defender Turlough Herbert came in for Barry Foley, whose rampant gallop had been halted by Larry O'Gorman. Limerick had now used all three permitted substitutes. In the last few minutes Wexford also introduced fresh legs as Billy Byrne, Paul Finn and Paul Codd came in for Larry Murphy, Rod Guiney and Garry Laffan. The Shannonsiders were now becoming frustrated as they threw everything at the Wexford defence. Cushe, Kehoe and Dunne were magnificent, as was John O'Connor who flung himself in front of a Limerick attacker to defy his scoring attempt. Finally, in the 66th minute, Dave Clarke, who was now the spare man, pointed when he found himself unmarked in the Limerick centre-forward position. Two minutes later, Carey plucked the ball from the sky and pointed once again. Martin Storey was seen clearing from the Wexford full-back line. It was heroic stuff as Limerick threw everything at Wexford, who refused to yield an inch. In time added-on, Ciaran Carey was fouled and Mike Houlihan took the free. The referee intimated that time was up. The ball was hit low and gathered by Larry O'Gorman as the long whistle sounded. O'Gorman and Colm Kehoe sprinted to the ecstatic thousands on Hill 16 and the rest of the Wexford team jumped with joy. At the whistle, George sank to his knees and an enterprising and alert *The Examiner* photographer got the shot of a lifetime as the big St Martin's man, at the end of his 18-year sojourn in the Wexford jersey, clasped his hands in silent and joyful prayer.

Wexford 1-13, Limerick 0-14.

Match Summary

It was not one of the great All-Ireland finals but the tension, the drama and the death defying refusal to concede by the Wexford backs, kept the capacity crowd enthralled to the end. Wexford had created 32 scoring opportunities and Limerick 26. Wexford did not appear to be disadvantaged by playing with 14 men. They deserved to win and their defence was simply heroic. The Limerick forward lines scored only one point, by T.J. Ryan, in the second half. Fitzhenry, as usual never put a foot wrong. Ger Cushe, Liam Dunne, John O'Connor and particularly Colm Kehoe were magnificent. Kehoe's last 15 minutes will never be forgotten, as he tigerishly snapped at the heels of every green-shirted opponent in his vicinity. Despite a badly damaged knee, he epitomised the fighting spirit of Wexford, coming away from much taller and heavier adversaries with the precious leather grasped safely in his hand. Dunne earned the RTE 'Man of the Match' award for his endeavours. Wexford people will never forget his sally from defence and subsequent run along by the Hogan Stand side line. He dodged opponent after opponent before bringing the sliotar over the halfway line. Rod Guiney played his part and Larry O'Gorman gave a faultless display of catching, running and striking. For long periods he looked the best player on the pitch – a complete hurler, who as well as defending superbly, found time to go forward and notch two valuable points. Adrian Fenlon had a remarkable match and his first time striking and linking was an invaluable asset to his team. He was well supported by the tireless George, who was still full of running at the final whistle.

Wexford had more opportunities in the second half but shot many wides. In the 70 minutes they shot 11 wides to Limerick's 9. In the forwards, Martin Storey played well, leading by example, and Tom Dempsey contributed 1-3 and played confidently and effectively. The real surprise packet was Garry Laffan. He won many balls and was a constant menace to the Limerick full-back line. He could and should have finished the game with a contribution of 1-5 but the incomparable Joe Quaid and some wayward shooting kept his tally down to a profitable 0-3. The ball did not run for Rory McCarthy. George, 18 years his senior, kept reassuring him during the game. 'Be patient. Be patient.' Before the Leinster final, for which George had been injured, he had approached Rory and encouraged him. 'We are both St. Martin's men and I'll be hitting every ball out there with you today. We'll win it together.'

Larry Murphy after his brilliant opening point, faded and was eventually substituted in the second half. He had been ill during the week leading up to the final and couldn't get Sonia O'Sullivan and her Olympic problems out of his mind. Eventually the inevitable happened and Larry was visited by the dreaded Big D.

The sending off of Eamonn Scallan was ironic. Tom Dempsey and Eamonn were the two Wexford players who were continually accused of not being physical enough. They were often goaded because they did not assert themselves. Scallan was unfortunate in picking the wrong occasion to lay these accusations to rest. Apart from his excellent contribution to Wexford's magical year from frees, the Liam Mellows man, a brilliant first-touch hurler, had played a largely unselfish part in the team plan. To a great degree, he had been sacrificed in the Leinster final, in order to drag his marker away from the edge of the square and create space for the rest of the full-forward line. He was one of only two Wexford forwards to score in all their championship matches. His contribution was clearly understood and appreciated by those with an inside knowledge of the game and its tactics, despite the fact that some commentators failed to fully comprehend his role.

Joe Quaid was mesmeric for Limerick, although his second half puck outs could have been better directed. His two saves, one in each half, were among the very best ever seen in Croke Park. Ciaran Carey, who scored three magnificent points, did everything that was expected of him. He never gave up and stormed through the second half, all the while frantically trying to rally his team. Stephen McDonagh, Declan Nash, Dave Clarke and Mark Foley played well but Wexford were on top at midfield, despite Mike Houlihan's defiant efforts. Among the Limerick forwards, only Barry Foley, before he was subdued, and occasionally Frankie Carroll, played up to form. Gary Kirby was obviously hampered by the unfortunate injury to his finger. He was later found to have broken the small finger of his right hand. He could not be blamed for the defeat and without his brilliance in the earlier rounds, Limerick would not have reached the All-Ireland final.

The Disallowed Limerick Goal

Some controversy arose, in the weeks after the game, concerning the disallowing of a Limerick goal in the second half. As late as the middle of October, Tom Ryan, the Limerick manager, in an interview in *The Title,* referred back to the incident. 'Why was it disallowed? Nobody seems to have a clue. It was a crucial decision which possibly cost us the All-Ireland final, yet the referee is under no obligation to comment on why he didn't allow it to stand. That's wrong', he commented. The video recording of the game clearly shows that the whistle had been blown seconds before Brian Tobin struck the ball to the Wexford net. It is also clear that the Limerick forwards and the Wexford backs heard the whistle and stopped playing, except for Tobin who hurled on. Referee Pat Horan later said that he blew the whistle because he saw a Limerick forward fouling a Wexford back. The forward appears to have been Gary Kirby, and the back, Liam Dunne. Tobin then broke away to his right and pulled on the ball. It went through Colm Kehoe's legs and into the net. None of the Limerick forwards protested, when the 'score' was ruled out.

Other Limerick Complaints

Tom Ryan was also critical of the referee and alluded to injuries sustained by Sean O'Neill, Gary Kirby and Owen O'Neill early in the game. '... I'm stating categorically that I thought the referee (Pat Horan) gave a poor performance in the All-Ireland final ...'

The conflict between John O'Connor and Owen O'Neill began and ended in similar fashion to the one between John's brother, George and Owen's brother, Sean, which took place seconds before the game began. Owen had carried an ankle injury into the game, suffered in a behind-closed-doors challenge game against Clare. His second-half substitution had more to do with this injury and his inability to round O'Connor, than to the damage sustained in the clash between the two.

In an interview in *The Limerick Leader* after the game, the Limerick manager said that his players were 'pushed, shoved and clobbered all over the field ... Maybe we will have to look at a more physical bunch of hurlers to complement the skilful players on our side'. Even allowing for the feeling of devastation brought on by defeat, it was a strange comment, when one considers that Limerick had four players (Carey, O'Neill, Houlihan and Tobin) booked by referee Pat Horan. Wexford, apart from Scallan's dismissal, had just two men booked, John O'Connor and Fenlon. Wexford earned fourteen frees and Limerick – just seven. Tom Ryan went on to complain about Wexford time wasting, fouling and not being penalised, the incursion of the Wexford mentors onto the field, the referee blowing for full time too early and two Wexford defenders 'lying down on the ball in their square'. A detailed examination of the video recording of the game fails to show up any justification for the awarding of further frees to Limerick. A further comment from Tom Ryan tottered on the edge of the credibility cliff and drew howls of laughter in Offaly, Kilkenny and Wexford. This was the assertion that Leinster hurling was much tougher than its Munster counterpart. Kilkenny hurling people particularly, could not believe what they were reading.

To be fair to Tom Ryan, he was most gracious in his after match congratulations to Wexford and admitted that Limerick had failed to avail of the extra man. He also apologised, in *The Limerick Leader* interview, for the behaviour of the Limerick players in the pre-match ceremonies.

In simple terms, the All-Ireland final witnessed Limerick up against a team who were more than capable of giving it and taking it, as well as the Shannonsiders. The Wexford men were willing to go through brick walls to gain possession and when heavily tackled, they just shook themselves and got on with the action. They were stronger than Limerick. They knew that they would have to be if the Kilmallock pattern was not to be repeated. The Wexford team's preparations were more detailed and the 'what if?' scenario, played out in the weeks leading up to the final, proved to be invaluable. In contrast, Dave Mahedy from the Limerick camp, admitted after the game that they had not catered for the possibility of a player being sent off and he accepted defeat with dignity.

Billy Rackard, the former-great Wexford centre half-back and now a successful writer, summoned it up very well when he wrote in his column in *The Wexford People*:

> *Figuratively speaking, Wexford started this game with 15 greyhounds, but ended with 14 rottweillers.'*

One Definitive Statistic

One definitive statistic underlined the reason why Wexford won the 1996 All-Ireland final. Surprisingly, it was not picked up by the national press. Throughout their campaign Wexford had paid particular attention to limiting the concession of frees within scoring range. In the Leinster final, the backs had given away two frees in the first half and none after the interval. The All-Ireland final saw the tigerish but controlled purple and gold-clad defenders chase and harry the Limerick forwards back and forth across Croke Park. Always, they were very aware of the absolute necessity of keeping their modus operandi strictly within the rules. During the first half, the Wexford backs conceded only one free, when Rod Guiney fouled Frankie Carroll. The second half, when the Slaneysiders were playing with only 14 men and against the wind, resulted in the concession of not a single free by the Model County backs. One free conceded by seven defenders, in 70 minutes of hurling, is a performance of rare discipline. When Limerick's extra man is taken into consideration, it borders on the impossible and makes the feat quite astonishing. The achievement has probably never been equalled in an All-Ireland hurling final. It was the main difference between victory and defeat.

The After-Match Scenes

At the final whistle, Seamus, Rory and Liam exploded from the dugout to embrace the Wexford team. It was chaotic and Seamus Barron fell in behind one of the Wexford substitutes, Declan 'Skippy' Ruth, a 6 ft. 2 ins. giant, whom he used as a shield, to enable him to get to the steps of the Hogan Stand.

Rory and Liam embraced one another with delight. Rory felt so happy for the people of Wexford and, together with his brother, Mick and John O'Leary, stayed on the Cusack Stand side of the pitch watching the presentation with tears in their eyes. The unbounded joy displayed by the fans was unforgettable. Two months after the final, the extent of their achievement has only begun to dawn on Rory Kinsella.

The pitch was a mass of surging heaving bodies as the purple and gold-clad throng swelled below the Hogan Stand. Many of the players were carried triumphantly to the steps, where Liam Dunne threw his arms around his Wexford colleague, Ger Cushe. Dunne had held Gary Kirby scoreless from play and Cushe, apart from heroically clearing ball after ball, had conceded only a solitary point to his immediate opponent, Damien Quigley.

'We showed them, Ger. We showed them today. This is the best day of all to have done it', shouted Liam Dunne.

Storey's speech was well delivered and he thanked everyone associated with the great victory. 'We have often been called the bridesmaids of hurling. Well – today we got married,' he proclaimed. The Wexford fans loved it.

The disappointed Limerick fans distinguished themselves by sportingly applauding from the Canal End.

After-Match Comments

Interviewed after the match, Liam Griffin was, in the words of Tom Humphries of *The Irish Times*, like 'a man with two hours of talk on his mind and just ten minutes of time in which to deliver it'. It was an apt description. Conscious of the huge disappointment in the Limerick camp he alluded to manager, Tom Ryan. 'I feel really sorry for him. He's a decent country man like myself, putting his heart into the game. I hope he's judged fairly; he's taken Limerick to two All-Ireland finals in three years.'

'Guts and determination is what won it. We paraded the full way round the pitch. We stood to attention for the President. We did everything we were supposed to do ... Mental preparation is so important. We were determined to be relaxed. We weren't going to be so tight-jawed that we couldn't perform. We were determined to enjoy the day. I described it to them as an under-15 hurling final. I told them to take that attitude. To face up to the responsibilities. To turn the ceremonies to our advantage...We had planned for it if a man was sent off. If we had an extra man. If they had an extra man. We wrote it and rewrote it ... Clare were an example to us all. We can be an example to others.'

He was questioned about his trip around Our Lady's Island, a revered place of pilgrimage in south Wexford. Reluctantly he responded:

'I hate doing this ... there is a pilgrimage season down there in Lady's Island where you have to go so many times between now and the 8th of September. My mother and myself have been marching all week. My mother has ten laps done, I've only five done, but I walked it last night and I felt peace and contentment. I said we are going to win this match. I'd looked at every aspect of this game. So I looked at that too ... I'm not some kind of latter day preacher or anything but I believe in those things. I don't want to come off folksy, so treat me well when you write this ... My fellow selectors Rory Kinsella and Seamus Barron have all been devoted to youth hurling for years and have come through the system. I believe that we have laid the foundation for the future of Wexford hurling.'

He did not mention that he had also visited his father, Mick Griffin's grave before every match.

The Players

Billy Byrne was in Heaven but still refused to give away his hurl to a young admirer, who requested it. His comment showed that there was life in the old dog yet. 'If I was retired I'd give it to you'. His two crucial goals had got Wexford to the final and Billy, now at the twilight of a fine career, was enjoying the most wonderful day of his life. Wexford fans swarmed all over him as he tried to come to terms with his new status in hurling. He kept thinking back to two years ago, when he had retired. He had missed the excitement and the rushes of adrenaline and was happy to return when asked by the selectors. Never in his wildest dreams, did he think that his comeback would culminate in this – an All-Ireland senior win. He thought of the great players who had given everything for the purple and gold and left the scene with nothing to show for years of unselfish effort. Players like Eamonn Cleary, John Conran, Jimmy Holohan, Martin Quigley, Padge Courtney and Seanie Kinsella. After the Leinster final, Billy had seen tears roll down the face of one of the toughest hurlers who had ever donned a Wexford shirt, Tony 'Sack' Walsh. He remembered watching *The Sunday Game* on the day, when D.J. Carey had scored the infamous winning goal in the Leinster semi-final of 1991. The camera had panned around Croke Park after the match and picked out the poignant figure of a young Wexford boy, still holding his purple and gold flag, standing in isolation on Hill 16. Billy had felt a lump in his throat as he watched the tears roll down the face of the young Wexford fan. That image had stayed embedded in his memory and now, in his mind's eye, he saw it again. He'd give anything to meet him now and see his reaction on this day of days.

Sean Flood may have been disappointed to miss the final, but he still won his All-Ireland medal and his pre-match speech had galvanised the Wexford team. He now had a distinction that marked him out as a man apart in Wexford. Sean Flood and his father Tim are the only father and son combination in the county to hold All-Ireland senior hurling medals.

Eamonn Scallan's All-Ireland day had not gone well. Large portions of the match passed him by as he sat despondently in the dugout. As the final whistle sounded he felt a surge of relief. His out-of-character pull would now be consigned to the dustbin of forgotten incidents.

The appreciation of the hurling skills of Adrian Fenlon is extremely high among his team mates. Throughout the campaign he was probably the team's most consistent player. The fact that he was not always given due credit by the media for his displays, can be put down to the fact that he rarely did the spectacular thing. His game is based on keeping the ball moving, with a brand of first-time hurling that warmed the hearts of the hurling men of old. His expertise on sideline cuts, his overhead striking and his workrate mark him out as the finest centre-field man in hurling. Many of the crucial scores obtained by Wexford originated with Fenlon. Both of the goals scored by Billy Byrne, as well as Tom Dempsey's goal in the Leinster final, came about as a result of precise deliveries from the man with the Rolls Royce engine who rampaged across Wexford's midfield.

How the Gap Was Bridged

Vincent Hogan of the *Irish Independent* was one of many sporting journalists who gracefully acknowledged that the epitaphs that had been written for Wexford hurling were premature. The team that 'like Ivan

Lendl, couldn't play on grass' had proved them wrong. Hogan, whose incisive writing had supplied Griffin with wonderful core phrases to motivate his forces, had to be complimented for his 100 per cent turn around in relation to his views on Wexford.

So how was the miracle achieved? What were the important elements in Wexford's hurling rebirth?

The portrayal of the state of hurling in County Wexford in the summer of 1995, as outlined in the Wexford Hurling Survey, was an accurate one. The foothold of the game was eroding and after the year 2000 it could well be lost. 1996 changed all that.

The readiness of the players to adapt to new and sometimes vastly different methods was central. Honesty, team spirit and trust were words that rang around the dressing room at Wexford Park. The players learned how to listen, how to think deeply about their game, how to improve their diet and how the intensive gym work was such a benefit. They learned to contribute at the team talks and they earned the trust of the manger and selectors. The players were informed of the exact line-out for the Leinster final, well in advance of the game. It was crucial to Wexford's plans that they kept it to themselves. The trust was not broken. The promise to refrain from alcohol was honoured. Old impulses to play the pattern of game that had formerly proved the team's downfall, were resisted. The players rarely reverted to type. The game plan was altered for each match and for each type of opposition. The old chestnut – 'We'll play our own game, so let the opposition worry about us' was cast aside and precise strategies were laid to counter the opposing team's strengths. Wexford became the chameleons of hurling and always adapted patterns that suited the occasion.

Griffin constantly used stories and incidents from the lives of great figures to illustrate and drive home his message. He reminded them of Mrs. Beaton, the famous cookery writer, whose jottings he remembered from his catering studies. She would invariably begin a recipe headed 'Chicken Casserole' with the sentence; 'First procure the chicken'. Similarly, Griffin would begin his talk with the forwards by stating the obvious. 'First procure the ball.' This exhortation was particularly aimed at one Wexford forward, who often played as if wearing roller skates on ice, such was his propensity for falling down when attempting to secure possession. The story of Stuart Pearce and his comeback from the trauma of the missed penalty was not forgotten. Neither was the anecdote relating to Alain Mimoun, the great French distance runner. A contemporary of the legendary Emil Zatopek, he had spent much of his career finishing second to the great Czechoslovakian. Finally, at the end of his career, in the Melbourne Olympic Games of 1956, Mimoun had run the entire marathon without stopping once for water. He won easily and Zatopek finished well in his wake. When Griffin returned to his Rosslare home one night before the Leinster final, following a long and arduous training session, he collapsed wearily into a chair and switched on the television. He saw an elderly Frenchman being interviewed. The fragile old man was sitting in a chair in his living room. Dramatically, he staggered to his feet and became extremely animated. 'I cross le line...derr is no Zatopek. I am le champion. Zatopek, I 'ave beaten 'im. I no longer am le shadow of Zatopek.' It was Alain Mimoun. Griffin was astonished. He thought that Mimoun had died years earlier. He was convinced that it was an omen. He couldn't get the incident out of his head. The next night he called the players together and told them the story. It became an inspiration for the Leinster final and the stimulus followed throughout the year. The team will never forget the manager's passion about Mimoun and his repudiation of his lifelong sporting demons.

This Wexford team became the Alain Mimoun of hurling.

Seamus Barron and Rory Kinsella continually came up with suggestions and fresh ideas. Griffin encouraged them to do so. It was always understood that the final decision lay with Griffin. Barron's astuteness and ability to read a game allied to Rory's mastery of the techniques of hurling skills were crucial factors. Their coolness and incisive decision-making on the sideline played seminal roles, especially in the Galway and Limerick games. The members of the backroom team knitted well together and it became a cohesive and harmonious unit. Lifelong friendships were forged and the unbreakable bond evident among the players applied, in like fashion, to the backup team. All played their part and those parts taken as a whole, formed a powerful and intrinsic weapon in Wexford's armoury.

Liam Griffin sought and received help from Bill Bowen, who had strong Enniscorthy connections. A world-renowned dental researcher in Rochester University in the USA, he was interested in sports coaching. Griffin met him in the United States and got access to up-to-date documentation on the techniques of psychological and physical preparation, visualisation and mental imagery. He acquired books and research papers on the topic and studied them intensively. He then introduced the methods to the players. They learned how to see, in advance, the type of game that they were about to play. To visualise the low ball. The forwards became mentally attuned to it and to anticipate the character of their game. They visualised sideline cuts and their immediate objectives. Damien Fitzhenry saw himself saving opponents' goal attempts and Billy Byrne visualised his goals being scored. It dramatically altered their concepts and increased their success rates.

The Wexford backroom team invented new types of physical preparation for hurling. Among these was circuit training with a hurl, where players ran and pulled on rows of tyres to increase speed and drive.

Plyometrics – exercises for exploding the muscles – were introduced and specially constructed wooden boxes used. The players hurdled these and bounded on and off them to put explosiveness into the legs. These new methods quickened reaction time and improved the standard of first time pulling. The original hand-outs given to the players had emphasised that the longer the time spent in preparation, the longer the ability to peak would continue. Griffin thinks that hurling has more to learn from the toughness, strength, muscular flexibility and particularly the discipline of Martial Arts, than other sports. Wexford met no team that was fitter than themselves.

John O'Leary's minutely detailed statistical reports on each player's performance were crucially important in the campaign. Every player became acutely aware of his particular strengths and weaknesses. The psychological end of the preparation was very important and Niamh Fitzpatrick and Liam Griffin made a powerful combination. The players responded enthusiastically and the altering of attitudes was a fulcrum point for the success that followed.

As far as the Wexford backroom team was concerned, the All-Ireland final was not just about winning a game of hurling. It was about doing everything correctly on the day and behaving with dignity and decorum, irrespective of the result. Sportsmanlike behaviour was always part of the 1996 Wexford hurling culture. They made it clear that they were totally opposed to thuggery in hurling. When Ger Cushe was seen to pull on Joe Erritty, after the Offaly full-forward had rounded him in the Leinster final, the action was not condoned by the Wexford bench. They were unhappy about it. The actions of George and John O'Connor in the All-Ireland final, on the other hand, were supported by the backroom team, because of the circumstances which prevailed in the lead-up to those incidents. The incident involving George needed no clarification in its initiation or conclusion, but John's altercation with Owen O'Neill, after which both players were booked, was not seen in its entirety by the Wexford bench. John O'Connor's explanation of the entire proceedings was deemed satisfactory.

Pat Murphy, the PRO to Wexford County Board, had been appointed by the Management Committee as liaison officer between themselves and the senior hurling selectors. He did his job with aplomb. Arriving in Croke Park for all matches well in advance of the team, he had every detail laid out in orderly fashion. Each jersey was on a hanger in its allotted place. Drinks and other specified requirements were placed neatly on a table. Initially, the dealings between the Management Committee of Wexford County Board and the selectors of the Wexford hurling team, had some tricky patches. Griffin found it wearying to deal with them early on, but when the successful run began, it got much easier. Towards the end of the championship they were very supportive. Previously, they demurred about the large panel that Griffin demanded. The expenses involved were a huge burden for the board. Griffin argued that being forced to practice with just backs and forwards was ridiculous and thirty players were required, otherwise they were designing their own failure. The manager also insisted on small incentives for the players after a major win. These incentives might include a track suit or a pair of new boots. He felt that the officials should not be petty with the players, who are after all, amateurs. Liam was mindful of the story told to him in 1995 by a well known ex-Irish rugby international. Following an international in Lansdowne Road, two of the Irish team, subsequent to the festivities in the Shelbourne Hotel, had ordered a copy of *The Irish Times* to be delivered to their room on the following morning. They were dumbfounded to receive a bill from the IRFU a few weeks later. They had each been invoiced for half of the cost of the newspaper by the IRFU. In 1996, this miserable attitude is put dramatically into perspective by the £30,000 per year being received by some international players.

All the angles were covered. Griffin was taking no chances with the spiritual side of things. His visit to Our Lady's Island was duplicated by some of the players. Jenny Griffin, Liam's elderly mother, whose determined genes had been inherited by her son, was resolute in leaving no stone unturned to help Wexford's cause. This cute, Wexford lady was aware that Matt Talbot was only a 'venerable'. She reckoned that he needed whatever help he could get to advance to sainthood. She would negotiate a quid pro quo with him. Before the Kilkenny match, she made straight for Gardiner Street church, where she spent several hours parleying directly. Matt Talbot, the long deceased Dublin docker, was requested to intercede on behalf of her son's charges. In return, she would pray for his sainthood. It must have been the first time that he had been subjected to such an unusual plea.

No one can say that he didn't comply.

It had been a long and winding road from the turning point of the apparently insignificant win over Offaly, in Birr, during the previous February. The watershed win in Thurles, in April, sowed further seeds of self-belief. Liam Griffin was central to everything and he added a new dimension to Wexford hurling. He regularly worked a seventeen-hour day and devoted nine of these hours to the Wexford hurling team. During 1996, in particular, he slept, ate and drank hurling and his co-selectors, Seamus Barron and Rory Kinsella, made the same sacrifices.

In the week coming up to the final, Griffin spoke to the players. He repeated a line that the players had frequently heard. They had not entirely understood the sentiments during the early part of Griffin's reign but now, all had grown to appreciate them fully. They practically knew the words by heart. 'A friend isn't necessarily the man who comes up to you and congratulates you after you've won a match. Some people like me and some people don't, but I am your friend. A friend is there through thick and thin. Through the good times and the bad. A friend is the man who tells you the honest truth about yourself – even when it is not complimentary. That's a real friend. Your best friend is the man who gets you to do the best you can.' He would invariably end his homily by looking directly at the cool laid-back, Sean Flood. 'Who's your best friend, Sean?'

'Oh, you are, Liam, you are', Sean would reply in a mock-bored fashion.

In the end, the outspoken honesty, passion and charisma of Liam Griffin, the hurling expertise of Rory and Seamus, the all-encompassing preparation, the attention to detail, the insistence on thinking, thinking and thinking again, the unflinching steadfastness of the Wexford followers, the will power, the loyalty, the trust and that forever friendship may have been too much for the teams that came up against the Wexford hurlers of 1996.

However, as Griffin never tired of repeating, 'managers do not win matches'. Nothing can ever compensate for not being on the field of play. The fulfilment level falls well short of that experienced by playing the game. While managers play an important role they do not defend or register scores. That is up to the 15 members of the team. It was their year and it was their bright September day. The day when they reached a summit last conquered on 1 September 1968. They exorcised all the bad memories and brought pride back to the Model County. The memory will live forever in the minds of Wexford people.

> *'An ash tree toppled when you died*
> *And scattered seeds at random.'*
>
> *Cuchulainn's Son*

The last line of the song written about Wexford hurling hero, Nick Rackard, could now apply to his successors. The lost ground of Bobby Rackard and the glamour hurling men of the 1950s had been reclaimed. The barren fields of Wexford hurling would once again be fertilised by the deeds of the hurling men of 1996.

It was Wexford's field of dreams.

ALL-IRELAND SENIOR HURLING FINAL
Croke Park, 1/9/1996

Referee:Pat Horan (Offaly)

WEXFORD

Damien Fitzhenry
(Duffry Rovers)

Colm Kehoe
(H.W.H. Bunclody)

Ger Cushe
(Naomh Eanna)

John O'Connor (0-1f)
(St Martin's)

Rod Guiney
(Rathnure)

Liam Dunne
(Oulart-The-Ballagh)

Larry O'Gorman (0-2)
(Faythe Harriers)

Adrian Fenlon
(Rapparees)

George O'Connor
(St Martin's)

Rory McCarthy (1-1)
(St Martin's)

Martin Storey (Capt.)(0-2)
(Oulart-The-Ballagh)

Larry Murphy(0-1)
(Cloughbawn)

Tom Dempsey (1-3,0-2f)
(Buffer's Alley)

Garry Laffan (0-3)
(Glynn-Barntown)

Eamonn Scallan (0-1f)
(Liam Mellows)

SUBS:Billy Byrne *(Naomh Eanna)* for Larry Murphy; Paul Finn *(Oulart-The-Ballagh)* for Rod Guiney; Paul Codd *(Rathnure)* for Garry Laffan; Seamus Kavanagh *(Buffer's Alley)*; Sean Flood *(Cloughbawn);* Shane Carley *(Glynn-Barntown)*; Jim Byrne *(Fethard)*; Declan Ruth *(Shamrocks)*; Tommy Kehoe *(Glynn-Barntown)*; Dave Guiney *(Rathnure)*.

LIMERICK

Joe Quaid
(Feohanagh)

Stephen McDonagh
(Bruree)

Mike Nash
(South Liberties)

Declan Nash
(South Liberties)

David Clarke (0-1)
(Kilmallock)

Ciaran Carey (Capt.) (0-3)
(Patrickswell)

Mark Foley
(Adare)

Michael Houlihan
(Kilmallock)

Sean O'Neill
(Murroe Boher)

Frankie Carroll (0-1)
(Garryspillane)

Gary Kirby (0-2f)
(Patrickswell)

Barry Foley (0-4)
(Patrickswell)

Owen O'Neill (0-1)
(Murroe Boher)

Damien Quigley (0-1)
(Na Piarsaigh)

T.J. Ryan (0-1)
(Garryspillane)

SUBS: Padraig Tobin *(Kilmallock)* for Owen O'Neill; Brian Tobin *(Mungret)* for T.J. Ryan; Turlough Herbert *(Ahane)* for Barry Foley.

STATISTICS
SCORE CHART

Player	v. Kilkenny	v. Dublin	v. Offaly	v. Galway	v. Limerick	TOTALS	FROM PLAY
Tom Dempsey		0-1	1-5	0-6(0-3f)	1-3 (02f)	2-15	2-10
Martin Storey	0-5	0-2	0-5	0-3	0-2	0-17	0-17
Eamonn Scallan	0-3 (0-2f)	0-4 (0-3f)	0-4 (0-3f)	0-1f	0-1f	0-13	0-3
Garry Laffan		1-2			0-3	1-5	1-5
Rory McCarthy	0-1		0-3	1-1		1-5	1-5
Larry Murphy		0-1	0-4	0-1	0-1	0-7	0-7
Billy Byrne	1-0			1-0		2-0	2-0
D. Fitzhenry		1-0f	1-0f			2-0	
L. O'Gorman	0-1		0-2		0-2	0-5	0-5
Adrian Fenlon	0-2	0-1				0-3	0-3
John O'Connor				0-1f	0-1f	0-2	
Liam Dunne	0-1f					0-1	
Paul Codd	0-1					0-1	0-1
Sean Flood		0-1				0-1	0-1
TOTALS	1-14	2-12	2-23	2-13	1-13	8-75	6-57

WIDES AND FREES CONCEDED

	wides	frees conceded by backs	frees conceded by rest of team		wides	frees conceded by backs	frees conceded by rest of team
v. Kilkenny	Leinster quarter-final			**v. Galway**	All-Ireland semi-final		
1st half	9	1	4	1st half	4	2	5
2nd half	3	3	3	2nd half	6	3	8
TOTAL	12	4	7	TOTAL	10	5	13
v. Dublin	Leinster semi-final			**v. Limerick**	All-Ireland final		
1st half	6	3	5	1st half	5	1	2
2nd half	9	4	3	2nd half	6	0	4
TOTAL	15	7	8	TOTAL	11	1	6
v. Offaly	Leinster final						
1st half	7	2	3				
2nd half	4	0	4				
TOTAL	11	2	7				

The rest of the Wexford panel in alphabetical order Tomas Codd (St Martin's); Mitch Jordan (Marshalstown); Joe Kearns (Faythe Harriers); M.J. Reck (Oylegate/Glenbrien); Liam Turley (St Martin's).

∞ CHAPTER 10 ∞

GLORY OH! GLORY OH!

The Malahide Celebrations

A rapture-fuelled celebration banquet took place in the Grand Hotel, Malahide on Sunday night of the All-Ireland final 1996. Demagogues and directors, government ministers and grocers, farmers and fishermen, businessmen and bankers, pensioners and publicans and the rollicking rank and file of Wexford GAA followers attended. Tears of jubilation and joy witnessed the Wexford panellists enjoying their release from the year-long training regime. The RTE cameras beamed Sean Flood's rendition of 'Purple and Gold' to the nation, as Liam Dunne received his 'Man of the Match' accolade. The revelry went on late into the night. 'If this is a dream, God help the fellow who wakes me up', Tom Dempsey remarked.

A Warning

Liam Griffin had told the members of the Wexford team, on the Wednesday before the final, that win, lose or draw there would be a meeting on the Monday morning after the match. Now everyone assembled for a private gathering. They were an exuberant bunch as they filed into the room. Enniscorthy Administrator, Fr John Sweetman led them in a quick prayer of thanks for their great victory and then the manager addressed them. He emphasised that they, the hurlers of Wexford, had won the All-Ireland – not the manager or selectors. He told them that they had behaved impeccably during their season of victory. Their conduct during the All-Ireland final ceremonies had done credit to Wexford and had drawn favourable comment from across the country. The team would now be looked upon as role models for the youth of County Wexford and further afield. During the homecoming they would be offered opportunities to imbibe with abandon. They would be exposed to massive adulation, hero-worship and a plethora of temptations. He asked them to refrain from drinking and copious carousing during the celebrations. They had responsibilities and they should continue to behave with ambassadorial dignity. The Wexford manager wanted the same standards of discipline that had distinguished their sporting behaviour to continue. It was to become a permanent part of their deportment from now on. It was Wexford's sixth All-Ireland win and these young men would be marked out by their achievement for the rest of their lives. They were now icons in Wexford and he wanted the young people of the county to have worthwhile symbols to look up to.

Not even the slightest demurral came from the players, who had already become aware of their responsibilities. To a man, they willingly accepted their new status and its attendant obligations. Throughout the coming months they were to set standards of behaviour which would be a benchmark for all to follow.

Martin Storey then made an emotional speech in which he thanked his fellow players for the privilige that they had afforded him in allowing him to be their captain. He would never forget how they had helped him to realize his boyhood dream. He said that all of them would remain friends forever.

Wicklow and Carlow Join In

The Wexford team attended the customary GAA lunch at the Burlington Hotel after which the two team buses set out for the south east. Wexford colours bedecked the pedestrian bridge across the Stillorgan dual carriageway. Through the Glen O' The Downs it was the same. People lined the route to Wexford, holding teddy bears and balloons. Klaxons and car horns trumpeted clarion calls for sporting heroes as the two buses sped on.

The people of Wicklow and Carlow showed tremendous enthusiasm for Wexford's All-Ireland win. Carlow-native, Mick Morrissey, had won three All-Ireland hurling medals with Wexford, as part of the great 1950s team. In an earlier era, Jim Byrne, a native of Ballymurphy, Co. Carlow, had participated in the four-in-a-row All-Ireland football winning side of 1915-18. Both counties are starved of success in Gaelic Games and their inhabitants entered with abandon into the excitement generated by the banner-embossed cavalcade of purple and gold that had regularly traversed their counties in the summer of 1996. They flew the Wexford flag as if it were their own. It was like the 1950s all over again, as the geographical county boundaries became blurred and the Sunday afternoon crowds lined the streets of Arklow, Ashford, Rathnew, Baltinglass, Rathvilly Castledermot and Tullow. Arklow Urban District Council even took the unprecedented step of giving a civic reception to the Wexford All-Ireland-winning team.

Now the people of Wicklow were showing their partiality for the deeds of their all-conquering neighbours. Near Ashford, a Garda escort joined the cavalcade. Rathnew had a blazing bonfire to indicate Wicklow had warmed to the victories of Wexford. Arklow was in festive mood and two bands turned out to rejoice with the elated crowds who lined the streets. A large banner read 'One Storey is worth fifteen Limericks'. The line of cars behind the buses had grown to an extended cordon of rejoicing. They reached Gorey at 6.30 p.m. and Martin Storey alighted on the edge of the town with the Liam McCarthy Cup. It was 28 years to the day since Dan Quigley had carried the revered old trophy into the Model County. The players and officials boarded an open-topped bus and continued into the town.

The Gorey Reception

The time you won your town the race

We chaired you through the market-place;

Man and boy stood cheering by,

And home we brought you shoulder-high.

(A.E. Housman, *A Shropshire Lad*)

The population of County Wexford is just over 100,000. It seemed that most of them turned out to welcome the team home. The pumping heart of the celebrations was the town of Gorey. A carpet of purple and gold greeted the cars that streamed into the main street after the final. Soon the traffic backed up and a two-mile queue of vehicles crawled along the Dublin road. A massive bonfire greeted the arrival of the team. The sight that met the players' eyes was awesome. The town was crammed, from the John Street intersection all the way past Christchurch, with 30,000 heaving bodies. The last time that Gorey had seen such a crowd was on 9 June 1798, when the Wexford insurgent army left Gorey Hill and marched through the town on their way to The Battle of Arklow. The tears streamed down Ger Cushe's face as he thanked the people of his town. Billy Byrne and Eamonn Scallan also spoke and these three were the real hometown heroes on that memorable night. Throughout the entire unrestrained celebrations, there was an affable and agreeable atmosphere. Although it took most people hours to get through Gorey's main thoroughfare, no one appeared discontented. Despite being severely buffeted, no one complained. A blanket of good humour and happiness descended on the county.

The Prodigal Sons of Wexford hurling had brought home the fatted calf.

Enniscorthy and Bill Peare

Then the procession moved onward through flag-waving thousands, through villages and by cross-roads. At Scarawalsh, just outside Enniscorthy, a huge bonfire blazed. One of those who had supervised its erection and conflagration was 89-year-old Bill Peare. Every player who had donned a Wexford jersey for the past 45 years knew Bill. He had been involved with Wexford hurling teams since the All-Ireland appearance against Tipperary in 1951, at the dawn of the Rackard era. He carried hurls, bags of oranges and generally, did anything that he could, in a life-long devotion to Wexford hurling. When Tony Doran had scored the winning goal against Kilkenny in the last minutes of the 1984 Leinster semi-final, Bill had been so overcome that he had dropped his bundle of hurls and ran on to the pitch to embrace Doran. Two of the best known hurling people in Wexford, the red-headed legend from Boolavogue and the then 77-year-old Bill Peare, were captured in a memorable bear hug by the RTE cameras. Doctor's orders prevented Bill from attending the 1996 series of matches. The team bus, on the journey to Croke Park for the All-Ireland final, had slowed down on Sunday morning as it neared his home at Island Road, Enniscorthy. There he was, sitting in a chair outside his house. The players recognised him and waved enthusiastically. Old Bill, with a lump in his throat, waved back. No person in Wexford was more devoted to Wexford hurling than Bill Peare. He admits that he cried with joy for two hours, with his head between his knees, after the All-Ireland final. His grand-children and his great grand-children had, at long last, seen his beloved Wexford triumph in an All-Ireland hurling final. Now he took his rightful place on the victory platform, as a crowd of 15,000 shouted themselves hoarse. The men of the hour in Enniscorthy were locals, Adrian Fenlon and Declan 'Skippy' Ruth. The banner which moved Griffin more than any other was held up by a well-dressed, elderly man in Enniscorthy. It read 'Thank you for your dignity'.

Wexford Town Dances at the Crossroads

The streets of the old Viking town of Wexford are narrow tentacles that reach out from the quays like the wrinkled fingers of an aged musician. The deep-powered Slaney sweeps by the salt-encrusted boardwalk where Celt, marauding Viking, bull-headed Norman, sartorial Georgian and stubborn Irish have left their indelible mark. Here, echo the terrors of rebellion, the glories of triumph, the failure of Ireland's first short Republic and the persuasive cant of a dozen pretenders. A curry of cultures in a frog spawn of memory. Here, the homeward odyssey of the victorious Wexford team ended.

A local pub, 'The Centenary Stores' had a massive banner stretching the whole length of the outside wall of the building. It read, '15 on the field and 50,000 subs. Good luck lads!'

The large car park beside Redmond Square was the venue for the Wexford homecoming. Mayor Dominic Kiernan intimated that he was organising 'the mother of all parties' which was to take place, together with another civic reception, on the Monday night. A star-studded bill of entertainers gave their services to entertain the crowd while they waited in anticipation for the arrival of the Wexford team bus. In the prevailing mood of celebration, it was expected that there would be huge delays while the bus passed through Gorey, Cloguh, Ferns and Enniscorthy. Like everything else associated with the 1996 Wexford hurling team, the team bus arrived in Wexford at the appointed time. The crowd was estimated at about 30,000. Just after 11 p.m., The Wild Swans took to the stage and performed *Dancing at The Crossroads* their celebratory Wexford hurling song, over and over again. Just before midnight, an unforgettable moment of magic occurred. A fireworks display turned the Wexford sky into a majestic hue of purple and gold as the victors rounded the corner into the square. A huge full moon shone down on the scene.

We were dancing at the crossroads

Underneath the silver moonlight

In the shadow of a bonfire

We were dancing until dawn

(The Wild Swans, *Dancing at the Crossroads*)

The song that had been on the lips of many Wexford people for the previous couple of months now became a hymn of déjà vu, as an electric current ripped through the crowd. The prophetic words of the song came true in a living moment of sheer sorcery.

Martin Storey and his team bounded on to a dignitary-laden Guinness Gig Rig and the assembled multitude went into rapture. Storey spoke well and then local hometown hero, Larry O'Gorman introduced each player, each panellist and each member of the backroom staff to a deafening ovation. The impromptu speech given by Griffin on that memorable night became a mini-hit on the Local Radio Stations and in the weeks that followed it became a much-requested item. It was beamed all over the south-east and many Wicklow, Waterford, Carlow and Kilkenny people heard the emotional words of 'The Rosslare Messiah':

'... *I've often said that Wexford's the flower of them all... but when you come tonight... and you look down through the streets of Gorey at about 30,000 people and you come on through the small places like Clough, Camolin, Ferns and into Enniscorthy and if you look back in Enniscorthy at that magnificent town, with the bridge in the background, the cathedral on the hill and the chapel and the spires, and you think to yourself what a beautiful place and what a beautiful part of the world. And then to come on to Ferrycarrig and a whole snake of cars, for something like ten miles and the two castles shining in the air, the moon on the water and then you can say about the blood in your veins and the county that you come from – this is a special place and the colours that you hold over your head are purple and gold.* (At this point the crowd could take it no more and were transported into thunderous acclaim) *I really would like to say something about Wexford. Wexford had a serious problem in hurling and in Gaelic Games for the last number of years. We didn't make the break through and we had been struggling for some time. Now that is always very difficult and as far as I was concerned we were looking at the death of a way of life. You, tonight, are looking at the beginning of a way of life. And that flag over your head is a symbol of everything that you stand for. That purple and gold isn't an accident. It's a fact and it's tangible and the people who wore it on their backs yesterday and marched behind the band with pride and stood with respect before their President carried your colours – of your county. (Applause) And I would ask everybody under the age of fifteen ... that colour is your colour... it represents everything that you stand for and all that went before you and people who died in the streets of this very town. This is your colour and don't forget it. (Applause) ... If you have pride in your own county, pride in the place that you come from, you become a special breed of people. This was always a special place and because of yesterday it's become a new place and a special place again. But it's up to you to keep that going for the future. Yesterday was only a beginning – not an end. So don't forget that...'*

The Wild Swans struck up again and as the players linked arms and danced, the entire panel sang the words of *Dancing at the Crossroads*. For the people who were present it was one of the most memorable experiences of their lives. An hour after the team had first mounted the platform, they departed for the Ferrycarrig Hotel, but the gala of revelry continued well into the night.

Christy Heffernan in Wexford

Christy Heffernan, the former Kilkenny star, feels a strong attachment with Wexford. He went to school in Good Counsel College in New Ross and the first county jersey he wore was purple and gold, when he lined out for a Wexford Vocational Schools' football team. He decided to drive to Wexford town to witness the team's homecoming. He had never seen a celebration of such magnitude.

'I thought that the celebrations were brilliant. There really was a great buzz. The players spoke so well, were turned out so well and behaved so well. There was no drunkenness. It was a credit to Wexford. In Kilkenny, there is not the same level of celebration. I suppose that we're more used to winning it. Sometimes, not all of the players would turn up for our celebrations. It is usually a lot more casual.'

The GOAL Match

John O'Shea of GOAL entered the respective dressing rooms of Wexford and Limerick immediately after the match and requested the presence of many of the players at the Annual Goal Challenge between the new All-Ireland champions and a Rest of Ireland selection. The game was played at Wexford Park on the Wednesday following the final and the proceeds were in aid of the street children of Calcutta. The occasion was a night to remember and the packed attendance watched the members of the Rest of Ireland team form a guard of honour for the Wexford players. The presence of Limerick players, Joe Quaid, Ciaran Carey, Mike Houlihan, Stephen McDonagh, Barry Foley and Frankie Carroll was a remarkable tribute to their sportsmanship and resilience. The game itself was played in a spirit of fun, as in excess of 10,000 people watched some of the finest exponents of the game jest their way through the proceedings. Some of the players even took calls on mobile phones during the match. The inimitable Micheál Ó Muircheartaigh supplied a side-splitting commentary and successfully engineered a draw by having Michael Walsh of Kilkenny stand alone in goal to face a Damien Fitzhenry penalty in the last few minutes. The final score was 4-16 to 3-19. The ecumenism of sport was in evidence, as Wexford Town-based North End Soccer Club opened its new pitch to be used as a car park and donated the proceeds to GOAL.

The Tour of the Schools

Liam Griffin and the Wexford players now set off on a hurling crusade. Complete with the Liam McCarthy and Bob O'Keeffe Cups they became hurling evangelists and embarked on a tour of all the schools in the county. All of the players had become proficient at addressing large crowds and many, like George O'Connor, Martin Storey, Billy Byrne, Rod Guiney, Tom Dempsey, Liam Dunne and John O'Connor had become excellent public speakers. Wherever they went they were received with unabated enthusiasm. Neither did the victorious cortège neglect the all-girls schools. Sometimes these visits resembled a reception given to a pop group, as Adrian Fenlon, Declan Ruth and particularly heart-throb, Rory McCarthy were mobbed by frenetic teenagers.

Griffin was fond of contrasting the dignity, self-sacrificing attitude and ambassadorial behaviour of his players to the conduct of the pampered professionals of other sports. The behaviour of superstars like Gazza, whose exploits take up large quantities of print, which are not always confined to the sports pages, created a disparity in demeanour and attitude which was in marked contrast to the hurling boys of Wexford. Athletics and its performance enhancing drug culture provided ample opportunity to contrast the pure amateur ethos and parish-based sense of identity of hurling. By the end of October, the team had visited over 150 schools.

Each visit was received with singular acclaim and the seeds of a county wide hurling rebirth were productively being sown.

The Hurling Survey had indicated to Griffin the precise areas where other sports had a strong foothold. A dramatic change in the results would occur if the survey was to be undertaken in Wexford following the 1996 hurling apocalypse. Some of the students at these schools had previously been less than enamoured by hurling. Now their conceptions were beginning to waver. Griffin knew that he was competing against the might of SKY TV and that it had all the appearances of an uneven match. This was never going to deter him from earnestly advocating a return to the hurling fold. He pulled no punches as he unleashed an avalanche of passionate prose:

> *How many of you will play for Liverpool or for Manchester United? How many of you, could reasonably expect even to play for Huddersfield? You can't ever aspire to that... But many of you could realistically play in Croke Park for Wexford. That's real. That's something worth aiming for. It's a great game – our game. Not a plastic far-away unrealisable dream. Look at Billy Byrne and compare him to Gazza. Billy plays for the honour of his county. Unpaid and unspoiled, a man who has given his life to bring pride back to the place of his birth. Gazza is an asshole. When you go home tonight put on your Newcastle Brown Ale shirt and take a good look in the mirror. Then take it off and put on your purple and gold Wexford jersey and look again. Ask yourself, "Which one am I?". The answer should be obvious.*

During one of these passionate proselytising incantations, Rod Guiney who was standing behind Griffin on the platform, got completely carried away. The Wexford manager could hear the tear-away, red-headed Wexford wing-back enthusiastically egging him on with a burning intensity. 'Go on Griffin boy! Give it to 'em.'

Waterford RTC

When Liam Griffin and the team took the McCarthy Cup to Waterford RTC, it was expected that 100 or so, all of them from Wexford, would turn out. It was the first time that the All-Ireland trophy had ever graced the establishment. The popularity of the Wexford team was seriously underestimated however, when 1,500 students, of both sexes, brought the college to a standstill. They listened intently as Griffin spoke poetically about hurling and his players. An enraptured audience watched as Griffin pointed at John O'Connor. 'Look at that man beside me here. If he were a rugby or soccer player you'd have to see his agent in order to get him here.' There was chaos later, as almost the entire student body queued up to have their photos taken with the guests.

Tom Dempsey on Network 2

A few weeks after the All-Ireland final, Tom Dempsey was the guest on RTE 2's *Echo Island*. Seven Wexford signed jerseys were to be given away in a phone-in competition. The results astonished the RTE personnel at the TV station, who had expected a few hundred callers. The switchboard was jammed as 4,723 calls were logged. 75 per cent of them came from girls. It was hard to blame the city-dwellers, who had failed to grasp the long-tailed significance of the purple and gold win on the nation. The producer could not believe what was happening.

Liam McCarthy's Grave

The players were in demand, not just in Wexford, but also in Britain where large numbers of Wexford people have gone in search of employment. The Liam McCarthy Cup was taken to London on quite a few occasions. On one of these trips, organised by the Wexford Association in London, Tom Dempsey, Larry O'Gorman and John O'Connor created a little bit of history when they brought the famous All-Ireland trophy into a graveyard. The grave of Liam McCarthy had been re-discovered in recent years. They were the first hurlers ever to have conveyed the Cup back to the man who had donated it in 1921. They were photographed holding the cup over the late Liam McCarthy's headstone.

Free Coffee for Life

On the wall of Murphy-Flood's Hotel in Enniscorthy stands the famous Guinness advertisement. 'This man can break hearts at 70 yards.' The management have substituted 'Tom Dempsey' for 'this man' and '7' for '70'. Underneath is another sign which reads, 'Tom Dempsey is entitled to free coffee in this hotel for the rest of his life'. A certificate to that effect was presented to Dempsey by the management of Murphy-Floods.

In Kilmuckridge, Hammel's pub, 'The Crosses' had a special section opened. It was called 'Dempsey's Den'.

Griffin Hailed as a Hurling Messiah

In Kilkenny, Griffin is seen as one of the greatest ambassadors that hurling has ever had. Their fondness for him and his hurling passions will do nothing to weaken their resolve to 'put one over' on the All-Ireland champions in their next championship encounter with Wexford. According to Kilkenny people, 1996 witnessed a level of support for Wexford's efforts which had never previously been seen by the Nore. The Wexford contingents who journeyed to the All-Ireland Under-21 final in Thurles were astonished and delighted by the large sign in the Kilkenny town of Thomastown. It read, 'Thomastown supports Wexford'.

During Martin Storey's victory speech from The Hogan Stand, he had referred to Griffin. 'He says that he's not the Messiah. But he is. He's our Messiah.' Larry O'Gorman referred to him as 'God'. He was now more in demand than ever and made an appearance on RTE's *The Late Late Show*. Columnist, Nell McCafferty and GAA President, Jack Boothman were his fellow panelists; while Martin Storey and his wife, Rosaleen were in the audience. Nell had become a late convert to GAA and hurling and she raved about the life style and tranquil ambience of the parts of Wexford that she had visited to gather information for a series of newspapers articles. Pat Kenny also interviewed Griffin. He was chosen as 'Philips Sports Manager of The Month' for September. He was interviewed on radio stations throughout the country. His unbridled passion for hurling and Wexford shone through every word that he uttered. Journalists searched for adjectives to describe him. Sue Mott of *The Daily Telegraph*, a Sports Feature Writer of the Year, was enthralled by the Rosslare man. She was probably OTT when she wrote:

> '...He possesses the charisma of the old parish priest, the cordiality of mine host (which he is, owning three hotels), the vision of a seer and the gift of the blarney in spades. Imagine the zeal of Alex Ferguson, the mischief of Bill Shankly and the dress-sense of George Graham and you are somewhere on the sun-drenched approach road to Griffin.'

Griffin had obviously won her over, as she wrote about hurling:

> '...Hurling is rooted in purity. No transfers, no money, nothing but straining every sinew and training five nights a week on behalf of the county you were born to...'

She went on to quote Griffin on hurling.

> 'This is a warrior game. As close to the old Coliseum as you can get – I find it difficult to sit in a bar and listen to a bloke having apoplexy over Liverpool, when there might be two fellas from Columbia in the team, three fellas from Spain, four from north Russia for all we know. To me that's the world of SKY TV, Dallas and fantasy. In our case, if we lose a match, then my friends and neighbours lose. My brothers and my family lose. So we won't have Asprilla playing for us and, if we did, they'd probably want the match called off. The soul of our game is not about artificial aids. It's pure amateurism. It's unique. This is 'Brigadoon' stuff. There is no perfect world. But hurling is as perfect as you can get.'

The shouts of 'Messiah' rang in his ears. 'I can not walk on water', he protested.

No one in Wexford was listening. As far as they were concerned he was omnipotent.

An Award-Laden Team

Wexford had won the Walsh Cup twice, the Oireachtais Cup, the Bob O'Keeffe Leinster trophy and the Liam McCarthy Cup. It was a fabulous return, from a two-year spell, for a county that had been written off, in hurling terms. At the end of October came the news that 14 of the Wexford team had been nominated for the Powerscreen All-Star awards. Limerick had nine nominations and Galway eight. The nominations for Hurler of The Year were Ciaran Carey of Limerick and Larry O'Gorman and Martin Storey of Wexford. Additionally, another Wexford player, Rory McCarthy, figured among the nominees for The Young Player of The Year, along with Liam Cahill of Tipperary and Mark Foley of Limerick. Larry O'Gorman received due recognition for his magical displays by duly being voted Hurler of The Year. Mark Foley won The Young Player of The Year Award. Tom Dempsey won the National Irish Bank-sponsored GAA Personality of the Month for September. Rory McCarthy had been named RTE's Man of The Match after the Galway game and he had also been voted *Irish Independent* Jury's Hotel Sports Star of the Week. Martin Storey had been honoured with the same award on two occasions – after the Kilkenny match and following the Offaly match.

An Omen

On the Wednesday night before the All-Ireland final, a little girl from Oulart, named Mythen, told her father that she was certain that Wexford was going to win the 1996 All-Ireland final. Her father asked her how she could be so sure. 'It's the registration number of Mr Griffin's jeep', she said, 'It is 6896'. The Wexford manager was astonished when the girl's father informed him of this obvious omen. He had never before noticed the significance. In fact, if he had been pressed he would have found it difficult to remember his own registration number, which was 93D 6896. 1968, Wexford's last win, 1996...could it be? Good God! – Why hadn't he seen it before?

Griffin Resigns

Liam Griffin resigned as manager of the Wexford hurling team on Monday the 30th of September. To those close to the team it was no real surprise. To the rest of the country, it came as a bombshell. His resignation statement however, made everything crystal clear. He had not wanted to impinge on the celebrations but now, four weeks after the All-Ireland final, it was time to go. He had served two of his three-year term as Wexford manager, but Mary Griffin's illness necessitated him devoting more time to domestic matters. He intimated that while he was leaving the job as Wexford hurling manager, he would continue a life-long involvement in the promotion of hurling.

Eulogies flowed from the national press. In the *Sunday Independent*, Galway's Peter Finnerty wrote:

'Last Tuesday the devastating news finally broke. Liam Griffin was stepping down as manager of the Wexford hurling team. The news overshadowed all other GAA titbits over the week. ... He is going to spend more time with his family at a very trying time... What you see is what he is. There is only one Liam Griffin. He spoke to the public in the same vein as he did to his players – calm, controlled and focused. When he had to make hard-line decisions he made them without losing the respect of the recipient...He frequently spoke of visiting his father's grave, a man he adored. He would ask for guidance and direction and, looking back on it, I feel his prayers were always answered.

... Putting the players first was always his priority. He gave them all the credit for bringing pride and honour back to the county, whereas, without Liam Griffin, Wexford would still be in the doldrums...It just goes to prove that there is an exception to every rule... and nice guys don't always finish second... I hope Wexford people understand Liam Griffin's situation.. Let him go and just be grateful that ye witnessed the realisation of his full potential... Hopefully, his father will answer his greatest need of all and restore Mary to full health.'

In the *Irish Independent*, Vincent Hogan wrote:

'...If Wexford's unstoppable will has illuminated the summer, Griffin's personality served to amplify the heartbeat. The flair of his oratory has bemused those inclined to see hurling as a crude, jumbled, often violent tap of rural self-expression...He has opened sleepy eyes to a modern picture of the ancient game. A picture of honour and wit and glowing self-esteem...Griffin is an interviewer's dream. A speeding lyricist who resists the structures imposed by commas, full-stops and deep breaths...'

Colm Keys of *The Title* wrote:

'There was something special in Liam Griffin which made men tick. The passion which escaped from his heart touched not just a county but a nation. Griffin is the GAA story of the year. A luminary who should not be lost to the game.'

Griffin had first told the team of his decision and team captain Martin Storey issued a statement:

'...When he made his announcement it was very emotional, but it wasn't a tearful affair. The emotion was there because, having got so close to him, we would love to have him stay, but his decision was accepted and respected by all. He had built up such a good relationship with all of us that he was one of the main reasons we

won the All-Ireland. He was so single-minded – and he let nothing stand in his way. Between the Galway match and the final he devoted an hour a day to work and the rest of his time to hurling – and he was a man who was running three hotels. In the end, he was just totally devoted to his goal. Thank God he achieved it. Winning the All-Ireland after 28 years was special and even if we won it again next year, it wouldn't be as special. In fact, if we won it every year for the next 28 years it would never be the same as it was this year. Outside of hurling he was a very loyal man to us all. If you wanted anything he was always available. Is he irreplaceable? Certainly, but that doesn't mean that someone else can't come in and do the job. But there is only one Liam Griffin. I can tell you that I'd hate to get on the wrong side of him, because he's so passionate and committed about what he sets out to do...I'll always be grateful to Liam for making my dream come true.'

The experience that the team had been through together, anchored them in trust, friendship and cast iron comradeship. The bonds will never be broken. Griffin was largely instrumental in securing employment for many of the players, while helping others to reach their potential in their careers outside of sport. He would continue to help any player who needed advice, or was worried about any aspect of his life outside of hurling.

A Well-Managed Transition

Seamus Barron of Rathnure also resigned his position as selector. For him, it had been a traumatic two years. His serious illness had brought anxiety to his family. His recovery from that illness and the triumphant march to victory had given him a cherished memory. He too, would continue his lifelong involvement with hurling, at his club, Rathnure. Great things were expected in the coming years from the little club in the shadow of the Blackstairs and many of the young players that Seamus had coached would now go on to play on a bigger stage.

A recommendation came from the entire group that Rory Kinsella be appointed as the new manager. It was a seamless and dignified transition as Rory took over. What greater tribute could be paid to Kinsella than to receive the backing of the players and the whole-hearted endorsement of his predecessor. The final say was with Wexford County Board and its members, who had the ultimate power in the matter. They accepted the recommendations of the team and the outgoing management, to the great benefit of everyone involved.

The Repercussions in County Wexford

'Start with an earthquake and move up from there'. The words of Sam Goldwyn come to mind when attempting to describe the repercussions of the All-Ireland win in County Wexford. It was 'goodly news, goodly news', as the consequences of the events in Croke Park turned a county on its head. This wasn't just about hurling. It was about the self-esteem of a people. Like the rest of the country, Wexford had entered into the atmosphere of unrestrained celebration, following the Jack Charlton-led exploits of the Irish soccer team. They had watched the green-shirted warriors bring joy to a nation. Wexford people had been boundless in their enthusiasm. But what followed in the wake of the events of the first Sunday of September put those feelings into perspective. Quite simply, Wexford went delirious. Everything else was forgotten as the winds of victory 'swept o'er the land like a mighty wave'.

On the Monday morning after the All-Ireland final the men, women and children of County Wexford opened their eyes to a dawn of euphoria. The county went into a tail spin of celebration. Flags, bunting and the Wexford colours flew everywhere. Before the All-Ireland final, Curracloe farmer, Nicky Doyle, resprayed his 17-year-old tractor from top to bottom in the purple and gold colours. Many others painted cars and houses and for months, vehicles with purple and gold streamers, were a common sight on the roads of Wexford. A county had salvaged its pride and the very core of Wexford was touched by it all. Even the defeat of the under-21 hurlers, when Galway triumphed in Thurles before a record attendance, failed to dampen the enthusiasm.

At times it seemed as if the whole of Ireland was celebrating with Wexford. Large numbers of Dublin people spend their leisure time in the sunny south-east. The county is dotted with Dublin registered cars during the months of summer and the long holiday week-ends. The laconic Wexford disposition allied to the wave-washed sands of Ballymoney, Courtown, Curracloe and Rosslare are powerful antidotes to the hustle and bustle of the city. These holiday-makers succumbed to the mass hysteria that swept across Wexford. They cheered and clapped with the natives.

After the Leinster final victory, a massive demand for Wexford jerseys manifested itself. Ned Buggy, the former intercounty hurler and All-Star, owns a sports shop in Wexford town. The demand for Wexford jerseys exceeded all his expectations. He was flabbergasted to receive orders not just from Wicklow, Carlow, Dublin, Galway, Donegal, Kerry and Cork, but Vancouver, Winnipeg, the USA and from Irish clubs all across England. Wexford track-suits, baby jerseys, small kids' jerseys, hurls and helmets, all-weather hurling balls, team photos, car stickers and Wexford souvenirs of every shape and size were despatched by the dozen. Eventually, the manufacturers could not keep up with the demand and orders had to be booked in advance. The suppliers went on holidays in the middle of Wexford's championship run. It was the biggest mistake that they ever made. Phil Doyle, a local hurl manufacturer was swamped with orders.

As co-commentator on Wexford's matches, with Liam Spratt, on South-East Radio, Ned Buggy had been enthralled by the unexpected year of triumph. After the All-Ireland final he had been booked into the Grand Hotel, Malahide, where a massive celebration was laid on. Despite the pleas of Liam Spratt, he decided to go back to Wexford to experience the journey and the unique occasion. He left Dublin at 6.45 p.m. and did not reach Wexford until midnight. It was unforgettable as he drove, at snail's pace, through County Wicklow surrounded by bonfires and jubilance.

Hurling in County Wexford was now thriving and County Board officials detected an immediate upsurge in interest among the youth of the county. The pool of available sponsors grew, bigger crowds turned out for club games and the following for, and interest in, the Wexford hurling team reached a record high, even for unimportant winter fixtures.

The anaesthetic of victory dulled the memory of all previous sporting disappointments. The despair and the tag of perennial losers, which had hung like a millstone around the necks of the Wexford hurling team and its followers, were banished. The repercussions were manifestly evident all over the county. There was a vibrancy in the air as the county entered into party mode. The purple and gold flew high from harbour and homestead, from village and valley and from haggard and hilltop. Tourists were overwhelmed at the sea of Wexford banners and viewed the kaleidoscopic carpet of county colours in astonishment, enquiring incredulously, 'What's happening? Is it Independence Day?' There was a smile on the face of Wexford people. The conversation in factory and farm, in supermarket and school, in household and hotel, centred around the hurling resurrection of the rejuvenated county standard bearers. A new spring was evident in the step of Slaneysiders. Even the cynics crawled back to the fold and joined in the prevalent air of celebration. The voice of the Rosslare Messiah was everywhere, as Martin Storey and his hurling soldiers took the county by storm. The ancient game of Cuchulainn underwent a massive resurgence. Cobwebbed hurls were taken out of hibernation and were swung joyously around parks and pitches. Jerseys of purple and gold swarmed around the honey-pot of a county in ecstasy.

The kids reeled off the names of their new champions. The radio stations hummed to the tunes of Wexford songs, hurling songs and paeans in praise of the hurling heroes. Heroes that had replaced the sterile TV images of Tyson and Hameed, of Cantona and Campese, of Christie and Gazza. These Wexford sportsmen were not flickering icons beamed from the almighty SKY. They were not tender-muscled prima donnas, whose earnings reflected greed and the worst aspects of crass commercialism, but real heroes, home-grown heroes, Wexford heroes, whom the kids could see and converse with, in the towns and villages of the county, at training sessions in Wexford Park and while engaged in their daily occupations. They behaved, not as pampered superstars, but as decent, ordinary, dedicated young athletes in the *Chariots of Fire* spirit of true Corinthians. There was no self-styled Prince among them, but to the young boys and girls of Wexford, throughout the memorable summer of '96, their champions walked as tall as kings. They did not, when tackled, gyrate on the ground like Oscar-winning actors, feigning counterfeited injury. They did not go missing before important matches and they were unlikely to jump into the Hogan Stand and assault spectators. Parents could be sure that their children's hurling heroes would not test positive for performance enhancing drugs and would not appear in sensational headlines across the tabloids. There would be no six-figure testimonial matches for these young men when their day of retirement came. For neither money nor riches were their spur. Rather the self-satisfaction of bringing honour and glory to their native place by playing, before their own people, the game of the ages, the game of the gods, the game of their forefathers, the game of the old timers of Crossabeg, Blackwater and the Bold Shelmaliers and the game of the Rackards, the Morrisseys and the men of the 1950s. For these were heroes who worked at everyday jobs and gave over their evenings and weekends to a torturous training regime – all for the glory of the little village, the glory of their parish, the glory of their club and the glory of their county.

Their dedication, their spirit, their skill and their determination ensured that the Summer of '96 would long be remembered in Wexford. Young people who had grown tired of their elders reminiscing on great Wexford teams of the past could now understand something of the feeling that grips the spirit when Wexford marches to victory. Talk of the magnificent fifties and the glorious sixties could now be better appreciated. If winning an All-Ireland final induced such a feeling of well-being from Broadway to Bunclody, then it must really have been something to savour when Wexford won three All-Irelands in a six-year spell from 1955 to 1960. And indeed it was! Those old enough to remember those days could see the same bountiful joy, the same contagious camaraderie, the same overwhelming pride and the same carefree happiness, as the county wallowed in the glorious exploits of the young men of Wexford. On the Friday before the final, a large card was delivered to Griffin by Eddie 'Dodo' Kelly, the full-back on the 1968 Wexford All-Ireland winning team. It was shown to the players in the Stillorgan Park before they departed for Croke Park on the morning of the match. It read 'We know you can do it. We are here cheering for you. Good luck in today's final. From the team of '68'. It was signed by all of the 1968 team.

Wexford people are fiercely proud of their history. Vast numbers of people have emigrated from the county, particularly during the employment-desolate 1950s. All over the world and particularly in Britain, men and women with Wexford blood in their veins were overcome with pride by the exploits of the hurlers. It wasn't just about winning, but the way it had been achieved, the dignified behaviour of the purple and gold-clad representatives on that memorable day. Outpourings of pride and joy in the form of over 3,000 letters and cards from all over the world arrived at Griffin's home. The majority carried the message that he had restored Wexford's pride.

One card came from a bank manager, who had recently been transferred from Wexford to Galway. He was a Mayo man and his county was about to face Meath in the 1996 All-Ireland football final. Written inside was the plaintive plea 'Please give this to Mrs Griffin and ask her to do a round of Our Lady's Island for Mayo'. Enclosed was a one pound coin.

Throughout Ireland there was rejoicing in hurling circles, that Wexford had, at long last, achieved a major breakthrough. Many other counties had cheered for Wexford in the All-Ireland final. Even the traditional hurling enemy, Kilkenny, had made it clear that they wanted Wexford to be victorious. Dozens of cards were received from famous and not so famous intercounty hurlers from all over Ireland. Many more arrived in the days after the final, congratulating them on their victory.

The hoodoo had been broken. The culmination of the magical march of 1996 had restored the self-belief and made everyone in Wexford, once again, proud to be part of an old and noble county, a place where unspoiled and unpaid young hurling men had unselfishly given their time and effort to play the best field game in the world, brilliantly and skilfully, and in the process created a special memory which will live for many a year.

Griffin's resignation signalled the end of one shining hour, when he became Arthur to the hurling Camelot of Wexford, and Martin Storey, George O'Connor, Billy Byrne and the others became the Lancelots. We are unlikely to see it again.

'I'm Glad that You're Not Over Us'

Following his resignation, Griffin resumed his activities in the youth game. One day, he was returning with a carload of young hurlers from an under-11 match. He pulled into a shop, on the edge of Wexford town, to get some refreshments for the youngsters. He was spotted by a young Faythe Harriers hurler. The Wexford town club had recently beaten St Mary's, Rosslare in an under-11 ground hurling tournament game. Griffin had attended the match as a spectator. The 10-year-old recognised Griffin and was blunt in his assessment of the famous Wexford hurling Messiah, whom he assumed was the manager of the beaten St Mary's team. 'I know you, boy. You're Liam Griffin. We beat yez. God, you're not much of a manager! You're really useless. I'm glad that you're not over us.'

Liam Griffin laughed. He was back where he started.

For the hurlers of Wexford however, things would never again be the same. After years of frustration and decades of defeat, they were back on top. That pinnacle had been achieved with style and panache. With courage and spirit.

With heart and hand.

Where The Slaney Waters Flow

Oft' times at night a memory came of golden days of yore
   And often in the mists of dawn I thought I saw once more
The Gold and Purple flying as it did long years ago
   From every home and flagpole where the Slaney waters flow.

But dreams are dreams and with the dawn the memory would fade
   I thought that here again I'd hear the music in the glade
Or see the flags and cheering crowds in the evening sunset glow
   As we welcomed home our heroes where the Slaney waters flow.

Then came that splendid Sunday when my heart began to sing
   And a victory ore Kilkenny made a tiny joybell ring
Then Dublin was defeated and it was all systems go
   To once more be Leinster champions where the Slaney waters flow.

When Offaly fell victims sure the joybells sounded free
   In every town and cottage from Bunclody to the sea
The barren years were swept away, their hearts with pride did glow
   As the lads prepared for Galway, where the Slaney waters flow.

What mattered who were favourites, what mattered who were odds
   The gallant sons of Wexford were like Olympian Gods
The country was behind them, and like the melting snow
   The Corrib throat was brushed aside by the Slaney waters flow.

The next step was the big one, the one through Heavens gate
   And the gallant sons of Wexford remembered '96.
A great tradition on your side, the pride of long ago.
   Made you set the heather blazing where the Slaney waters flow.

One that first day of September in the year of '96
   You walked with pride behind the band the full round of the pitch
An omen that you'd stay the pace where others failed to go
   And our hopes were riding with you from where Slaney waters flow.

The game was hard, you fell behind, yet no man would give in
   And when Dempsey crashed it to the net we made the Blackstairs ring
The second half was tension-packed, the play swung to and fro
   But you brought McCarthy back to stay where the Slaney waters flow.

You lit a flame for our native game with your sportsmanship and pride
   Like heroes bold in your Purple and Gold you swept like the Slaney's tide
All doubts away with your great display, and your names will always glow
   Like the bonfires on that evening, where the Slaney waters flow.

Willie White
Clonegal, Co. Carlow

Index